TRANSFORMERS

Therese — We are both driven by the same need to help, to EMPOWER others!

D1379628

TRANSFORMERS

Creative Teachers for the 21st Century

MARY KIM SCHRECK

CORWIN
A SAGE Company

Copyright © 2009 by Corwin

All rights reserved. When forms and sample documents are included, their use is authorized only by educators, local school sites, and/or noncommercial or nonprofit entities that have purchased the book. Except for that usage, no part of this book may be reproduced or utilized in any form or by any means, electronic or mechanical, including photocopying, recording, or by any information storage and retrieval system, without permission in writing from the publisher.

All drawings by Leslie Smith.

For information:

Corwin
A SAGE Company
2455 Teller Road
Thousand Oaks, California 91320
(800) 233-9936
Fax: (800) 417-2466
www.corwinpress.com

SAGE India Pvt. Ltd.
B 1/I 1 Mohan Cooperative
  Industrial Area
Mathura Road, New Delhi 110 044
India

SAGE Ltd.
1 Oliver's Yard
55 City Road
London EC1Y 1SP
United Kingdom

SAGE Asia-Pacific Pte. Ltd.
33 Pekin Street #02-01
Far East Square
Singapore 048763

Printed in the United States of America

Library of Congress Cataloging-in-Publication Data

Schreck, Mary Kim.
Transformers : creative teachers for the 21st century/Mary Kim Schreck.
    p. cm.
Includes bibliographical references and index.
ISBN 978-1-4129-7111-9 (cloth)
ISBN 978-1-4129-7112-6 (pbk.)
   1. Creative ability—Study and teaching. 2. Creative thinking—Study and teaching.
3. Creative ability in children. I. Title.

LB1590.5S36 2009
370.15'7—dc22   2009007517

This book is printed on acid-free paper.

09   10   11   12   13   10 9 8 7 6 5 4 3 2 1

Acquisitions Editor:	Dan Alpert
Associate Editor:	Megan Bedell
Production Editor:	Jane Haenel
Copy Editor:	Sarah J. Duffy
Typesetter:	C&M Digitals (P) Ltd.
Proofreader:	Gail Fay
Indexer:	Wendy Allex
Cover and Graphic Designer:	Scott Van Atta

Contents

Preface

THE ELEVATOR TALK VERSION

Elevator talk is a common business term. It means to concisely convey what you're up to in the time it takes an elevator to go from the ground floor to an upper-level floor. A real "cut to the chase" articulation of subject, purpose, intent—everything—in 30 seconds or so. Here's mine:

   A. This book is about building in its readers an awareness and a desire for seeing creativity as a part of living for everyone but, more important, as a necessary part of teaching and learning.

   B. This book is an interactive experience in learning, thinking, reflecting, playing with the types of thought patterns and structures that initiate creativity.

   C. This book is an attempt to both inspire and help transform all teachers into becoming more creative and thus more engaging and effective in their delivery of information, skills, and understanding.

   D. This book provides current research that explains why creativity is not an add-on but rather a necessary element in effective teaching for the 21st century.

THE VERSION THAT TAKES THE
STEPS INSTEAD OF THE ELEVATOR

It was only in the last 10 years that I can remember taking the time to read the introductions or prefaces in the professional development books I would buy. I was usually in too much of a hurry and would go through the table of contents looking for whatever I might be most interested in reading. How did I pick a book? Well, if the topic was one I was interested in and the format was appealing, I would consider buying it. But for the most part, a friend's strong and enthusiastic suggestion was usually the best recommendation.

The book that had the most effect on me and consequently on my teaching wasn't even a professional development book per se; it was Julia Cameron's (1992) *The Artist's Way* that dramatically unblocked my creativity that I hadn't known was even blocked. This book was recommended by a workshop presenter. She had her favorite books on display for all of us to page through. I do that now myself—bring whatever books space allows for show and tell. For example, when giving a workshop on mind mapping, I have all of Tony Buzan's books to pass around for teachers to examine. When giving a workshop on the power of multiple intelligences, I pass around *Math for Humans* (Wahl, 1999) or the Sir Cumference series by Cindy Neuschwander and Wayne Geehan.

I envision a teacher at some point in time holding up this book during a workshop or faculty meeting and saying, "If you think you are a creative teacher, this book is for you! If you *don't* think you are a creative teacher but would like to be, this book is for you! This book will empower you to put the life and joy into your teaching that you know belongs there. This book is a mix of concrete teaching ideas, steps to improve your own creativity, philosophical musings on what role creativity plays in your own development. This book speaks to your longing as an individual to express yourself authentically as well as your longing to help your students do the same."

I hope teachers would find the whimsical sketches that punctuate the book to be delightful markers for important concepts and examples included. I hope teachers would enjoy the wisdom of master educators who have taken their time to give advice or a slice of their hard earned experience for us to think about. I'd like that. Personally, I think this book should serve as a cheerleader for the creative soul in each of us. The attitude that "if it can't be bubbled in, it isn't worth teaching" is short-sighted and dangerous. I hope that an open discussion on what creative teaching looks like and the energy and empowerment it produces will help change that mentality. I hope these discussions will move the fulcrum to provide a more balanced environment in which to teach and learn. While working through this book, you will find evidence of why you entered the profession in the first place as well as a way to keep you in it—a way to secure a sense of meaning and joy in your teaching.

With this book as the vehicle, you and your administrators and colleagues should begin the discussion on how a school's atmosphere and culture can strangle or nurture creative teaching. I want to make the case that creativity is the fuel, the juice, that should propel the educational focus of the 21st century. I give concrete steps on how all teachers, no matter what the level or course, can increase their innate ability to think and act more creatively in the classroom—and all while raising test scores rather than jeopardizing them. This is not the book to buy if you just want someone to tell you to do more coloring, cutting and pasting, and poster making with your students. That's not what creativity will look like here.

This book is an interactive experience in transformation through learning, thinking, reflecting, playing with the types of thought patterns and structures that initiate creativity. By talking with others about the material and working through the suggested activities, you will be tempted, if not positively motivated, to stretch and exercise your creative muscles. And we all know that once a creative muscle is stretched, it never goes back to its original size again. But most important, you will find yourself in this book—a self filled with the energy to try new approaches and bring serious play into the curriculum delivery equation. No matter how restrictive the educational environment you move in has become, there is room for you to be a creative teacher. In fact, the more restrictive the situation, the more necessary it is for you to constantly inject creative approaches and procedures. Let this book be just the invitation you need to begin.

Acknowledgments

Corwin gratefully acknowledges the contributions of the following reviewers:

Julie Duford, Fifth-Grade Teacher
Polson Middle School, Polson, MT

Debbie Halcomb, Teacher
R. W. Combs Elementary School, Happy, KY

Karen Kersey, Teacher
Alban Elementary School, St. Albans, WV

Lisa B. Lucius, Principal
North Pontotoc Elementary, Ecru, MS

Renee Ponce-Nealon, Kindergarten Teacher
McDowell Elementary School, Petaluma, CA

Beth Madison, Principal
George Middle School, Portland, OR

Wendy S. Miner, Department Chair of Education
Truman State University, Kirksville, MO

Richelle C. Talbert, Principal
Brader Elementary School, Newark, DE

About the Author

**Mary Kim Schreck,** after 36 years in the classroom, currently serves as an education consultant for districts in Missouri, Maryland, and Texas as well as for the National Writing Project and the National Education Association. She has published four books of poetry, served as editor of *Missouri Teachers Write*, and written articles for national and state education journals. She lives with her husband, Bernard, at the Lake of the Ozarks, in Missouri.

During her career as a classroom teacher, Mary Kim spent years in almost every possible teaching setting available. She taught at an all-girls private academy, then in a small 270-student rural school that served Grades 6–12. From here she worked in a public school of over 4,000 students in three grades on a split-shift schedule. She also spent years tutoring for the St. Louis (Missouri) Special School District while teaching full time in another district. She later taught classes at Brown's Business College and served as a literacy coach at Vashon High School, an inner-city school in St. Louis. Most of her teaching career has been spent in the Francis Howell School District, in St. Charles County, Missouri, where a rural school district was forced to transform into a suburban district within a few years.

In the past eight years, Mary Kim has taught hundreds of teachers through various workshops and consulting opportunities. Among these opportunities, she has been an instructor for the Literacy Academies, a partnership program between the Missouri National Writing Project and the state department of education, and for the I Can Do It Beginning Teachers Assistance Program offered through the Missouri National Education Association. She is currently fulfilling a consultant contract at North East High School, in Kansas City, Missouri.

An Elementary Teacher Speaks Out About Creativity

by Stephanie Kinser

In the elementary setting, you often hear teachers saying things like "I allow children to be creative in my class. They get to choose the order in which they complete their centers" or "I promote creative thinking by offering choice in how students present what they know about a given topic." These are common thoughts and, in my opinion, misconceptions about what it means to be a creative teacher.

As educators of the very young, we are not simply called to be creative in our teaching processes and styles, in our lesson plans, and in our projects; I believe that the task in front of us each day is much greater than that. The students in our care still love to play, have make-believe friends, and get excited about the Tooth Fairy visiting. Our job is not only to be creative in our interactions with our students; it is also to encourage, foster, and intentionally allow *their* creativity to flourish.

I believe that we must teach creativity in the same way that we teach math or any other "academic" subject. We must start with basic exercises in creative thought and scaffold the subject just as we would anything else. We must view creativity in the young classroom as essential, and we must be intentional in how we encourage creativity among our students. It is not enough to simply allow students to use their imaginations within our class walls; we must provide practice so that they learn to harness and use their creativity to solve problems in real-life settings.

In my second-grade class, I encourage creativity in the way that I structure my entire year. In working with children and observing their learning, I have come to believe that artistic thought leads to scientific inquiry. This is to say that thinking as an artist thinks encourages great innovations in the areas of research, design, and experimentation within the context of every scientific capacity. I believe that every great scientist is also a great artist and that every great artist has a greater command of the scientific process than many realize.

Artists and scientists have much in common. They both create, encourage change, find better ways to solve the problem in front of them, envision a solution, seek answers, explain the world around them, predict, plan, change their plan as needed, ask questions, and contemplate. In other words, they have both learned to harness their childlike creativity into a productive way of seeing and working with the world. This idea has become the framework for my classroom interactions with students.

In my classroom, I teach children to be *ArtScientists* (a term coined by Professor David Edwards at Harvard University), scientists who see the world through creative, open eyes and who can see the innovative solutions to problems set before them in ways that others cannot. To be more creative thinkers, we must attack problems from the viewpoints of both an artist and a scientist. The integration of these two distinct views allows profound creative thought to occur in the minds of children.

My classroom is not a classroom, but rather an ArtScience lab with science equipment and famous artwork framed on the walls. Students add paintings to their own frames in our art gallery and are taught to look at all problems (math, reading, social issues, current events, etc.) by using the scientific method. Second graders do research and form hypotheses and conclusions to learn how to add two-digit numbers. They sculpt answers to test items such as "Explain what is happening during evaporation." They even use their ArtScience base when dealing with class rules by gathering evidence, creating charts, and coming up with better, innovative ways to solve class problems.

As a teacher, once you teach an eight-year-old to think in this open-minded, open-ended manner, it is astonishing to see how capable he or she really becomes in the classroom. Every situation becomes an opportunity for students to exercise their newfound understanding of the scientific method. Many of the best ideas that come out of my classroom have not come from me but from the students in my care because I have allowed them to think and work like ArtScientists.

Do I think this is the answer for every elementary classroom? Of course not! This is what I have found works for me and my teaching style. My hope is that all elementary teachers not only begin to see the importance of being creative in their practices, but also begin to be intentional in their teaching of creativity. It is only when we tap into this incredible potential in our students, and guide them through experiences that will strengthen this skill, that students' problem-solving capabilities will be fully realized.

Stephanie Kinser has taught second grade at Shamrock Springs Elementary School, in Indiana, for the past five years. She was the recipient of the Lilly Endowment Teacher Creativity Fellowship in 2007 and 2008. She is currently researching and working toward improved science education for elementary students through the use of the arts in the classroom.

1

What Teachers and Students Have to Say About Creativity

An Introduction

41 CREATIVE IDEAS

While considering just how to start this book, I searched for an appropriate metaphor that would resonate with teachers. I thought about the challenge of introducing a new topic or an important unit or lesson to students. How do we begin a journey through unfamiliar terrain? How do we keep students from succumbing to fear or, even worse, boredom? I concluded that a good way to introduce the subject of creativity would be to present ideas from actual teachers on what creativity looks like in the classroom.

We begin, therefore, with what we know about our own creativity and move on to new information for consideration. During the journey through this book, we will dig into what experts have to say about what creativity really is and how it manifests itself in teaching. I offer a chapter on the personal evolution of my own creative growth as a teacher, after which the focus shifts to why it seems so hard to be creative and still function successfully under the pressure to prepare students to take high-stakes tests and raise scores. Because of the explosion of new information on the workings of the brain, I devote a chapter to how creativity can flourish by tapping into that world of knowledge. The next chapter explores how personal transition comes about—from the inside out. Most teachers are aware that administrative attitudes set the tone for what is honored, expected, valued, so I present a chapter written by a superintendent who not only nurtures creative efforts in her staff but leads them through her example. This is followed by suggestions on how to strengthen the creative abilities that each of us has as our birthright. The last two chapters look at the future by considering the technology available to us now and how creativity is so integral to preparing our students and ourselves for a very different educational landscape.

Let's start with how most of us view creativity in our classrooms now. The creative activities listed here are samples from the nearly one thousand cards I asked teachers to fill out during a year's worth of workshops, keynotes, and presentations. Topics that these teachers commented about include major blocks to their creativity, what they think their administrators' opinion is about creativity, and when they usually get their best ideas. After reading card after card, I began to see similarities rising to the top and patterns beginning to form. Of course, the situations in which teachers are teaching will impact how they perceive their own circumstances, but many of the patterns seemed to cross geographical, age, and economic lines.

If you look closely at this sampling of creative ideas, the most obvious commonality is the fact that they are all examples of what researchers would call *effective strategies*. They may not technically fit under the title of creativity as defined by experts, and they might better fit under a column labeled Stimulating and Engaging Methodology. One other important commonality I invite you to observe is that these teachers give students the opportunity to make their own choices. One of the fastest ways to assure student buy-in is to create an opportunity for them to make a choice or many choices throughout the progression of the assignment. The very act of choosing results in students' developing a vested interest in how things will turn out.

In looking at the examples, you can also see that many teachers are applying content to their students' personal experiences, drawing on students' background knowledge, while others are using multiple intelligence pathways to build understanding, and still others are embedding authentic performances to "uncover" the material rather than simply to "cover" it. Teachers are using supplementary materials to better cement concepts for children. Another observation might be that many of these examples lead to a celebration of the products children have created—photographs on walls outside the classroom, speeches over the PA system. Children are manipulating content in these examples and coming up with new ideas and products. They are involved and enjoying themselves; they are engaged in learning. Teachers are proud of their efforts and the results of these efforts.

To make them more intelligible, I charted these creative examples using nine divisions: allowing for choice, use of novelty, authentic tasks, tapping multiple intelligences, visual presentations, application of knowledge, celebration of products, personal references, and problem solving (see Table 1.1). All of the examples reflect at least a couple of these categories, and most, even more.

These activities should be the rule, not the exception. I think this is the nagging realization that began to haunt me as I read card after card. These were considered the events that could only occur if there was enough time after the drill and worksheets and constant testing was completed . . . after "real" school work was amply attended to. Yet these are examples of those points in time when content and understanding and emotion collide in a child's brain and learning happens. As I read one card after another, I wanted to do two things simultaneously to these teachers: shake them and hug them. Shake them and shout that they should be doing this *all the time,* planning this kind of engagement with students and content all the time. Then hug them because I realize they are often fearful that they are straying from the pacing guidelines and could somehow be damaging their students. Although their gut feeling is that they know both their students and themselves are suffering from too heavy a dose of boredom from tedious prepackaged programs, the teachers also suffer from an artificial conscience that inadequate methodology has imposed on their sensibilities.

One interesting result of reading so many of these cards is the cumulative understanding of what teachers seem to imagine creativity looks like: students moving around, using outside materials, giving more choice to learners, breaking the normal routine, igniting spirited reactions from participants, allowing themselves to get involved and even get laughed at. I like this mix of ingredients to cook up a creative stew. Not a bad combination at any level.

---

41 Teachers' Input: Tell Me Something Creative You've Done in the Past Few Weeks

1. *Elementary School (general):* I have a baton that lights up—my "magic wand"—I let kids who are doing a good job hold it in line.

2. *High School (language arts):* Students wrote and recorded radio shows about a "teen theme," including personal stories and interviews of peers that related to them.

3. *High School (physics):* Students had to come up with their own ideas on how to make an air duct move the same each time.

4. *Middle School (literature):* After reading four short stories, students created an object using play dough symbolizing each of the main characters. Then they explained their choices to the class.

5. *Middle School (history):* We read about quilts used during the time of the Underground Railroad. We found and made patterns from paper, then actually made quilts in our class free time. I have quilt frames set up in my room. We use famous historical patterns, measure for math, learn about textiles for science. I want to teach my students an almost lost art and give them something to always do with their hands and time.

6. *High School (family and consumer science [FACS]):* My Level 1 FACS students design an adaptive device for a person with a disability. They could draw, write, or use actual materials. They also designed a room for the year 2108 using technology ideas.

(Continued)

(Continued)

7. *Elementary School (Grade 1):* As a group we made a chart of as many characters, settings, and events as we could think of. We chose two characters, one setting, and an event. We wrote a class story together using our choices with a beginning, middle, and end. We reread it, counted how many words we used (108), the number of spelling words we used, and contractions (our skill learned that week).

   The next writing day, I told them they could choose two characters, a setting, and an event. I asked them to write at least three to five sentences. This was a week ago, and I've had students write on this assignment all week when they had an opportunity. I was amazed at their enthusiasm.

8. *Elementary School (kindergarten):* I recently took sight words for kindergarten and created a fun new game. I cut stars out of yellow construction paper and wrote our sight words on them. I had them laminated and pinned them to the ceiling in my classroom. We turn out our lights and the students begin to sing "Star Light, Star Bright." I shine a flashlight on a sight word, and the students shout out the word!

9. *High School (biology):* We cut out images from *Missouri Conservationist* magazines of different living organisms. Then we hung them around the classroom and connected them with yarn to form a food web. The students had fun trying to make me knock things over as I crawled through the yarn spread all around my room.

10. *Elementary School (Grades 1–2):* I had puppets have a conversation about what makes a gold-star paper. The students compared a messy paper to a gold-star paper and came up with a list of things that made it a gold-star paper and then told the puppets.

11. *Elementary School (K–6 art):* Each month I've been painting a new Missouri bird somewhere on the walls at school. The first person to find and identify the new bird gets a prize. I want them to *look* at the world around them, to be observers.

12. *Elementary School (Grade 2):* We write a letter to the president as a gift for president's day, then I also make a silhouette of the kids' heads and place them on the wall of Past Greats/Future Greats with Washington and Lincoln. The president always sends a picture and a letter back.

13. *Middle School (literacy):* We watch an episode of *SpongeBob SquarePants* and discuss character traits of SpongeBob and Patrick. We write traits on the board and check as we go along which would go with which character. We make a Venn diagram for this.

14. *Middle School (history):* Our bulletin board has all 44 presidents' pictures. I ask students to find names of presidents in fiction books and write the title and president on a star by the picture. We celebrate at the end of February with a special day when everyone can wear or carry something that hints at who their favorite president is. We have an election for the favorite president after students give persuasive speeches for their choices over the PA system.

15. *Elementary School (Grades 4–6):* We hold a Living History Museum where the students research a famous person in history and prepare a speech. On museum day, they dress as their famous persons, bring posters, and have props. The lower elementary [students] come to see them "come alive" to tell about themselves.

16. *Elementary School (Grade 3):* When working on multiplication, we learn our facts using stories and rhymes. Example: 8 x 8 fell on the floor, picked it up it was 64.

17. *Middle School (science):* I have students summarize by writing a text message . . . 25 words or less, has to be comprehendible.

18. *High School (Grade 9 language arts):* The entire class went into the hall on the staircase to read the balcony scene in *Romeo and Juliet.* While Juliet stood at the top, the rest of us watched from Romeo's view.

19. *High School (language arts):* Teaching *Huckleberry Finn* and the theme appearance vs. reality, on the large paper doll body we put who the character *really* is, and on the paper doll clothes we write who they pretend to be and why.

20. *Middle and High School (language arts):* I have students cut out 20 random words and phrases from magazines, then have them put these words and phrases into a poem.

21. *High School (science):* I wrote my name on a T-shirt in permanent markers and then let my students put alcohol on it to separate the colors (chromatography). It came out looking tie-dyed, and they loved it.

22. *Elementary School (K–2):* As a transition sound from one activity to the next, I turn a kitchen pot lid upside down and scrape a whisk around the inside edge. (It sounds like the Disney Magic Wand sound.)

23. *Elementary School (kindergarten):* The students each stated a sentence. They then went to their seats and wrote their sentences. We corrected them and then rewrote them and traced the words with markers. They drew speech balloons around each sentence, cut them out, and I took a photo of each child holding their speech balloon by their mouth as if they were saying the words. I posted the photos in the hall for all to see.

24. *Middle School (science):* We learned weather symbols and drew them on a large map of the United States, then we did weather forecasts.

25. *Elementary School (Grade 5):* We wrote a story called "A Day in the Life of a Water Drop" after learning about the water cycle. As a prewriting activity, we acted it out and talked about how it would "feel" at each stage.

(Continued)

(Continued)

26. *Elementary School (special education):* My kids need sensory activities. We use shaving cream on the table to practice spelling words. We also make our own books to understand there is a purpose for reading.

27. *Elementary School (math):* For math lessons about money, we involve a real-life focus. The students have wallets, checkbooks, earn money, and spend money in the classroom.

28. *Elementary School (general):* To review for a test, I put A B C D on the four walls, and when I read the question they have to go stand by the answer they think is right.

29. *High School (special education):* I teach a Life Skills elective in Health to all my special education students. We have been talking about the food pyramid and nutrition, so I gave them the yellow pages and had them order two balanced meals from take-out menus and compare the two to find the healthier meal.

30. *Elementary School (general):* I use two huge ropes to form a Venn diagram in my classroom. Students then stand in the appropriate space when I call out the specific characteristic, color, data we are using to compare and contrast.

31. *Middle School (language arts):* After reading the short story "The Jacket," students choose one of their favorite or least favorite articles of clothing, write a description, and then illustrate it. I always receive very interesting responses.

32. *Middle School (history):* We make Pizza Biographies. We pick persons to research, then on each slice of "pizza" we write specific segments of information: accomplishments, dates, where they lived, etc. We put them inside a pizza box and decorate the outside with the name and pictures and sources of our information. Then we have a pizza party and share our information.

33. *High School (poetry/writing):* During a poetry unit, I have my students record one or more lines from each poem we read. I tell them to choose lines which move them, impress them, sound nice, etc. When we finish the unit, I put the students into groups of three or four and have them write a 5- to 10-minute play, complete with exposition, character development, conflict, climax, and resolution. They are to include as many of the lines they have collected as possible and still make sense.

34. *Elementary School (math):* The Human Multiplication Table. Students in groups of 10, each with a poster-sized number on their chests, form the answers for various problems.

35. *Elementary School (kindergarten):* While putting numbers 1–10 in the right order on the smart board, I pretend I am a four-year-old and ask them to teach me how to do it. They love to help me out.

36. *High School (Grade 9 history):* My students create Amendment Storybooks for a second-grade audience, with appropriate language, illustrations, explanations that a little kid could understand. We try them out on little kids.

37. *High School (algebra):* In Algebra we acted out the Associative Property of Addition by making an analogy of the property to students' calling each other to arrange a trip to the movies.

38. *Elementary School (literacy):* After reading the story "The Grouchy Ladybug," I took pictures of each of their grouchy faces and had them write about times when they felt grouchy. I put them together and hung them in the hall.

39. *Elementary and Middle School (general):* Many times I offer students options, and one of the options is to make it up as we go along. We have a Choose Your Adventure Day. When we finish one activity, I offer students the opportunity to choose the next activity—of course, I have a series of activities from which they can choose. We've gone from learning affixes to an onomatopoeia dance that the kids made up. They leave happy, and I don't mind taking work home.

40. *Middle and High School (history/communication arts):* I bury a group of "artifacts" from a specific age or time period outside on the school grounds. I bring in an "old map" to begin the unit and say we need to investigate what this map might reveal. . . . We go out and students follow the map until they can dig up these lost items just like they would do if they were archeologists. We then research the objects and deduct what they have to tell us about the time period we are now studying.

41. *All Levels (drumming, chanting):* While teaching *Things Fall Apart,* I showed them a drumming/chanting sequence we would do between discussions of the chapters. With the lights off and all heads down on desks, one person goes around the room randomly tapping each student on the shoulder. When a student is tapped, he or she begins either making a rhythmic drumming sound on the desk or with their mouth, or chants a phrase over and over or makes any other repeated sound. When all are drumming/chanting, the "tapper" goes back and taps each student again, but this time it is a sign to stop. . . . The volume decreases until the last person is tapped. Then the lights are turned on again and the class proceeds with the next section of the book. Surely this could be done with other material as well.

It's resourcefulness, not resources, that counts!

Table 1.1 Effective Teaching Strategies in Teachers' Creative Ideas

Example #	Choices	Novelty	Authentic Task	Multi Intelligence	Visual	Application	Celebrate	About Me	Problem Solving
1		×			×				
2	×			×				×	×
3	×		×			×			×
4	×			×	×		×		×
5			×	×		×			×
6	×		×			×			×
7	×					×			
8		×		×	×				×
9		×		×	×	×			
10		×			×				
11		×			×		×		
12			×				×	×	
13	×	×				×			
14	×		×	×		×	×		
15			×	×	×		×		
16				×		×			
17								×	
18				×	×				
19		×		×	×				
20	×	×		×					×
21		×			×				
22		×		×					
23	×			×	×		×		
24			×	×	×	×			

Example #	Choices	Novelty	Authentic Task	Multi Intelligence	Visual	Application	Celebrate	About Me	Problem Solving
25				×					
26	×			×	×				
27			×			×			×
28	×			×	×				
29	×		×		×	×			×
30		×		×	×				
31	×			×					
32	×	×							
33	×			×		×	×		×
34		×		×	×				
35			×	×	×			×	×
36			×	×		×	×		×
37				×				×	
38					×		×	×	
39	×			×				×	
40			×	×					×
41	×	×		×					

11

YOUR TURN

As an individual:

1. Look through the 41 examples and find a couple that deal with your students' level(s).

2. What are your thoughts about these suggested activities? Feasible? Too hard to duplicate? Write down your reaction to two of them.

3. What have you done in the past couple of weeks that you would consider creative?

4. If this isn't a sample of how you teach the majority of the time, why isn't it? How could it be? What do you need to do to see that it is a more frequent occurrence?

5. Check out the list of strategies in Table 1.1. Which check marks would fit your idea? Which of the categories do you embed in your planning? Which ones seem to be rarely utilized in your classroom?

6. Pick one of the categories that seldom get practiced in your classroom and plan a way to integrate an activity into one of your upcoming lessons.

As a teacher team:

1. Look through the 41 examples and find a couple that deal with your students' level(s).

2. What are your thoughts about these suggested activities? Feasible? Too hard to duplicate? Write down your reaction to two of them and then share with your team.

3. What have you done in the past couple of weeks that you would consider creative? Write down your answer and share with each other.

4. Check out the chart of strategies. Which check marks would fit your ideas? Which of the categories do you embed in your planning? Which ones seem to be rarely utilized in your classrooms?

5. Pick one of the categories that seldom get practiced in your classroom and plan a way to integrate an activity into one of your upcoming lessons. Share your plans.

TEACHERS VOICE THEIR CREATIVE BLOCKS

I wanted to give you a broad sampling of teacher-generated ideas on creative activities for a few reasons. I hope these examples will help you build a visual picture of teacher-perceived creativity across a spectrum of both age and subject matter. And I hope that seeing just how activities like these, which traditionally have been labeled "creative," are actually the very kinds of methods that increase understanding, memory, skill building, and engagement in our students. I also hope that you will garner the courage and enthusiasm to pepper your lessons with far more similar activities as an integral part of your everyday planning and lesson execution.

I urge you to look outside your own level or discipline to see how some of these ideas could be adapted for use in your own arena. I didn't include these simply for the purpose of having you replicate them in your classroom, though. I want you begin to recognize the patterns that they formed, the themes that prompted them. Being able to generate your own creative behaviors is a far better goal than just being content to mimic what I or anyone else hands you.

From the one thousand teacher input cards I collected, these questions probably produced the best gauge of teachers' current creative fever or lack thereof: What keeps you from being more creative in the classroom? Or what are the major blocks to your creativity? *Fear* is one of the most often expressed states of mind voiced by teachers. We will discuss this further in a chapter on strengthening one's creative abilities, but for now let's look at all the other various reasons teachers give for getting "blocked."

In front of fear as a factor is a lack of time—to plan, to think, to breathe. Those who have never had a full-time teaching job have no idea what demands are made on one's time. More than a few teachers remarked that strictly enforced pacing guides and the push for everyone to be on the same page at the same time leaves no room for creativity. One teacher described her situation like this: "Our district's curriculum gives you a step-by-step set of instructions. You are NOT allowed to deviate from the goals or activities in the unit. We are given six days to complete each unit. Each day is laid out at 10-, 15-, 20-, 30-minute intervals with specifics for each section. This really limits creativity!" Need I add that this also strips the teacher of any sense of empowerment or flexibility?

Even the most restrictive environment doesn't negate the possibility for creativity in implementation. Look at the teachers in Plano, Texas, whose curriculum is online; they have found ways to combine both the prescripted and the creative worlds, and the academic success in that district is outstanding.

Another often-expressed concern is the unbelievable amount of content that needs to be covered. I read this complaint on many cards. I keep thinking of the plea of most education researchers to look at content as something to be "uncovered" rather than "covered"—the plea to shift content into its reasonable place as a tool rather than a goal in itself. This message is not the one many teachers seem to be getting from the educational leaders in their districts.

Other teachers blamed their inability to be creative on a lack of resources. Despite all the studies that have come to the conclusion that students need to be exposed to a wide variety of materials, I often read that teachers find administrative restrictions on supplemental materials outside of the adopted curriculum to be one of the most frustrating blocks to creative teaching. As one teacher wrote, "When a district spends money on textbooks and corresponding workbooks, they expect us to use them." It is the state of fear, though, that we have the best opportunity to confront and change.

What dragon is keeping you from being more creative?

Although some teachers blame their lack of creativity on the students—they're too apathetic, too unmanageable, or there are just too many of them in a room at once—many went to the heart of the cause: themselves. As one teacher said, "I am the biggest block to myself. Laziness and not having confidence, being afraid of failure." Another wrote, "I often reinforce the idea, my idea, that I'm not a creative person because I'm not spontaneous. I realize that this isn't what creativity is all about, though." Another admitted, "I'm afraid of the chaos created by creativity. My left-brain dominance is strongly ingrained in my background, leaving me with an overwhelming lack of confidence in my creative abilities."

One high school math teacher found that this question about her own creativity peeled back a world of feeling and realization: "My block has always been the fear of failing and of looking foolish. I grew up in a 'dysfunctional' family before the term was ever coined—I could never do anything right, according to my Mom. My only worth was as a free housekeeper and a tax deduction. I still feel the effects (and so do my students), even though I'm 51 years old." Another teacher echoed this comment: "I fear not getting to the heart of the grade-level objectives and among other things is my fear of what other teachers will think or say about my creative techniques." One said it this way: "I fear being misunderstood. Sometimes a principal or other teacher passing by my room might think I am 'goofing off' rather than really teaching. I am afraid to trust myself." Each one of these blocks is a dragon guarding the castle doors to teacher creativity. It's not just those mythical knights in shining armor who needed courage to slay dragons; it's our human lot day after day.

YOUR TURN

As an individual:

1. What blocks to creativity do you experience in your own teaching? Write down as many as you can.

2. Put a check mark in front of those blocks that originate with you rather than come from the outside.

3. What small steps can you devise to face those blocks and perhaps diminish them? Write down two or three small, concrete actions you can take. Try one today.

As a teacher team:

1. What blocks to creativity do you experience in your own teaching? Write down as many as you can, and share your lists.

2. Put a check mark in front of those blocks that originate with you rather than come from the outside.

3. What small steps can you devise to face those blocks and perhaps diminish them? Write down two or three small, concrete actions you can take. Try one today.

4. Take an informal poll of your staff members on the subject of creativity. Ask them two of the same questions I asked the thousand teachers I came into contact with: What have you done in the past two weeks that you consider creative? What blocks you from being more creative?

5. Compile the good creative ideas and share with everyone. Use the list of blocks as the source of discussion at a faculty meeting.

JUMP STARTING STUDENT CREATIVITY: MAKING MIND MAPS

Before providing samples of what students have to say, I should first provide you with an activity that allows teachers and students to both discuss and experiment with the creative process in any content area or grade level. Probably one of the most foolproof strategies for jump-starting student creativity is instruction in the art of making and using concept or mind maps. While working for my state affiliate of the National Writing Project, I have had the pleasure of introducing mind mapping to hundreds of teachers in Grades 4–12. The majority of these teachers work in middle schools where this technique is being embraced with a great deal of enthusiasm. By googling "mind maps" you can gain access to a ton of examples and references.

As a brief introduction, let me say that my familiarity with mind mapping comes from the material of Tony Buzan. His path to developing his process is as fascinating as the process itself. His main goals were to find out how to use his brain more efficiently, remember material better, be able to problem solve more efficiently and with more creativity. In his search for answers, Tony, along with his brother Barry, made some very interesting discoveries. These discoveries, bolstered by brain research, convinced him that we think and remember far better if we use color, pictures, variety—all the right-brain functions—in concert with the usual left-brain functions. A whole mind is better than half, which should seem logical. He makes an impelling case in his books—specifically, *Mind Maps for Kids* (Buzan, 2003) is a great starting place for examples and an explanation of his process "as the easiest way to get the answers out of your head." This method also serves to "track down lost information," make projects "more creative, more organized, easier to keep control of, and will save you loads of time" (p. 97). Because we don't think in straight lines, the mind map contours our thoughts on paper with more accuracy and authenticity, which then delights the brain. In reflection papers about their projects, my students have echoed most if not all of these results of having used mind maps.

In *Mind Maps for Kids*, Buzan (2003) lists five easy steps to get students going. The following steps are not word for word, but do capture Buzan's directions:

1. Use a blank sheet of unlined paper—preferably larger than 8" × 11"—and some colored pens. Make sure the paper is placed sideways.

2. In the middle of the page, draw a picture that sums up your main subject. This is the main topic.

3. Draw some thick, curved, connected lines coming away from the picture in the middle, one for each of the main ideas you have about your subject. These central branches represent subtopics.

4. Name each of these ideas, and draw a little picture of each.

5. Now draw other connected lines like tree branches, and add thoughts on each. These represent details. Continue drawing pictures. Use a different dominating color for each "tree."

My use of mind mapping was twofold: as a vehicle for reviewing the material we had covered during the semester and to satisfy the requirements of an alternate assessment, which was to serve as one half of the semester's exam grade. I taught students the principles of mind mapping using Steinbeck's novel *Of Mice and Men* as the content. Since a first and even second try at mind mapping usually yields very poor products, I strongly urge teachers to whom I introduce this system to promise to allow students more than one or two opportunities to create mind maps. They aren't able to discover the freedom and sense of style that this activity demands until they hit the third or fourth try.

My assignment consisted of having the students prepare and turn in a manila folder with seven mind maps—two we did in class together, and the rest were done on their own time. The inside of the manila folder was to be used for their personal mind map containing four areas of their life and associations connected with them (family, friends, school, personality, preferences, hobbies, goals, etc.). The other five covered the material we studied in the semester: *The Adventures of Huckleberry Finn* (focusing on four of his aliases, why he needed them, the circumstances, and whether these aliases were effective); *The Catcher in the Rye* (focusing on Holden's relationships—categories of people, quality of relationships, symbols that would represent each relationship); stories by Edgar Allan Poe (focusing on his four story types, with examples and characteristics of each); and Miller's *The Crucible* (displaying each main character's motivation and subsequent actions along with the repercussions of those actions).

Student comments about this assignment provided an interesting peek inside their minds, for example: "I loved doing the personal mind map. I just love to see what I like and what I dislike. When I was working on it, my parents saw some elements that they have never seen before. Some I have been keeping a secret until now. I never knew how much fun it was. After doing them all, I felt that I understood the material really well." Another girl wrote, "I loved this assignment. Not only did I enjoy reading the books, but I also got to work on a project I love doing. Art is one of my hobbies and special interests. Whenever I get to incorporate art into anything, I get excited because I can be as free and creative as I want. I found that these mind maps reinforced what happened in each book's storyline and gave me visual ideas of the plots, helping me to distinguish among characters." One young person commented, "The pictures and colors used helped to relax the mind to not have to concentrate on reading words. Looking at a picture that has description is much easier than remembering what you got out of taking notes or reading a paper. It's colorful and bright—therefore interesting to the mind." A young man admitted, "I really enjoyed making these because they actually did help me remember things and also pushed me to be creative, which doesn't happen much."

Mind maps take more time to do than average assignments, and perhaps it is the very time they take that allows students to think over the subject in more depth and cement the major ideas more effectively in long-term memory. One student admitted, "I remember one night I stayed up until 2:30 a.m. working on these, but I'm not complaining, this assignment was SO MUCH FUN! And yes, I feel I have a good grasp on the material from this semester." Another student added, "Although it took so long, this was a very good assignment. It helped me understand and remember the material. It was something I looked forward to doing. All I have to do is glance at a mind map and the whole book flashes into my memory." And finally, "This assignment was a relief. It took time (lots of time) but it allowed us to show what we know, still having to think, without the pain and torment some teachers think is so necessary."

I gave students my aims for this assignment and asked if they had

- unleashed the enormous power of the visual cortex;
- enhanced the memory's storage and recalling capabilities through the use of images for emphasis and association;
- increased aesthetic pleasure—simple enjoyment of the images themselves;
- broken down resistance to the use of images and color in learning; or
- aided mental relaxation.

A young man noted, "I don't know what a visual cortex is, but I'm pretty sure I got some of the aesthetic pleasure and breaking down of my resistance to the use of color." Another student responded, "I experienced all of them. No, seriously, I did! It was fun spending hours at a time drawing and coloring. I haven't done that since I was little. It forced me to remove the cobwebs out of my 'creative' section in my brain and use it! I haven't done that since I was in the gifted program in elementary school, and I miss it." One boy said, "I experienced all of these and totally agree with these aims. For a few of the maps, I drew what I saw and I saw alone. That is the pleasure of this project; it lets one express his thoughts in a way that cannot be counted wrong or incorrect, it gave me rules and directions that I could bend and still do them right." And a last comment comes from a young lady who was initially skeptical: "At first I didn't like this assignment, but then I was surprised that drawing the pictures and mapping them out did make it much easier to remember little things about the stories that I otherwise would not have remembered, and it also made the project very enjoyable."

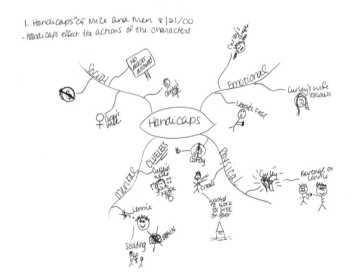

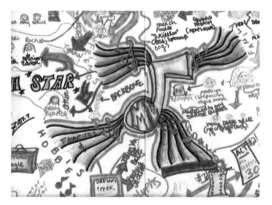

THIS IS NOT THE "CRAYOLA CURRICULUM"

I think that this is as good as any place in the book to make my distinction between creative drawing and coloring that has a precise focus and Mike Schmoker's (2001) nightmare account of what is occurring in many literacy classrooms across the country, which he aptly coined the "Crayola Curriculum." Touring hundreds and hundreds of classrooms primarily in the lower grades, Schmoker and his companions found that time which was set aside for literacy instruction was more often spent coloring than anything else. He quotes Kati Haycock, director of an education improvement nonprofit, as saying, "I can only summarize the findings by saying we've been stunned [that] . . . kids are given more coloring assignments than mathematics and writing assignments. I want to repeat that, because I'm not joking, nor am I exaggerating" (¶ 12). This situation is not an example of creativity in the classroom, but rather is a good reason why both administrators and teachers should be leery whenever the boxes of crayons are brought out more often than the reading or writing materials.

So how do we walk the line and balance the time we are given to do so much teaching? Many of the most engaging assignments my students were given that involved lots of multiple intelligence opportunities and hands-on application were what they did as homework. I gave ample time for completion, periodic accounts on what progress was being made, plenty of checks and balances and conferencing. I did not, however, use up an inordinate amount of class time. When I did these types of activities in the classroom, they adhered to a strict timeline and what didn't get finished in class went home for completion.

Now I can imagine many of your eyes rolling at me already, and under your breath I can hear you murmuring to your neighbor, "She didn't have *my* kids. There's no way I could expect to see anything turned in if I sent it home to do." I am well aware that doing work at home, or after school, or even in study halls is a hard sell for some teachers to make to their students. Much of that has to do with what expectations have or haven't been articulated, what longstanding cultural or simply neighborhood attitudes exist toward education in general, what age group we are speaking about. However, it is possible to change cultural attitudes within a school, or within your classroom at the very least. I've seen it done. There is far too much to be said and discussed about that animal named homework to be dealt with here. I simply want each of you to know that the black hole coined the "Crayola Curriculum" is not what I want you to fall into in the name of creativity. Creative thinking is not learned by wielding crayons alone.

YOUR TURN

As an individual:

1. Look up the available Web sites that give explanations and examples of mind mapping (the sample images that I include in this book will not be adequate in black and white to show their richness), or order a copy of Buzan's (2003) *Mind Maps for Kids.*

2. Go back and review the way I kept control of students' mind maps by supplying the focus of what I wanted them to contain.

3. As the material for a mind map, choose a unit of study, a point in your curriculum during which you will be reviewing, or a topic you are covering.

4. Show students samples of mind maps that are appropriate for their age group.

5. Try a couple!

6. What are your thoughts on the "Crayola Curriculum"? Do a private investigation to see whether your school would be on Schmoker's (2001) list.

As a teacher team:

1. Look up the available Web sites that give explanations and examples of mind mapping (the sample images that I include in this book will not be adequate in black and white to show their richness), or order a copy of Buzan's (2003) *Mind Maps for Kids.*

2. Go back and review the way I kept control of students' mind maps by supplying the focus of what I wanted them to contain. Discuss my assignment.

3. As the material for a mind map, choose a unit of study, a point in your curriculum during which you will be reviewing, or a topic you are covering. Share your choices.

4. Collect and show students samples of mind maps that are appropriate for their age group.

5. Try a couple!

6. Discuss the problem of the "Crayola Curriculum," and do a private investigation of your own school to see whether it would be on Schmoker's (2001) good or bad list. Discuss your results.

STUDENT BLOCKS TO CREATIVITY

Basically the same blocks that hamper teachers are the ones that hold back students as well. Students are terribly afraid of the judgments of others, especially their peers. A teacher who pronounces judgment on a fledgling attempt at creativity can cut the artistic legs right out from under a student. We all can remember someone in our past that did just that. Few of us are ever strong enough to ignore the authoritative negative reaction of a teacher when we are young. So nudging the artistically bruised student into taking risks is no easy venture.

One of the finest results of an in-depth professional development program that allowed teachers to meet consistently over time, to grow and develop together and actually try out the activities and assignments they give to their students, is the empathy and sensitivity that they develop for their students. If teachers don't write with students but assign writing, even frequently as is suggested, they have no idea what some of their requests feel like from the students' point of view.

Fear of being wrong, of not following teachers' directions precisely, of not giving them "what they want" are all blocking attitudes that grow year after year if they are continually justified by teachers' behaviors and expectations. We can easily cut into these blocks through our relationships with students and by providing an atmosphere in which we are seen to value taking a risk, asking a question, trying something new.

Another block experienced by students and related to the fear of not giving teachers what they want can be generated by teachers who consider themselves quite creative teachers. I've seen some of the most wonderful ideas and assignments teachers came up with ruined by the directions. If too much is decided beforehand and dictated with every possible variation covered, there's nothing left for students to do but follow orders. All the creativity has been taken up by the teacher; there's nothing left for students to choose, or solve, or create. Beware of directions that leave nothing to chance. They only stimulate conformity and squelch creativity.

As teachers, perhaps one of our jobs that I haven't really seen written down for consideration in the mainstream classroom is directly teaching students ways to unblock their creativity. Since I happily believe that the purpose of the universe is to bring you answers, I urge students to open their senses to what is all around them all the time: signs on buildings, bumper stickers, conversations overheard in the lunchroom, magazines casually flipped through, surfing the Web, an MP3 player on random dishing out a song you haven't heard for awhile, a chance statement a teacher makes that sparks curiosity. I introduce them to what Jung called *synchronicity*.

Over time, those of us who have grown to trust the competency of our subconscious tend to take for granted the kind of leap of faith this implies. Having young people discover this on their own is a giant step in crushing blocks. A student commenting on how her mind mapping developed wrote, "I also was able to just start putting pictures on the page, and when I finished drawing one, another picture immediately placed itself in my head." After reading this, I brought in an E. L. Doctorow quote about the creative process: "It's like driving a car at night. You never see further than your headlights, but you can make the whole trip that way." The young student felt that she was indeed experiencing the same phenomenon that one of those "really creative people" experiences. How empowering!

Another technique that students need to be taught is the art of "marinating." Most students haven't had enough experience to know that time is necessary for the subconscious to do its work on problems and challenges—time away from the problem, time to let the ideas simmer. The more they learn to trust their subconscious to serve up a good answer, the better they will be at accessing their intuitive abilities on a regular basis. One of the problems we have in the way we structure lessons is that we seldom allow for this simmering or marinating time. We say, "Think up an idea, now write, and turn it in tomorrow." We tend to get nervous if it looks as if a student is daydreaming. We don't often allow for thinking, do we? "Quit daydreaming and get to work."

Students need help in seeing past the first idea that bubbles up. This is one of the areas where teachers can be of such great value. When assigning anything, whenever possible, we should embed the opportunity to come up with many options, to consider a wide variety of possible paths to follow before settling in on one. Often when I was teaching writing, I had students write three or four variations on the topic and place their best one on top for close grading. They got credit for the other drafts but didn't take up my time by requiring me to scrutinize them closely. This way students got more writing practice, chose their finest piece, and I worked on one instead of four pieces per student.

I know this is addressed by the term *brainstorming*, but I think that the way we tend to implement brainstorming sessions is usually too quick and too isolated from the rest of the process. Often I find myself revisiting the brainstorming step in a creative endeavor far more than once. Students should experience that flexibility in doubling back and know that dumping an idea that isn't going anywhere is a natural and healthy process. In fact, I've found that if you are serious about helping students unblock their creativity, you need to spend much more quality time really teaching them what productive brainstorming feels and looks like. Consider just going through the brainstorming process by itself. You don't always have to write the paper, or construct the solution, or work out the problem; simply generating possible ways of doing something is a valuable lesson in its own right.

I want to address one particular group of students who seem to suffer from blocked creativity. These are our strongly left-brained students. As a teacher of honors-level students for many years, my rosters would always read like a who's who of science project winners, math quiz bowl giants, winners of scholarships from the top engineering schools, and national merit scholars. As you can probably tell by now, my teaching style would often tend to curl the hair of my rigidly academic scientific and mathematic thinkers for the first couple of weeks. Every year I would have the duty and privilege of "selling" them on the necessity as well as the validity of implementing creativity into instruction. I had great answers for the "Why do I have to do this?" and "How will this help me?" types of questions.

Appealing to these students' already overstuffed logical brains, I draw the picture of how they will be competing later on for a place in the best schools, for selection by the best companies or firms, and so on. I show how there are hundreds of students just as good as they are. So what would give them an edge? What would make them the better candidate than those who are as good at math or science or logical reasoning as they are? The ability to use both sides of their brain, not just counting on that one hefty left side to get them through. Then I promise that this is the year, and I am just the person to help stretch and strengthen their right-brain abilities in a safe environment. I know how uncomfortable this will be for them at times, and I assure them that I will be there to give support and guidance. No, their "grade point" will not suffer by the possible missteps they make as they take risks in areas that aren't their strong suits. We have a goal and purpose as we begin the year's work. I am going to prepare them to be far better equipped to maneuver in the competitive marketplace that is surely in their future. They give me a chance to do this for them.

The school year is like a runner's marathon, and I help them exercise *both* legs. It makes for smoother running!

A PAST STUDENT'S E-MAIL ON CREATIVITY

The following e-mail came from a woman I taught 10 years ago as a sophomore and junior in high school. We had resumed contact after she purchased a couple of poetry books I had published. I invited her response to Chapters 2, 3, and 5 of this book while it was in rough form.

> Your chapters really got me thinking about creativity, especially the difference between truly creative assignments and fluff. Definitely have a lot to learn about the research done on learning, etc., although what comes out above all in your book is that good teaching takes into account the research but also relies on your own instinct and life experiences when dealing with people. I loved the story about your pink hair! It made me miss my grandma, who totally would have done that. Told my husband about your race around the track with the kid who wouldn't sit in his seat, and he got a big kick out of it.
>
> I closely read the section on the analytical honors kids because that most related to my own experience, and I have been thinking a lot about challenges for that group. What creative projects did for me was to help me broaden my identity. School can feed smart kids' addiction to success, which is not helpful for real life. Our identity can easily become tied to academic achievement, and we need ways to cultivate other parts of ourselves. After being very successful at Wash U, I suddenly found myself not accepted to any of the graduate

school programs I applied for, married, working as a receptionist in Chicago. Had to quickly remember that writing A papers and reading complicated articles was not all of who I was. It was a very hard time (think you had a poem about finding a Plan B that is along this theme). We need more in school that builds identity around who we are, not what we do. Also I'm thinking about another of my classmates, who you may remember. He is a computer programmer now but also one of the most creative people I've ever met—how sad if he had never had a chance to cultivate that part of himself. He and my husband still laugh about some game they made up for your class about a security guard in a mall.

A. B.

YOUR TURN

As an individual:

1. What are the signs of creative blocks that you see in your students? What do you do to counteract them?

2. Do you ever ask your students how *you* are doing? What you could change to make an assignment better? What to keep? Write down what you could possibly learn from doing this with your students.

3. Make your own template questionnaire for students to "talk to themselves" about how they handled an assignment and what changes they would have made if they'd had the time or inspiration.

4. What observations can you make about my former student's e-mail? How can this relate to your relationships with your current students?

As a teacher team:

1. What are the signs of creative blocks that you see in your students? What do you do to counteract them? Share concrete ways that you do this.

2. Do any of you ask your students how *you* are doing? What you could change to make an assignment better? What to keep? Discuss what you could possibly learn from doing this with your students.

3. Make your own template questionnaires for students to "talk to themselves" about how they handled an assignment and what changes they would have made if they'd had the time or inspiration.

4. What observations can you make about my former student's e-mail? How can this relate to your relationships with your current students?

PROLOGUE #2

Before We Begin . . .
Get Out Your Notebook!

Your participation in this book is important. Creativity isn't the kind of information that goes into the brain very easily. It needs to go through the body, heart, and soul then swirl around for a while until it feels comfortable and at home. You don't memorize creativity like you did the times tables as a small child. You already have seen a set of questions to consider, activities to try out. These are set up for you to use by yourself (as an individual) or with a small group of fellow teachers (as a team). Both sets are similar but arranged for the opportunity to share and discuss if working with others. Before we begin, here is your first opportunity to "participate" in this journey:

YOUR TURN

As an individual:

1. After reading about what others think creativity is or should be, it is probably best for you to think through just what your initial ideas on the subject are at this point. Please set a timer or check your watch, and take at least 10 minutes to freewrite your ideas on what you think of when you hear the word *creativity*, especially as it relates to education.

   A freewrite is an unstructured writing experience during which you aren't at all concerned about the order in which ideas flow out onto the page, what form they take, what possible mistakes you might be making in conventions. It's an exercise in generating ideas and digging up what you think about a given topic. If the 10 minutes aren't over and you find you can't think of anything else to say, just write about how you can't think of anything else to say! Keep your pen or pencil moving for the whole duration.

2. Go over your freewrite, and underline the words or sections that seem to really say what you feel about creativity. Sometimes these fundamental feelings on a topic don't actually appear until you have written for 5–10 minutes.

As a teacher team:

1. After reading about what others think creativity is or should be, it is probably best for you to think through just what your initial ideas on the subject are at this point. Please set a timer or check your watch and take at least 10 minutes to freewrite your ideas on what you think of when you hear the word *creativity*, especially as it relates to education.

   A freewrite is an unstructured writing experience during which you aren't at all concerned about the order in which ideas flow out onto the page, what form they take, what

(Continued)

(Continued)

possible mistakes you might be making in conventions. It's an exercise in generating ideas and digging up what you think about a given topic. If the 10 minutes aren't over and you find you can't think of anything else to say, just write about how you can't think of anything else to say! Keep your pen or pencil moving for the whole duration.

2. Find a partner. Either read each other's paper or talk about them with each other. What common ideas do the two of you share? What different ideas do the two of you hold?

3. Thank your partner for sharing, then find another person to partner with and repeat the discussion of freewrites.

4. As a whole group, have one person chart out the most commonly used phrases and attitudes that tend to bubble up from the group. Be sure to make room and include ideas that don't seem to fit with the majority of opinions.

2

What Is, What Isn't Creativity?

AN OVERVIEW OF PRECONCEPTIONS

Recently, a young teacher was interviewing for a job as an administrator in a large school district. One of the people from the 10-member panel asked him, "When it comes down to it, which is the more important, creativity or instruction? Which would you choose?" He immediately replied that you don't choose between the two—they coexist. Creativity doesn't stand alone outside of instruction as an add-on; rather, it's the vehicle for good instruction.

The panelist didn't seem to get it, and the teacher didn't "get it" either—the job, that is. He had dared to utter the *c* word as a necessity in engaging middle school students and counteracting the school's dismal rate of student failure and classroom management issues. He dared to suggest that instead of stricter guidelines on student behavior, perhaps it might help to focus on helping teachers examine their style of delivery and build their creative tool chests with options that line up with best practices and current brain research findings. He suggested that teachers don't need to work harder but rather smarter, and creativity is a big part of that smarter approach. All teachers can be helped to utilize the energetic power of their own creativity more effectively.

Discussing the false conception of what creativity is, Edward de Bono (1988) writes, "Serious Creativity will seem a contradiction in terms for many people. Everyone knows that creativity has to be fun, lively, and crazy—so how can we have serious creativity? It is precisely this misconception about creativity that has done so much damage and has held back the development of creativity for at least two decades. There are far too many practitioners out there who believe that creativity is just brainstorming and being free to suggest crazy ideas" (¶ 1–2). This misconception exists not only in the professional worlds of research, business, economics, and medicine but also, most important, in the world of education at all levels.

Fluff. Administrators hate fluff, and with good reason. The teacher who offers "fun" activities that have no basis on or relationship to the curriculum goals or standards is the teacher who destroys the safe environment for true creative teaching for everyone. Good, effective teaching has every strategy and activity thoroughly embedded into the unit or lesson for a specific purpose. Many times I used to cringe when a fellow teacher took an activity of mine that had a high level of engagement for students and used it with his or her class in a totally out-of-context manner, just because it seemed like a "fun" activity.

The effective, innovative, creative teacher is the one who knows *why* this project or strategy is valuable and can explain and defend its worth to anyone wishing to know, can cite the research-based findings that encourage it, and can show how it reinforces the central purpose of the lesson. Most negative attitudes concerning creativity flow from a prior knowledge of someone who misuses and misdirects creativity without a legitimate purpose. Other negative attitudes stem from a sense of uneasiness at how messy creative activities can appear to be, how a classroom may seem to be on the verge of chaos from an outsider's point of view. And the truth is that some classrooms are and some aren't on that verge of chaos at times. To many, it seems so much more efficient to tell students something than to allow them to discover it for themselves. A quiet room seems so much more disciplined than a noisy one. Disciplined, yes, but not always educationally alive.

If this book does anything, I hope it strips the word *creativity* of those connotations of fluff, eccentric, extra, artsy, warm and fuzzy, some mysterious talent and instead forms a picture of creativity as a serious thinking tool that facilitates problem solving and problem discovering for a new and untested future. Pann Baltz, who is involved in the Creative Classroom Project, a collaboration between Project Zero and the Disney Worldwide Outreach project, has said, "Although most people might look for signs of creativity in the appearance of the bulletin boards, student made projects, centers and displays in the classroom, I feel the truly creative classroom goes way beyond what can be seen with the eyes. It is a place where bodies and minds actively pursue new knowledge. Having a creative classroom means that the teacher takes risks on a daily basis and encourages his/her students to do the same" (quoted in Morris, 2006, p. 2). Seeking out and recognizing true creativity and what copious rewards it can bring to your classroom are perhaps the most important results you should aim for while considering the material in this book.

The Creativity Matters Campaign was the outcome of a summit held October 30, 2007, in Tacoma, Washington. At this summit, close to two hundred educators and leaders addressed the importance of creativity and imagination in the education of Washington's students. This group offers the following definition of *creativity*:

> Creativity is the capacity to make or express things that didn't exist before or to solve problems in new ways. It's different from imagination, which is the ability to conceive of new things; creativity is about the doing of what is conceived. Creativity is also distinguishable from innovation: innovation is the product of creativity; an innovation advances a form or the state of a field of knowledge or endeavor. The chain of concepts flows as follows: creativity is imagination applied; innovation, in turn, is creativity applied. (¶ 2)

From Rudolf Flesch we get this definition: "Creative thinking may mean simply the realization that there is no particular virtue in doing things the way they have always been done," which touches on the role of creative thought in questioning the status quo. In today's changing world, our students depend on all of us to question the status quo of educational structures and ideas in order to prepare them for a tomorrow that will be very different from yesterday.

And finally, a bottom-line basic definition for creativity is . . . a new idea that works. There are plenty of new off-the-wall ideas that people can and do generate, but that doesn't make them creative. Those ideas should be useful and able to move the learning forward productively. Those ideas should be a lovely mix of a reach into the fresh, the different with a firm grasp of the pragmatic and useful.

YOUR TURN

As an individual:

Looking at your written piece on what you think of when you hear the word *creativity,* highlight any of your descriptors that are also mentioned in this section. Consider just where your attitudes fall in relation to this opening piece.

As a teacher team:

Looking at your written pieces on what you think of when you hear the word *creativity,* highlight any of your descriptors that are also mentioned in this section. Have someone highlight those terms on the chart as well. Consider the team's principal attitudes on the whole topic of creativity so that you have a baseline before you begin this investigation.

WORSHIPPING AT THE ALTAR OF RIGHT ANSWERS

What the book *Lateral Thinking,* by Edward de Bono (1970), has given me are the labels, the words I needed to wrap around my own experiences so that I can explain them with more clarity. Just as most research-based information often resonates as the truth that teachers know already in their gut, so de Bono's language serves as the gift I needed to better explain what is true and worth sharing with fellow teachers.

More important, is the explanation that vertical (critical) thinking is contingent on being right all the time and excluding anything that isn't right along the path, whereas lateral (creative) thinking is about being right in the end—not necessarily along the way. Lateral thinking is concerned more with change than with proof. The best scenario is to use both methods in concert and to teach students to do the same.

As you are probably aware, there are many who think that creativity is only for special brainstorming sessions or that creativity is not for them but for artists, designers, and inventors. de Bono (1970) cites this as a dangerous and limiting attitude, especially for educators. As he aptly points out,

THE ALMIGHTY RIGHT ANSWER

A dangerous mind-set for students and teachers alike!

education is soundly based on the *need to be right all the time*. Throughout education one is taught the correct facts, the correct deductions. . . . One learns to be correct by being made very sensitive to what is incorrect. . . . This sort of thing is the very essence of vertical thinking. [Yet] exclusive emphasis on the need to be right all the time completely shuts out creativity and progress. This need to be right all the time is the biggest bar there is to new ideas. (p. 108)

MAKING MISTAKES

One of the drawbacks of this emphasis on being right, which incidentally has been fueled even more directly by the current focus on scoring well on high-stakes tests, is the fear of making mistakes. This fear is generated in both teachers and students. We teachers need to be conscious of how this toxic attitude can build in our classrooms. If we begin wondering why class discussions are growing flatter and flatter, why fewer students are willing to ask questions or offer ideas that aren't always found in the text, if we begin to find our students more comfortable with mediocre output rather than ignited with the desire to try a different approach, if we are getting bored with the stale cookie-cutter papers we bring home to grade, we need to do something about it! What do we do? We make risk taking one of our priorities. Awareness of a problem is always the first step to solving it.

Our students are afraid of giving us wrong answers. Continuous drill and whole-school emphasis on high-stakes testing has built a shrine to the Right Answer. Students grow to see that education is a hunt for the Holy Grail named Right. One teacher counteracts this by beginning the school year using *Mistakes That Worked: 40 Familiar Inventions and How They Came to Be*, by Charlotte Foltz Jones (1991). In it are short reader-friendly stories accompanied by great cartoons of the mistakes that brought about dozens of objects we use every day. The teacher cuts up a couple of copies of the book and has pairs of students choose the mistake they want to work with and report on. They make large posters that are then taped up around the classroom. As students explain the strange beginnings of everything from Coca-Cola to cheese, from aspirin to X-rays, from the Frisbee to glass, from Levi's jeans to VELCRO, the concept seeps in: in this class, you are expected to take chances, make mistakes, try out ideas; risk-taking attitudes and behaviors are valued. Of course, as the year goes on, the products that this teacher receives from her students prove the validity of this concept. The students know that not only are they safe, but they are urged to try things, to reach out in the unknown and see what they can discover.

One interesting finding in current brain research is the fact that the brain is not naturally concerned with right answers at all, but rather is taken up with the processes of arriving at answers (Nadia, 1993). The difference between these two offers an intriguing insight into students' motivation and at times their seeming inability to get excited about right answers in the first place. When I give Beginning Teacher Assistance Workshops—a Missouri requirement for certification—to new teachers, one of the ideas I emphasize is the need to make sure everyone in the class is "playing school." By which I mean being an active, thinking participant in what is going on—no heads on desks, no blank daydreaming stares, no text messaging, no giving attention to anything besides what is going on in the lesson—I'm talking about full engagement.

Who Knows the Answer?

Students grow to know that teachers hate silence after they ask a question. When we ask, "Does anyone know the answer, or have an idea?" there is always a sprinkling of students that know their names aren't *Who* or *Anyone* and never even consider trying to think up an answer to our questions. And we often fold and call on that sweet little girl in the front row who always has her hand up. What is happening in these classrooms and particularly to these nonparticipating students is the building of the habit of non-thinking. If we feel that the goal of the questioning segment is to arrive at the answer, instead of everyone going through the process, we will be satisfied with the recitation of those students we can count on who always answer correctly. But later we will be frustrated by the fact that so many don't seem to remember what had been covered in those discussions. The fact is those students weren't playing school.

So what do we do? This creativity is geared toward seeing that all students think. So never ask for *who* or *anyone.* In fact, don't call on students by name until you have given them all a chance to play school, to think. Hand out scrap paper, and have students jot down what they feel would be a good response. Then have them exchange with their neighbor. Now you can ask if anyone read a good answer; everyone should have something to say with no fear of being wrong. I find that if the answer or response is a good one, the student who reads it takes full credit, but if the answer or response isn't quite on the mark, the student will point to the student who wrote it and put the blame there—but most important, everyone is thinking. This isn't really a flashy show of creativity, but much of what we do day in and day out won't be the flashy, in-your-face, fireworks display kind of creativity. It will pull students into the lesson and get them thinking—it will be a new idea that works!

YOUR TURN

As an individual:

1. Have you ever found yourself questioning this "right answer" emphasis? Have you ever seen students whose need to be right has kept them from being able to take a chance and trust in what they really think? What do you do, or can you do, to counteract this?

2. I use the phrase *playing school* to mean student engagement. What do you do, or can you do, to see that students play school with you? Make a list of what you already do to tease them into joining the group and participating.

As a teacher team:

1. In your group, discuss how this "right answer" emphasis plays out in your classrooms. Have you ever seen students whose need to be right has kept them from being able to take a chance and trust in what they really think? Share what each of you does to counteract this.

2. I use the phrase *playing school* to mean student engagement. What do you do, or can you do, to see that students play school with you? Make a list of what you already do to tease them into joining the group and participating. Share lists, and add these cools ideas to your individual lists.

SPECIFIC METHODS OF CREATIVE BEHAVIOR

As I mentioned earlier, de Bono gave me the labels I need to more easily explain what I've found to be methods for generating my own creativity over the years. Three of those labels are (1) cross-disciplinary fertilization, (2) using an alternate entry point into the material, and (3) the power of randomness to stimulate fresh pattern making. In this segment, I translate these techniques into more readily accessible examples from personal experience. These are techniques that every teacher can use to improve both the quality of their students' performance and their own understanding and grasp of creativity in their classrooms.

Cross-Disciplinary Fertilization

In my list of 20 Keys to Creativity, which appears in the prologue to Chapter 3, I call this my Mixing and Matching key. This is one of the most successful structures you can use to develop lessons and units that produce engagement and quality products. This mixing also has the effect of subtly shifting the content into its rightful place as a vehicle for thinking about larger, more important ideas and questions. The textbook is a tool, not the curriculum and not the driving force of the teacher's purpose in drawing out students' understanding of important issues.

By cross-disciplinary fertilization, I mean taking two different disciplines (mix math with language arts, cooking with math, etc.) or two different fields of information such as Joseph Campbell's (1991) stages of the hero's journey applied to Steinbeck's short story "Flight," or Art Costa's (1995) 12 indicators of intelligent behavior applied to the main character in Orson Scott Card's (1991) science fiction bestseller *Ender's Game*, or Shakespeare's "Seven Stages of Man" sonnet applied to Poe's rooms in "The Masque of the Red Death." The pattern or structure is to match up the given curriculum with something that wouldn't usually be used with it but that presents a totally novel and interesting source of comparison and avenue for study. The effect of this mixing of two pieces of information that are not often matched together is a fresh approach to a more traditional method of studying material— one that grabs students' interest and curiosity, throwing a brighter light on what the teacher wants the them to consider, think about, understand.

Periodic Table of the Presidents

A good example is this twist on the periodic table of elements, which mixes history with science. This table was the brainstorming result of a young history teacher as he was driving home with his wife one evening and started playing with the idea of just how the presidents would fit into the periodic table. As always seems to happen, a creative idea generates a great deal of energy and enthusiasm in the creator. To the drawing board he went and developed this amazingly complex, thoughtful chart. Being a young teacher in this technologically advancing world, he also went right to e-Bay and offered his table for sale to anyone who was interested.

Periodic Table of the Presidents

KEY:

Franklin Delano Roosevelt — President's Name
32 — Number of President
Fdr — Name Abbreviation
1933–1945 — Year(s) in Office

Died in Office of Natural Causes
Assassinated
Resigned
(i) Impeached

PARTY (while in office):

No Party
Federalist
Democratic Republican
Democratic
Whig
Republican

Major U.S. Wars:
*indicates periods of U.S. involvement

Major U.S. Wars:
- War of 1812 (1812–1815)
- Mexican-American War (1846–1848)
- Civil War (1861–1865)
- Spanish-American War (1898)
- World War I (1917–1918*)
- World War II (1941–1945*)
- Korean War (1950–1953)
- Vietnam War (~1964–1975*)
- Persian Gulf War (1990–1991)
- Iraq War (2003–)

Founding Fathers

| George Washington 1 **GW** 1789–1797 | | | | John Adams 2 **Ja** 1797–1801 |
| Thomas Jefferson 3 **Tj** 1801–1809 | James Madison 4 **Jma** 1809–1817 | | James Monroe 5 **Jmo** 1817–1825 | |

Young Nationhood

| John Quincy Adams 6 **Jqa** 1825–1829 | Andrew Jackson 7 **Aja** 1829–1837 | Martin Van Buren 8 **Mvb** 1837–1841 | William Henry Harrison 9 **Whh** 1841 | John Tyler 10 **Jt** 1841–1845 | James K. Polk 11 **Jkp** 1845–1849 | Zachary Taylor 12 **Zt** 1849–1850 | Millard Fillmore 13 **Mf** 1850–1853 | Franklin Pierce 14 **Fp** 1853–1857 | James Buchanan 15 **Jb** 1857–1861 | Abraham Lincoln 16 **Al** 1861–1865 | Andrew Johnson 17 (i) **Ajo** 1865–1869 |

Gilded Age

| Ulysses S. Grant 18 **Usg** 1869–1877 | Rutherford B. Hayes 19 **Rbh** 1877–1881 | James A. Garfield 20 **Jag** 1881 | Chester A. Arthur 21 **Caa** 1881–1885 | Grover Cleveland 22 **Gc** 1885–1889 | Benjamin Harrison 23 **Bh** 1889–1893 | Grover Cleveland 24 **Gc** 1893–1897 | William Mckinley 25 **Wm** 1897–1901 |

Early 20th Century

| Theodore Roosevelt 26 **Tr** 1901–1909 | William Howard Taft 27 **Wht** 1909–1913 | Woodrow Wilson 28 **Ww** 1913–1921 | Warren G. Harding 29 **Wgh** 1921–1923 | Calvin Coolidge 30 **Cc** 1923–1929 | Herbert Hoover 31 **Hh** 1929–1933 | Franklin Delano Roosevelt 32 **Fdr** 1933–1945 | Harry S. Truman 33 **Hst** 1945–1953 |

Global Power

| Harry S. Truman 33 **Hst** 1945–1953 | Dwight D. Eisenhower 34 **Dde** 1953–1961 | John F. Kennedy 35 **Jfk** 1961–1963 | Lyndon B. Johnson 36 **Lbj** 1963–1969 | Richard Nixon 37 **Rn** 1969–1974 | Gerald Ford 38 **Gf** 1974–1977 | Jimmy Carter 39 **Jc** 1977–1981 | Ronald Reagan 40 **Rr** 1981–1989 | George H.W. Bush 41 **Gb** 1989–1993 | Bill Clinton 42 (i) **Bc** 1993–2001 | George W. Bush 43 **Gwb** 2001–2009 | Barack H. Obama 44 **Bho** 2009– |

Used with permission from P. J. Creek.

34

Cooking Up Lessons

Another example that teachers use successfully from early grades on up is taking a vocabulary list specific to a given field and using it to serve as an overlay for another purpose. I took a cookbook and began listing all the verbs used to describe methods of cooking. Then I gave students a generic list of what is commonly found in a recipe and had them make their own recipes. The vocabulary list in Table 2.1 is from just such an assignment that was used to open a discussion of expectations on the part of both the teacher and the students in a math class.

Table 2.1   Words for Processing Foods, for Use in Recipe Writing: The Verbs

Add	Caramelize	Drain	Leaven	Pare	Score
Arrange	Chill	Dredge	Marinate	Pasteurize	Simmer
Bake	Chop	Fold in	Mash	Peel	Skewer
Baste	Combine	Fricassee	Mask	Place	Steam
Beat	Cover	Fry	Melt	Poach	Stew
Blanch	Cream	Garnish	Mince	Pour	Stir
Blend	Crumb	Glaze	Mix	Render	Thicken
Boil	Cut	Grate	Mold	Roast	Toss
Braise	Devil	Grind	Pan-broil	Roll	
Brown	Dice	Knead	Parboil	Sauté	
Candy	Dissolve	Lard	Parch	Scald	

Classroom Radio Talk Shows

I, like many of you, am always on the lookout for interesting outside texts, structures, examples to better present the material I have been given to teach. Many of my assignments begin with taking structures students are most familiar with and "cross-pollinating" them to manipulate the course work. Radio talk shows, for example, make good structures for discussion of material familiar to the whole class or, even better, for a front-loading activity before studying the material. Take a topic or theme that will soon show up in the students' reading or that has just been in their reading and make it the topic of the radio talk show segment. Give out cheat-sheet questions for call-in participants the first time you use this strategy so students see what it will sound and look like. The panel includes three roles: an expert on the subject, the host, and a guest from the book.

An example would be having a talk show while reading the first few chapters of *The Adventures of Huckleberry Finn* and focusing on the theme of child abuse. I would have an expert (a social worker perhaps) who comes prepared with statistics and expert information to present; this is a great job for those students who need to be stretched, differentiated with challenge activities. The other guest is Pap; his job is to defend his behavior.

Students are urged to ask their own questions after those from the cheat sheet have all been covered. I suggest that you serve as the host and moderator the first time. Later, let go and hand that part over to students. We use a microphone (props are always easy engagement tools) and keep the segment to a strict time limit, around 15–20 minutes. This way it doesn't drag on, students want to do it again, and it doesn't absorb too much of your precious class time. You can schedule a few of these over the course of the unit and have students sign up to prepare the various roles.

The secret is in keeping it short and compact. If you spend too much time on these kinds of activities, you jeopardize your focus on the major goals you are trying to reach and fall into the stereotyped group of creative teachers whose kids have fun but never really learn anything. It's this that scares administrators and diminishes the role of creativity in everyone's classroom.

If you would like more information about these types of activities that students of all ages adore and respond to positively, order any of the wonderful books by Jeffrey Wilhelm. Some of his most well-known titles are *"You Gotta BE the Book"* (1997), *Action Strategies for Deepening Comprehension* (2002), *Engaging Readers and Writers With Inquiry* (2007b), and *Going With the Flow* (2006; cowritten with Michael Smith). Wilhelm has written over 16 in all, and in each one he makes a consistent bridge between his activities and good teaching research. Creative teachers have these books in their personal libraries. The more we learn about the body and the brain, the more we find the need to teach students of all ages through their bodies and to drop the notion that learning is a "heady" and passive experience. Embracing this single fact and allowing it to guide your planning will move you to more and more productively creative teaching experiences. Ah, the preacher in me is surfacing! And I know I'm preaching to the choir.

Ender's Game

Since the purpose of school-based learning is ultimately, according to Bransford, Brown, and Cocking (2000), the transfer of knowledge from school to the everyday environment, one of the best methods of accomplishing this transfer is in the context of a performance project. John W. Thomas (2000) explains that projects enable students to be able to make immediate connections between content and application. He emphasizes that "learning is maximized if the context for learning resembles the real-life context in which the to-be-learned material will be used" (p. 7), which is the fundamental basis for project-based learning.

As Eric Liu was quoted as saying in a *Teacher Magazine* article, "students need to be taught to use their imaginations to solve problems, to connect the dots. . . . Good teachers are already doing this, but the idea needs to be given a higher priority, and project-based and experiential learning should replace some book work and tests" ("Courting Creativity," 2007, ¶ 6). What I like about Grant Wiggins and Jay McTighe's (2005)

Understanding by Design is the discipline it exerts on the teacher to keep a main focus on the final goal—the articulated understandings that are at the heart of learning. This discipline protects the teacher from getting so involved in the activities and projects that the reason for doing them in the first place is ultimately lost on the students.

I developed my favorite example of cross-disciplinary fertilization in conjunction with the Show-Me Classroom Performance Assessment Project, utilizing the work of Wiggins and McTighe (2005) through a Pattonville School District Grant. I used Arthur Costa's (1995) 12 indicators of intelligent behavior: persistence; decreasing impulsivity; listening to others; flexibility in thinking; metacognition; checking for accuracy; questioning; drawing on past knowledge; precision of language and thought; using all senses; ingenuity, originality, and creativity; and wonderment, enjoyment, and curiosity.

In an online interview for the *Journal of Advanced Academics*, Costa explains how he began compiling these Habits of Mind:

> We have identified numerous habits that people have, and these are the habits that cause them to be successful in life in careers, in marriage and family, as well as in academic pursuits such as college. These habits include persisting, managing impulsivity, thinking about their own thinking, being conscious of their actions, understanding the implications of behaviors and their effects on others, and using clear and concise language to adequately communicate. This means knowing how to ask questions, surface the problems, be creative, and be innovative. (Richards, 2007, p. 313, reprinted with permission)

I felt this was a perfect element to insert into my teaching. Students are always fascinated with any information that sheds light on how they think, why they act the way they do, and how to get a handle on bettering themselves. Anytime I learn anything that relates to current research on the brain, the body, the world we live in, I share it with my students.

So my big idea was this: successful individuals act intelligently. My essential questions were: What are traits of intelligent behavior? How can one identify intelligent behavior? These served as the fulcrum for adjusting the springboard of activities and strategies I would be assigning and employing throughout the unit. I love the focus on understanding that is emphasized in *Understanding by Design* (Wiggins & McTighe, 2005), not only for its discipline but also because it asks planners to anticipate students' misunderstandings. No topic is more misunderstood by students than intelligence, and our schools are often to blame. A reliance on single test assessments to inform students about their success or failure has many children thinking they don't possess the intelligence to do well in the future. This unit is geared to dispel that narrowed notion of intelligence for students.

The other element I used was *Ender's Game* (Card, 1991) because it is such a compelling read. My assignments therefore would be designed to really put students through their paces and stretch them. In my later years as a teacher, I have been all about processes and giving students experiences that would build the skills necessary for them to succeed as adults. I saturated students with Costa's (1995) 12 indicators. They made posters, gave explanations of what these indicators meant and looked like in everyday life, and wrote which ones were their strengths and how they applied to their lives. The students were amazed that these were the things that measured whether they were intelligent. Nothing on the list had a thing to do with grades or testing. They were simply amazed. Then we read the book once for fun. One girl who had sworn she could never enjoy a science fiction book—she was an honors student and enjoyed more philosophical material—came to my room three hours after I had handed out copies of *Ender's Game* and told me she had finished it already. She told me it couldn't really be science fiction because she absolutely loved it!

Next, students went through the book, charting examples of each of the 12 indicators that were exhibited by the main character. I gave them removable dots to put in the book as they went through it again and two charts—one to put page numbers on and another to write down the specific examples.

Students don't get enough practice speaking orally for any measurable duration, nor do they understand the difference between writing an in-depth paper and presenting it. They are also used to looking for their weaknesses instead of their strengths; this experience was one of mapping out strengths—their own and the main character's. As the language arts department chair, I had access to a tiny office next to my classroom. I set the room up to hold a presentation desk, a panel of four adults (I was not one of these), one ex-student who had read the book, and a video camera. In here, each of my 126 juniors would deliver their persuasive report on why Ender should be chosen as head commander. They were to use their formal paper as the basis for their report, but not read it to the panel; they were to use visuals (posters, pictures, graphs) to support their arguments, which came from the 12 indicators of intelligent behavior. They were to choose any 5 of the 12 to use as the bases of their report. Since each student entered the room to meet the panel and shut the door behind him or her, no one saw or heard any of the presentations except those in the room. This solved that problem we have all experienced of the first couple of students having the hardest time and the rest of the class learning from their mistakes as the reports are given. In this case, everyone went first!

My students had their first experience of facing a panel of adults they didn't know and keeping their composure while trying to present their case. Some came out feeling they had done a terrible job because they had forgotten to say some of the things they had planned. I told them that this is a common feeling most of us have had during job interviews, that the people on the panel didn't know if a student had forgotten anything; they only heard what was presented. I sent the videotapes home for students to see just what their presentation really looked and sounded like. Often they would return surprised that it seemed pretty good and not nearly as bad as they had previously thought, which was a good lesson for each of them. Those whose performances were marred by poor body language, reading more than speaking to the panel, or rolling the chair in and out of the view of the camera all saw this as they viewed their tapes and didn't need me or anyone else to point it out to them. Watching the tapes was the immediate feedback that is so often lacking but so vital to student improvement.

When each student was finished, I had him or her sit down and eat a clementine before returning to class—time to calm down the jitters. These days, I can't look at a box of clementines without thinking of those presentations. Whenever I bump into students I've taught in the past, this unit is brought up more often than any other as the one they remember most vividly. Some are young teachers now themselves and are teaching this unit to their students.

Taking an outside piece of information or strategy usually not found within the normal course work and applying it to material covered within the discipline has the potential to spark curiosity, new insights into the course material, motivation, novelty, and a fresh approach to the structure of the content delivery. This technique of cross-disciplinary fertilization brings a richness to the learning experience, which leads to more depth of thinking and expansion of learning. It certainly served as one of the strongest techniques that I used, allowing my creativity to flourish.

YOUR TURN

As an individual:

1. This section focuses on the creative technique of cross-disciplinary fertilization. It deserves a page in your journal. After labeling a page, write down a definition for this concept in your own words.

2. I gave three types of examples: mixing two different fields of information, applying a familiar "pop" structure to traditional material, and pulling in another thought structure to direct the focus of the text. Use these as subtitles on your journal page, and write down the examples I gave as samples.

3. Think back to any examples you can give from your own teaching, times when you applied this technique successfully, and add them to your list.

4. When teachers work together from different disciplines to form lessons, this is the creativity technique they use. Is this done on a regular basis in your school? If so, has it been successful? Why or why not?

(Continued)

(Continued)

As a teacher team:

1. This section focuses on the creative technique of cross-disciplinary fertilization. It deserves a page in your journal. After labeling a page, write down a definition for this in your own words. Share with your group.

2. I gave three types of examples: mixing two different fields of information, applying a familiar "pop" structure to traditional material, and pulling in another thought structure to direct the focus of the text. Use these as subtitles on your journal page, and write down the examples I gave as samples.

3. Think back to any examples you can give from your own teaching, times when you applied this technique successfully, and add them to your list. Share your past experiences with the teachers in your group. Jot down any of their ideas that you might find useful in the future.

4. When teachers work together from different disciplines to form lessons, this is the creativity technique they use. Is this done on a regular basis in your school? If so, has it been successful? Why or why not?

Using an Alternate Entry Point

This second method of creative behavior has worked for me in more ways than simply seeing that my students are engaged. This is the method that also gives a purpose to their work, gives meaning, which focuses them on a goal that is larger than the material itself.

Kindergarten Style

A close-to-home example is my husband's granddaughter, Charley, a kindergartener who was studying maps in school. The final project was to send her Flat Stanley paper doll that she had colored to someone who lived in a different town. Many of you may be familiar with Flat Stanley projects and the series of children's books by Jeff Brown and Scott Nash. For those of you who aren't, Flat Stanley is the main character who was flattened by a bulletin board that fell on him while he was sleeping. He discovers many advantages to being flat. He can go anywhere by sliding under doors, getting folded up and mailed away, flying in a breeze like a kite. Charley's Flat Stanley arrived in the mail at our house with the instructions that he was to stay a week and then be returned to the class with a letter describing what he had seen and done and what this new place he was visiting was like. What a cute assignment and a great entry point into the concept of maps for little learners! It was as much fun for me to do as it was for Charley to report on once her Flat Stanley was returned. The teacher would locate our house at the Lake of the Ozarks, Missouri, on the map and read what an interesting adventure this place afforded Flat Stanley.

High School Style

If you or any of your fellow teachers aren't convinced about the power of identifying purpose and an alternate entry point as a means of producing that purpose, one of the best activities a teachers' group can try out during a professional development meeting is found in Chris Tovani's (2000) *I Read It, but I Don't Get It.* Included is a narrative titled "The House," which describes what a boy sees as he walks around his friend's house. The piece is approximately six short paragraphs in length. Students (or teachers) are requested to read the piece and circle with a pencil any words or phrases they find important. As Tovani comments, no one ever asks a question but rather jumps right in and begins finding important words to circle. Then readers are asked to use a highlighter to highlight any words or phrases in the text that a robber would find important. Readers find this read-through much easier because they have identified a specific purpose. Then they are instructed to use a highlighter of a different color to find those words and phrases that a potential home buyer would find important. Again, the task is easy and everyone vividly sees the point of just how important it is to set a purpose for reading a text.

Until students are able to create or recognize a purpose for reading a piece on their own, it is our job as teachers to help set their course and make the reading experience more likely to yield comprehension. This is where using an alternate entry point comes in for me. If students are not offered a "reason" to read a particular piece, they almost always slip into the mind-set of a default purpose: Do I like this material, or don't I like it? This was never brought home to me so clearly as when I was teaching Salinger's *Catcher in the Rye.* When I started the novel with students without any outside purpose (alternate entry point), I fought the continual complaints from a few students about how weird Holden was, how they didn't like his language, how offended they were by the book. These students were in the default mode of finding a reason for how they felt about the book.

The next time I taught it, I went about it altogether differently. This time I set up the book as a case study, gave the students the role of psychological evaluator and the job to determine by studying his case just what was wrong with Holden, what professional observations led to that determination, and what recommendations they would make to facilitate his recovery. They would hold discussions over his file, interviews, research possible causes and suggested treatments. As they read, they kept a journal, answering a couple of questions about each section and answering the following two questions each time as well: What did you find out about Holden in this section that you hadn't known before? What unanswered questions do you still have? While completing this focused assignment, none of my students complained once about the language, the crazy behavior, anything. They were mentally in the mode of psychologists and expected abnormal behavior. Their job was to analyze and come up with solutions and causes. Nothing is a better alternate entry point than giving a student a role and consequently a purpose for reading. It always works. This is a portion of the set of ongoing activities that the students do as they read. I must confess this activity isn't my "creation," but it sure is the kind of project-based unit I love to write myself. I found this unit by David Grant in Grant Wiggins's (1998) *Educative Assessment: Designing Assessments to Inform and Improve Student Performance.*

Some of you might recognize this type of prompt writing as role-audience-format-technique (RAFT). It gives students not only an entry into better writing, but also a purpose for more comprehensive reading. The idea of easy material/difficult activity can always be brought about when you use the RAFT prompt method.

YOUR TURN

As an individual or as a teacher team:

1. The RAFT writing strategy involves four elements:

   R—Role of the writer (Who or what are you?)

   A—Audience for the writer (To whom or what are you writing?)

   F—Format of the writing (What form will your writing assume?)

   T—Topic + a strong verb (What are you writing about?)

   What was the RAFT assignment that Charley's teacher gave me to do? What was the gist of the RAFT assignment that I gave to my students reading *Catcher in the Rye*?

> 2. Type "R.A.F.T. writing" into Google. Check out the many sites that give examples of this writing strategy in various curriculum areas. Hopefully you can see how easily this format can be adapted to any age group and any discipline.
>
> 3. Write a mock-up RAFT assignment for material you are presently teaching.

The Power of Randomness

Of the three methods of stimulating creative thinking we are examining here, the power of randomness might seem the most unusual. The brain, this pattern-making machine, is constantly trying to make sense of the information that floods our senses and grabs our attention. And that "making sense of it all" results in patterns that we construct to explain the reality around us. Although the brain takes great pleasure in taking random and chaotic information and ordering it, deviating from those patterns we originally constructed is not always easy or comfortable. Creative thinking is deviating from the patterns we expect to see, which makes creative thinking an act of stepping out of the brain's normal way of processing information. Not always easy. We are reminded that "the brain is not designed to think creatively but to set up routine patterns of perception and behavior and to make sure we do not deviate from these" (de Bono, 1988, ¶ 5). Yet once there is group or personal awareness of the need for creative thinking, once there is an expectation and value placed on it, anyone can become more adept at strengthening this ability.

One way to fool the patterning system of our brains into taking a different path is to insert a random word, phrase, idea into the mix. What our brains then do is try to assimilate this new mental object with the patterns that already exist and to then serve up an altered pattern for our consideration. In an active (patterning) system, the random word provides a new entry point. As we work back from the new entry point, we increase the chances of using patterns we would never have used if we had worked outward from the subject area (de Bono, 1992).

In Chapter 4 I will have you work with novelty items—tiny unrelated things that you use to start up or insert as part of your own lessons. It will be an exercise in using this concept of random stimulation. But for now, I offer an illustration of just how our brains deal with random words to come up with interesting ideas by using a set of random word chunks as the basis for a dynamic writing activity. It is important to stress the fact that anyone can build a similar list of word chunks just by opening up a book and pulling unrelated words and phrases out and typing them into short lists. Try hunting for descriptive words and interesting verbs, of course; but other than that, it doesn't matter what the words are or how unrelated they might seem at first glance. Take a look at the page of lists that I created:

Writing From Word Chunks

blue swan	sugar bowls	signal
lake	cloudy glasses	reach
ceramics	coffee cups	steal
morning sun	ashtrays	follow
window sill	gray aprons	turn
curtains	cash register	stretch
Mother	open for business	leap
		yell
clouds	car	branching
scrape	Grandpa	stream
granite	chrome	underfoot
rocks	shine	shadow
ledges	polish	conscious
gray movements	creak	smoke
brown voices	Sunday	Mary
white light	smile	
happiness	roads	radiant moon
July	twist	raging
wading pool	scramble	wheeled
beach towel	confuse	only a dream
building blocks	voices	dot of sweetness
Tonka trucks	tangle	hushed
two arms	dissolve	cheek
Jonathan		border
wicker rocker	glaze over	remember
slow hands	assume	giggle
whittle	new way	slouched
carvings	woman	colored squares
green years	Muslim	pots and jars
yesterday	hero	stampede
tomorrow	talk	splinter
hawk	free to go	rendezvous
black on blue	cigarette	swallowed
shadows	credit	manners
follow	abnormal thought	hopscotch
circle	Why do this?	giant birds
settle	money	macaroni
scream	electric rain	whisper

Students and teachers are instructed to look over the word lists and choose any set that seems of interest. They are to use these words/phrases in a short narrative—one with a beginning, middle, and end. The point is not to get the words into the narrative as fast as they can, but to use them when they seem appropriate. The pieces that are generated from this activity are always such a surprise to the writers. It's a perfect exercise to show students just how their brains work overtime to make patterns from unrelated material.

Another variation on this would be to take a paragraph or a poem and, using a spreadsheet application, type each word on a separate line and then click on the program's "alphabetize" feature. Hand out the alphabetized list of words to students with the instructions that they are to use as many of them as they can to come up with a paragraph or a poem of their own. Then have them compare theirs with the original. Doing this, they can feel their brains working to put meaning into a random list of words. It's really interesting. Basically, as Lackey (n.d.) puts it, "the implications for learning and instruction [are] that presenting a learner with random and unordered information provides the maximum opportunity for the brain to order this information and form meaningful patterns that will be remembered, that will be learned. Setting up a learning environment in this way mirrors real life that is often random and chaotic" (¶ 15).

In any curriculum—science, math, history—a great assignment is to comb the chapter or unit for about 15–20 words that will be key to the meaning of the material. Have students write sentences embedding no more than 2 or 3 of these words in each. As the unit progresses, have students reread their sentences and mark whether they are accurate or not. At the end of the unit have them rewrite all their sentences, making corrections where needed, and turn in both the original set and the reworked set.

YOUR TURN

As an individual:

1. Try out the word chunk exercise. See what you come up with!

2. Make a set of word chunks from material you have just studied with your students. Have students choose a few of them to write about in order to show what they have learned.

3. Take a paragraph or poem on a topic you will be introducing and alphabetize the words contained in it. Have students write using the words. This can serve as a preloading activity before beginning work on a particular unit of study.

(Continued)

(Continued)

As a teacher team:

1. Try out the word chunk exercise. Give yourselves around 15–20 minutes to complete your pieces.

2. Read your creations to each other. Discuss the process and how you arrived at the choice of word chunks as well as the narrative you produced. Discuss how you could use this in your various fields.

3. Discuss how you could take a paragraph or poem on a topic you will be introducing, alphabetize it, and have students write using the list, serving as a preloading activity before beginning work on a particular unit of study.

20 Keys to a More Creative Classroom

1. Relearning to Pretend, to Imagine

   Imagination is more important than knowledge.

   —Albert Einstein

2. Using Action

   We learn to do something by doing it. There is no other way.

   —Robert Holt

3. Finding Your Cheerleaders

   Creativity flourishes when we have a sense of safety and self-acceptance.

   —Julia Cameron

4. Challenging Ourselves

   It is more important to ask one good question than to settle for easy questions with obvious answers.

   —Beverly Nance

5. Mixing and Matching

   Creativity generally involves crossing the boundaries of domains, so that, for instance, a chemist who adopts quantum mechanics from physics and applies it to molecular bonds can make a more substantive contribution to chemistry than one who stays exclusively within the bounds of chemistry.

   —Mihaly Csikszentmihalyi

6. Following Your Passions

   Creativity is available to all of us. We need only reach for it. Choose it. Embrace it. Life is too brief not to follow our passion and live in the fullness of our creativity.

   —Michael Toms

7. Welcoming Humor

   Humor has been found to liberate creativity and provoke such higher-level thinking skills as anticipating, finding novel relationships, visual imaging, and making analogies.

   —Arthur Costa

8. Creating Multi-Multi-Multi Options

   When everyone has more choices in their lives, they accept more choices and flexibility in others.

   —NLP [Neuro-Linguistic Programming] Manual

9. Discovering Surprise and Curiosity

   Without awe life becomes routine. . . . [T]ry to be surprised by something every day. . . . [T]ry to surprise at least one person every day.

   —Mihaly Csikszentmihalyi

10. Practicing Adaptability and Flexibility

Flexible thinkers display confidence in their intuition. They tolerate confusion and ambiguity up to a point, and they are willing to let go of a problem, trusting their subconscious to continue creative and productive work on it. Flexibility is the cradle of humor, creativity, and repertoire.

—Arthur Costa

11. Listening to Your Body

The mind is the flow of information, via neuropeptides among the cells, organs and systems of the body, body and mind are inseparable and would be more aptly called the *bodymind*.

—Candace Pert

12. Knowing You Are Enough

The authority in the classroom is and must be the teacher. As a teacher, I don't want some outside agency or publisher creating my agenda. I am the world's only expert on my students at this point in time in my particular school and classroom. Therefore, the ultimate professional decision-making power must rest with me. But to wield this decision-making power effectively, I must deeply understand pedagogy and I must know my own students.

—Jeffrey Wilhelm

13. Allowing Yourself Big Thoughts for Innovation

Creative thinking may be simply the realization that there is no particular virtue in doing things the way they have always been done.

—Rudolf Flesch

14. Developing the Courage to Take Risks

To live a creative life, we must lose our fear of being wrong.

—Joseph Hilton Pearce

15. Thinking With Metaphor

Metaphor is the right brain's unique contribution to the left brain's language capability. Metaphors beget poetry and myth, and are essential to the parables of religion and the wisdom of folktales.

—Leonard Shlain

16. Playing and Mimicking

The creation of something new is not accomplished by the intellect but by the play instinct acting from inner necessity. The creative mind plays with the objects it loves.

—Carl Jung

17. Finding Novelty and Props

Overall, you'll want to provide a rich balance of novelty and ritual. Novelty ensures attentional bias. . . . [P]rops, noisemakers, bells, whistles, costumes, music, or singing can get attention.

—Eric Jensen

18. Knowing Your Critic and Your Creator

   One of our problems is that we mix them up so that while we're trying to create, the critic is tapping at our shoulder saying, "Don't do that. Don't say this." We freeze. So it's [writing without stopping] a way of separating it out.

   —Natalie Goldberg

19. Honoring Creativity in Yourself, Others, and Your Environment

   One needs to demonstrate tolerance and appreciation of unusual thoughts, original ideas, or creative projects, teach students to accept, acknowledge and appreciate their own creative thinking behavior and production.

   —Arthur Copley

20. Walking, Writing, and Water

   If you are seeking creative ideas go out walking.

   —Raymond Inmon

   Writing can take you to a place inside yourself—the true source of creative power.

   —Natalie Goldberg

   Thinking, problem solving, and creative processes are slowed when the body is low on fluids.

   —Eric Jensen

3

Memoir of a Creative Career (Abridged)

MY FIRST CREATIVE TEACHER

This autobiographical piece is a short set of segments about my personal dance with creativity during my teaching career, my own ongoing transformation as an educator. I do need to set the stage, though, by painting a picture of just how creativity came to be such a valued commodity in my outlook on life. My mother was my most influential teacher. She died a week after my 16th birthday, but not before instilling in me the compass I would need to guide me through life. I grew up in a home environment that honored risk taking, took delight in everything that was fresh, curious, and unusual. Conformity was considered a fault. I was taught that I was the sculptor of my own life, that quality didn't necessarily mean expensive. We never worshipped at the altar of consumer labels, although many of our friends did. Nothing received a sneer in our household like the phrases "everyone else is doing it" or "everyone else has one." Our only competition was always ourselves, even our school grades were looked at with only mild interest—school was our job and ours alone, our parents never became overly involved or interfered.

I grew up knowing there were tons of options just waiting to be called upon to solve any problem. If I came home with a boring, stilted topic for an essay, we would sit around thinking up all the possible ways we could put life into the paper, make it fun to write. Everything was a challenge just waiting for us to twist into something interesting. As a 15-year-old, I put a rinse on my hair in preparation for a big dance. It was a disaster. My hair was pink, and it wasn't going to change anytime soon. My mother put me in the car, and off we went to buy a new dress to match it. We found the perfect dress in the perfect shade of pink. I went to that dance with my pink head held high as if I had planned the whole look weeks earlier. She gifted me with courage, an unlimited supply of options, and a delight in the originality of life.

YOUR TURN

As an individual:

1. Write about how creativity was viewed in your household as a child. Can you recall examples of when you and your family created your own family rituals or special days? Talk about evidence of creative thinking in your growing-up years when you were urged to do things your own way.

2. Pick out a sentence or phrase in my piece that particularly speaks to you. Explain why you chose this and how it relates to your experience.

As a teacher team:

1. Working in groups of four, have someone designated as the timekeeper. Each person is to talk for two uninterrupted minutes about his or her family experience with creativity. No one is to comment or add to anyone's remarks until all four have finished their two minutes of talk.

2. Discuss among yourselves how your early experiences have colored your attitudes toward creativity as an adult. From this short segment, discuss how my early experiences have probably influenced my attitudes in the classroom.

A FIRST-YEAR TEACHER

I began teaching in an all-girls' private high school in Illinois. Being new, I got the classes that weren't snapped up by more experienced teachers: the low-level English literature class and all the religion classes for the freshmen and sophomores. I was also the newspaper sponsor after school. My roster ran way over 225 students, but the new modular schedule allowed us to sandwich counts like this into a five-day week and still see that each course covered the required number of minutes. Sometimes I would see a class of more than 100 students at a time for an hour. Other times I would see small groups in 30- or 45-minute segments. If I ever lost my color-coded schedule, I would never have been able to function. I never could memorize it; it was too random to even wrap my brain around.

But this was my first year of teaching, and I didn't know any better to worry—I was definitely a young, eager, romantic idealist much like many new teachers I meet today. Curriculum? For my one section of English literature, I was shown the school book room, had the English literature novels pointed out to me, and was handed a textbook. For all my religion classes I was given a flyer from a Catholic weekly bulletin distributor, which had five quotes from the Bible—one for every day of the school week. That flyer appeared in my mailbox every Friday and was the sole material and manual I was given.

Pressure is a serious producer of creativity. I was pressured indeed to rely on my own resourcefulness to keep those classes of chatty, wiggling teenagers engaged and somehow learning what my little sheet of Bible quotes had to offer. I was left to invent the wheel. We used cooperative learning before it had a name; we took ideas from whole chapters of Jeffrey Wilhelm's books before he had even learned to print in school. We kept journals, interviewed people on religious concepts, invented character education before it was in vogue. We did projects using music, art, oral presentations, poetry, research. We were savvy about multiple intelligences before Gardner (2006) had formulated his thesis. We had to be. The only other option was chaos or, worse, anarchy. This is when I first came to see the immediate value of writing as a tool for digging out ideas and seeing what students were thinking. I saw my job as to create opportunities to revisit and take a new look at old ideas, to see anew and with more thoughtfulness, to broaden the horizon and landscape of the mind through the manipulation of information. As I think back, I can see now that I have never changed my initial view on what my job in education was—not in 36 years.

There were no expectations placed on me except to keep students busy and in the room. A different era completely, it was the most wonderful training ground for a young teacher to try things, take risks, learn what a classroom's dynamics felt like, and never feel guilty that she was not doing what was expected. I was the manual.

YOUR TURN

As an individual:

1. Write about the pressures you experienced as a first-year teacher and how you found your own creativity bubbling up to solve your problems. Give an example of one particular episode in which your creativity served you well.

2. Name a new teacher in your building now who could use a little support. Surprise him or her with an offer of assistance, or a surprise package of extra supplies that you have, or a set of lessons that really worked for you. Be creative in reaching out!

As a teacher team:

1. Share with your group what your first-year of teaching was like now that you have a little distance from it. Talk about the pressures you experienced, and give an example of one particular episode in which your creativity served you well.

2. New teachers seldom have much in the way of money or supplies. Pretend your team is in charge of throwing a "New Teacher Shower." Make a wish list of all the supplies that a new teacher could use that aren't issued by the district. Talk your Parent Teacher Organization into funding this endeavor.

MY HOME TEACHING DAYS

I produced four children in five years in the early 1970s. Because it was financially impossible for me to stay home, I took on part-time work home teaching for the Special School District of St. Louis County, a unique district that serviced the special education needs of the surrounding public school districts. They gave me as many cases as I could reasonably handle. I would go to students' houses or institutions—mental or detention—anywhere from two to four days a week for an average of three to six months depending on the individual circumstances. I tutored students in Grades 7–12 in English, math, social studies, and literature. Many were pregnant, while others were dying of cancer, suffering from anorexia, or saddled with extreme behavioral problems, mental illnesses, paranoia, or broken legs. Anything that would keep a child at home for a few weeks qualified as a case for home teaching.

During these years I honed my teaching skills and came away with a foundation that would have taken three times as many years to acquire in a traditional classroom setting. I found out I could teach anyone anything if I broke it down enough, allowed ample time, and was able to find the right metaphor for a student to link new material to what was already known.

When I received a case, I'd visit the school to see what courses I would be responsible for, pick up the course description and any text books they could give me (often the teachers didn't have enough books to send one home). Usually the school only wanted a grade at the end of a grading period and no other paperwork. I never met with the student's teachers, but I did see to it that each child had a portfolio of work to give the teacher upon reentering the class. Basically, I was once more free to do anything I wanted within the thin boundaries of the course description. I loved this arrangement. I would have been in heaven if only there had been Internet access back then.

I discovered that far more time is taken up with discipline, management, and housekeeping tasks in the regular classroom than when teaching one on one. In our hour to hour-and-a-half sessions, we covered three or four times as much as I ever could have under regular classroom circumstances. Upon returning to the classroom, my students always either were weeks ahead of the others or had covered the topics in far more depth and with much more reading and writing under their belts. I was always conscious of this time discrepancy later when I went back to a regular classroom. I always tried to cut down on the time that wasn't taken up with teaching and use every minute, bell to bell, for instruction.

In the home teaching situation, I had the luxury of allowing students to follow their curiosity. If we were doing a unit on the short story, instead of simply reading the stories in the anthology, we'd read everything I could find for them by authors who piqued their interest. I would be reading new material right along with them. A student and I would become experts on Flannery O'Connor's work. Another student and I would become experts on Jack London. Curiosity fueled our choices. We would talk style and patterns, make connections from one story to another. It was so much fun, and I was learning so much! In 1976 one student gave me a book to read by a new young author who wrote really weird stuff; it was *Carrie,* by Stephen King. Another guided me to some great science fiction writers I would never had tried otherwise. I read what they recommended; they read what I recommended.

One seventh-grade boy was home because he exhibited such behavioral problems in class. My job was to teach him basic math and reading. From him I learned the value of "out of the box" strategies, of hands-on learning. Since he wasn't sick, I didn't see the need to stay in the house, so I made every visit a field trip. This was an opportunity to make every lesson real and dynamic, what we now call an experience in authentic learning. We went dumpster diving for soda bottles one day. Each was worth 5–10 cents if returned to a grocery store. We collected enough to fill the trunk of my car, added up our treasures, turned them in for cash. We brainstormed and calculated what we could buy with our new money. We figured out how many bottles we'd have to collect to purchase big-ticket items. Other days we measured public parks, the widest a person's bottom could be to use the swing sets. We went on sign-reading excursions trying to find words we couldn't make out; we found pages of words in museum descriptions of art, on movie marquees, on fancy restaurant menus. Each session turned out to be a work of art for both of us. We laughed a lot. A heavy dose of novelty was the prescription I found most successful for him. No, I don't advocate dumpster diving with a class of sixth graders, but I include this anecdote because it was an important learning step in my development. It ingrained in me the need for reaching across the textbook for just the right hook to catch every student.

I could fill a book with just my home teaching adventures—the times I drove young girls in labor to the hospital to have their babies; the boy who never said a word the whole time I taught him, and that was well over 75 hours; the girl who was thrown out of her house because she was pregnant, and I had her living with us until she delivered her baby; the mother who served me sassafras tea in a washed-out orange juice can—abject poverty; the father who stood outside the door guarding my car from theft or vandalism the whole time I taught his daughter. I learned firsthand what the worlds of our charges look and feel like.

YOUR TURN

As an individual:

Underline or highlight 10 words or phrases that seem important to this section as they apply to creativity. Use these words or phrases in a paragraph of your own. You don't need to write about my experiences, but rather your own. The point is not to get as many words in as few sentences as possible, but rather to let them guide your thoughts as you write. Try to use most of them. Change any forms of words to fit your needs.

As a teacher team:

Do the same activity that is written above. Read your paragraphs to each other and discuss which words you chose in common. Discuss how easy or difficult it was to do this activity and why it felt this way.

BACK TO THE TRADITIONAL CLASSROOM

I got a full-time job once more in junior high teaching language arts. Here I learned again what being the new teacher meant and felt like. In my career I was the "new teacher" more than seven times. I was always assigned classes no one else wanted and given the worst room in the building, if any room at all. I became an expert in New Teacher Survival. My foremost strategy was to make anyone in my classes the envy of the school. My classes were to be the ones everyone wished they were in, the finest place to be, the most exciting place to be. When teaching Repeater 9th Grade English in one school later on, I'd have students ask how they could enroll in one of my classes. I'd say, "Well, you would've had to have flunked your English class and since you passed it already, you're not eligible." I had a board member angry that I was wasting my talents on "those kids," saying I should be teaching the honors classes where his children were. As a mother of a child with learning disabilities, I saw in those early days just how prevalent that mentality was and how it steered strong teachers away from the "low achiever" classes. I only wish my son had been the recipient of the upgraded special education with professional personnel that I see in schools today. We have come a long way in this area.

Let me talk about one specific seventh-grade low-achieving language arts class. This was in the years before letters and labels were attached to student files—no LD, BD, ADD. Nothing except "low," so they were all placed in one class: mine. Talking, jiggling, dropping things, throwing things, shouting to others across the room were the rule of behavior. I turned to that old favorite, behavioral modification strategy, for help. Armed with a large timer and an even larger box of malted milk balls, I began the process of taking back the classroom.

They reacted just like the books said they would. We moved from 30 seconds of quiet to 45; from 45 seconds to a minute. Each segment was accompanied by malted milk balls for those who could stay still for the duration. When we finally got to a couple of minutes, I taught frantically, telling them all the while that this is what everyone else's classrooms feels like. Telling them that now they were acting like all the other students in the school. Everyone wants this no matter what the disability, the handicap. We were finally on a roll.

One student, however, never earned one malted milk ball. He was in continual motion around the room. I found out that he was the fastest runner in the class and won all the races in last year's end-of-the-year school picnic. I told him I didn't believe he was very fast at all, that I could beat him hands down. I said that if he would stay in his seat the entire week, on Friday the whole class could go out to the track and I would race him and embarrass him in front of everyone. He stayed in his seat. We went to the track. He beat me by a mile. But I was the real winner. He was my buddy now, and with the promise of a rematch later in the year, he tried his best to stay put.

I learned that if I could teach these sweethearts, I could teach anyone. We did kinesthetic grammar. I had them write an S on the top of their left hands, an O on the top of their right. I told them that their bodies were verbs. By finding a noun on the left and one on the right, they would usually be right in properly labeling them subjects and objects respectively. That's our sentence pattern!

Most of my students at this level had no clue when they should start another paragraph, so they never indented at all. I got sick of these long blocks of writing and developed the two-inch rule: "I don't care if you know anything about how to determine when you need a new paragraph. When you get to around two inches, indent anyway! Fake it until you get it!" Our state tests give partial credit to students who "attempt paragraphing," and what happens after a little while of using the two-inch rule is that many students kind of figure out what it all means and eventually add another sentence when it makes better sense. The rule simply takes the pressure off of them, and in reality they usually change topics about that time anyway.

I cut my creative teeth teaching those who needed teaching rather than assigning. I stretched my brain to find ways to make concepts clear and understandable. Ways to have them repeat skills without getting bored. Each success was such a thrill and an impetus to think up more and better strategies that would work. My later years saw my honors students benefiting from the same teaching skills that I had learned in those early years.

Remember: everything you need to know is within you.

YOUR TURN

As an individual:

Pretend you were me and it was you taking your class out to the track to race one of your students. On your return, your principal stops you and asks you to come into his office after school for a short talk.

1. Write down what goes through your head as you wait for the end of the day to go by.

2. Write a short dialogue on how that conversation goes. How do you explain to the principal what you were doing with your class?

3. Check your dialogue. Did you use a confident tone of voice, or did you sound guilty and caught in the act? How did your principal respond to your explanation? How does your tone and confidence make a difference in the way efforts at creativity are received by others?

As a teacher team:

Pretend you were me and it was you taking your class out to the track to race one of your students. On your return, your principal stops you and asks you to come in to his office after school for a short talk.

1. Divide your team into pairs.

2. Pair 1: Role-play the afterschool conversation between you and the principal. The person playing the teacher should use a confident, excited tone explaining her success.

3. Pair 2: Role-play the same conversation, but this time the teacher uses a guilty tone of voice and lots of apologies and regrets.

4. Discuss the difference in the principal's responses to the two teachers. What does this say about how we project our own creative efforts?

EARLY YEARS AT FRANCIS HOWELL SCHOOL DISTRICT

Even in 1969, while interviewing for jobs, I avoided those districts that proudly announced "every ninth-grade teacher will be on the same page on the same day in the entire building." I felt that those people never taught in the classrooms I was in. Who were these people? Didn't they ever experience fire drills? Unexpected assemblies? Early dismissal that cancelled the last two classes of the day? Groups than needed more time or less time to cover the material? How about the flu season, when a whole section of a class would be missing? Of course I recognize the Herculean need in some areas for methods such as pacing guides, even for scripted learning that can provide a structure for teachers and students who sorely need it. But I've always felt this should never be the norm or the goal of a professional teaching community.

So I sought out districts that considered their teachers to be collaborating professionals who should rightfully take for granted that the administration, curriculum, book room, librarians, tech department were all there to assist them in their jobs as teachers. Not as groups to dictate to them the best strategy, product, proof of a student's learning. We were always interested in collecting data to inform us about our students' learning as well as the effectiveness of our own teaching, but it never overshadowed the primary need to teach the students first.

Ten years later, in 1979, I began teaching in a district that was quickly moving from rural to suburban status. Its growth far outstripped its ability to build and staff and equip classrooms adequately. My student load was 180—the state cap—and I traveled to my six different classrooms in four different buildings on campus. Needless to say, I was exhausted by the end of the day.

My first principal here reveled in nurturing creative teaching. I found my place to grow. Let me note here one of the milestones during this period that opened my eyes and made profound changes in my ability to be a better teacher. It was an all-day workshop given by a young researcher by the name of Anthony Gregoric. It was held in an auditorium, and it was the only time on record I can remember no one moving from their seats, whispering to others, complaining, or grading papers. We were being introduced to how differently each one of us learns and teaches; we were being introduced to learning styles for the first time, and we were mesmerized.

I never looked at my students the same way again. I had always thought my freewheeling creative right-brained approach was by far more valuable than any other method. I had gone about trying to change people, hoping to have them "see the light." After that day with Gregoric, I was the beneficiary of a whole new mind-set. I was more respectful of student differences, I added layers of explanations in different learning modes to my lessons, I gave outlines to those who needed to see my structure, I explained where my activities were headed to those who needed answers to that old "Why are we doing this?" question. I was patient with those who found organization difficult. I never failed to answer a question even if I had already answered it four times already. I had had my eyes opened. My creativity had a focused mission now—accommodate all the needs in front of me. Previously, I had never taken those needs seriously or, worse yet, had made fun of them and dismissed them as trivial.

YOUR TURN

As an individual:

1. Jot down a list of the best professional development experiences you have had in the past few years.

2. Explain one item on your list and how it influenced your teaching or gave you a strategy you have used with success more than once.

As a teacher team:

1. Jot down a list of the best professional development experiences you have had in the past few years.

2. Share with each other one item on your list that has influenced your teaching or given you a strategy you have used with success more than once.

3. From listening to each other's examples and sharing each other's lists, draw a few conclusions as to what types of professional development opportunities really help teachers improve their teaching.

TEACHING SKILLS AS WELL AS CONTENT

One of the best educational movements that would resonate with me for years to come was the one that highlighted the necessity for a teacher to be able to point to the skill building as well as the content coverage that goes on in the classroom. This move toward a dual emphasis had a greater impact on high school teachers than those in lower grades because, for the most part, we at the high school level saw ourselves as content deliverers—experts in specific content areas. If anyone asked us what skills we were building in our students, he or she would first be greeted with blank stares and then flooded with a thorough explanation of the content in that individual course. In those early days, we were probably building skills but never focused on that as one of our priorities. I never remember talking about skill building at faculty meetings or among my peers.

I found this whole concept delightfully appealing and a license for creativity. I could now point to many of the activities I was embedding into the traditional content and delivery and rattle off lists of skills that they were strengthening. I found this new way of looking at my instructional methods both vindicating and liberating. Armed with Bloom's (1956) Taxonomy, I could develop opportunities and situations in which my students could practice them. These tools gave my creative planning a strong framework in which to function. The following is an example.

Learning Bloom's Taxonomy: The Test

A fundamental tenet of learning stemming back to John Dewey, and probably back to the days of the apprentices and master craftsmen, is the fact that you learn best by doing it yourself. So I set up a situation in which students learn how to take tests more efficiently by making them. My students were to make up an end-of-unit test on the material we had covered—in this case, a novel—using the levels of Bloom's (1956) Taxonomy (Figure 3.1). Now, the verbs had been changed on this taxonomy, which incidentally places creativity at the top of the pyramid. Then I explained how these levels built on one another, how they became more and more complex, and how the last ones were considered the higher-order thinking skills that all students should be practicing and becoming proficient in so that they could utilize their brain power more effectively. Students love to learn about how their brains operate, their thinking/learning styles, anything that deals with themselves. This lesson played into that curiosity and interest. I typed up the verbs associated with each level and attached a point value for each level: 1 point for knowledge verbs, 2 points for comprehension, and so on.

Figure 3.1   Bloom's Taxonomy Pyramid

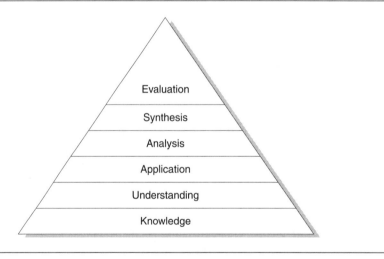

1. *Knowledge*: arrange, define, duplicate, label, list, memorize, name, order, recognize, relate, recall, repeat, reproduce, state

2. *Understanding*: classify, describe, discuss, explain, express, identify, indicate, locate, recognize, report, restate, review, select, translate

3. *Application*: apply, choose, demonstrate, dramatize, employ, illustrate, interpret, operate, practice, schedule, sketch, solve, use, write

4. *Analysis*: analyze, appraise, calculate, categorize, compare, contrast, criticize, differentiate, discriminate, distinguish, examine, experiment, question, test

5. *Synthesis*: arrange, assemble, collect, compose, construct, create, design, develop, formulate, invent, manage, organize, plan, prepare, propose, set up, write

6. *Evaluation*: appraise, argue, assess, attach, choose, compare, defend, estimate, judge, predict, rate, core, select, support, value, evaluate

Students were to create the test using no more than five Level 1 (Knowledge) verbs in their questions and at least one from the other levels. They were to formulate an appropriate question and then answer it. At first, students who always sought the path of least resistance thought that this was right up their alley. But when I showed them how they could actually flunk their own test by asking a question using one verb but not answering it appropriately, they changed their tune.

What happened then was a teacher's dream—we were actually talking about what those verbs really meant, what implications they had for their answers. "Does 'compare and contrast' mean I have to give both likenesses and differences?" It sure does!

The results were often even more astounding than the conversations. I had students ask and answer questions I would never think to ask them. They went into more detail than I had gotten on any previous test questions I had asked in the past.

So I would see 4-point questions about the novel *Fahrenheit 451* such as this: "*Compare* Montag's state of mind at the beginning of the book with that at the end of the book." For 5 points: "*Invent* a title for a sequel to this book giving a plausible explanation for your choice based on the text." (I loved the fancy tone to this question, "plausible . . . text" from a 16-year-old.) And for 6 points: "*Predict* what might have happened to Montag if he had never met Clarisse or Faber." Each answer had to have reasons that were based on the text and applicable to the question in order to qualify for the points.

Best of all were the discussions on why those upper-level questions were worth more than the factual questions since it was so much more fun making up and answering the higher-level ones. I would tell students that the reason the higher-level thinking experiences were "more fun" was because our brains are built for that—we thrive on stimulating our brains with opportunities to think this way! Memory questions, those resulting in tiny bits and pieces of information, offer our brains nowhere to go; they stop right at the answer. No challenge there.

The only drawback with this activity was the resulting criticism aimed at other teachers' tests. I had produced a group of test makers who felt qualified to judge the quality of other people's test-making skills. I'd hear comments like, "That history test asked only low-level questions. Did you see that?" or "I bet I could have made up some really great higher-order thinking questions for that test!" I had to warn them not to share their newfound abilities with their other instructors if they wanted to stay on their good sides! Ironically, what they were saying was in some cases right.

So movements such as these served to bring out not only my creativity but that of my students as well. One student used the test he had made as part of his application to Harvard. He was asked to include an assignment that really stretched him, really made him think and go far beyond what effort he usually would put into an assignment. I was so proud that he chose to include one of mine.

YOUR TURN

As an individual:

Again and again we are told that we as teachers do too much and that students should be doing more. Often in our desire to plan for all possibilities, we tend to overplan lessons to the point that students are left with few choices and, consequently, less mind stimulation and less buy-in.

1. Think of ways that you can give your students more room for planning and executing one of your favorite activities. Write down possible options you can give them.

2. Try out the Bloom's Taxonomy test with your students. Feel free to offer more verbs or any version of Bloom's Taxonomy that you currently are using. I suggest the latest version, which places creativity at the top of the pyramid.

As a teacher team:

1. Jot down the exercise, activity, or lesson in which students are making most of the choices within your framework. How do the products of these activities usually turn out?

2. Share your favorite student choice activity with your team.

3. Can any of the examples from fellow team members be adapted to your specific classroom? If so, be sure to write it down in your idea journal.

4. Try out the Bloom's Taxonomy test with your students. Feel free to offer more verbs or any version of Bloom's Taxonomy that you currently are using. I suggest the latest version, which places creativity at the top of the pyramid.

MY REPEATERS ON GRAMMAR PATROL

Here's one final episode to round out this collection of teaching experiences. Anyone who flunked ninth-grade English had to repeat the course in order to graduate. A special section was built into the schedule to accommodate those students needing to fulfill this requirement, and I was the teacher. Typically, the class consisted of an even distribution of 10th, 11th, and 12th graders, mostly boys. Expectations for these students weren't set very high. Attend class, and do enough work to pass the course. No one was concerned about GPA; competition was centered on who was the funniest, never on who was getting the highest grades. I was surprised when it first dawned on me that most of these students were really bright, above average in intelligence. They had flunked because of their attendance, behavior, lack of motivation, or outright refusal to cooperate. None were in this class because they couldn't do the work. I loved teaching them.

One class in particular looked like a pretty rough bunch from the outset: chains connecting wallets to blue jeans, tattoos before they became more acceptable, leather jackets (no letter jackets on this crowd), heavy motorcycle boots with steel toes, rock band T-shirts, worn circles on the back pockets from tins of chewing tobacco, long hair—the uniform of those who didn't enjoy school. I'm spending precious space on their description because it has a significant impact on this episode.

Since grammar was the primary focus of this class's curriculum, I asked the class just what they would like to learn—especially since they had proudly agreed they knew very little or even nothing at all about the subject. This began as a dead discussion until someone asked what would be the hardest thing to learn. Now, that piqued everyone's interest, including my own. I had just come off three years of moonlighting in a business college teaching grammar and knew the 32 reasons for using the comma appropriately. In other words, I was quite fluent in grammatical trivia. I told them the grammatical errors that most irritated me are the misuses of the apostrophe. I said these mistakes are made by everyone—businesses, students, adults, everyone. I said if they learned to use the apostrophe correctly, they would be part of a very elite minority. They could even catch teachers making mistakes. This sounded very appealing indeed.

Around the same time I had read about a national contest being sponsored by Kodak/NEA in which cameras were to be used in lesson plans to facilitate learning. The creative wheels began turning. How can I blend the contest regulations with the instruction about apostrophes and come out with a unit that would stimulate my student skeptics into getting interested enough to participate. A potent key of creativity is the mixing of two unrelated entities to come up with something new—cross-disciplinary fertilization. That's what I did. The goal was shifted from learning for learning's sake—a hard sell in itself for any class—to winning that contest. We were going to prove that the business sector doesn't know its grammar when it comes to possessive case and forming plurals—both the territory of the esteemed apostrophe. We would take pictures of the errors, write letters to the companies explaining how sweet, impressionable students need them to serve as role models of correct grammar constructions and not lead them astray. We called ourselves the Quality Seekers and created letterhead and business cards.

Quality Seekers in action

The lessons I taught focused on how to identify incorrect constructions. I scheduled a field trip for this class of camera-carrying, chain-dangling teenagers. We would visit two local shopping malls and look for grammar errors on their signs. We were greeted by store employees terrified that we came to loot, vandalize, or just start general mayhem in their stores. One store was a virtual gold mine of mistakes. A couple of students and I were snapping picture after picture when the manager asked why we were there. He promptly got a security guard to escort us out. In fact, we were asked to leave one of the two malls altogether. The students were ecstatic. Their teacher was having a run-in with the cops! This was something many could relate to and empathize with.

The letters to store owners that we composed on our return simply steamed and melted with our wrongful treatment at the hands of their employees. We received apologetic letters in return, copious promises to change signs, gratitude at our observant skills, and even a coupon for discounted merchandise from one. Oh yes, and we won first place at the state level and second place at the national level for our project.

As a follow-up, I took each student's picture and, with a class-written article covering the contest success, sent them out to any small-town newspaper where my students had relatives. Small-town papers are always looking for news, and many of the ones I contacted put us on the front page. What a shock it was for some of these students' grandparents to open up their paper and see their gangly teenage grandson or granddaughter smiling out at them.

YOUR TURN

As an individual:

1. I could write down the lessons I learned from this experience, but I would rather have you make this list. What do you think I took away that I could use in future classes to motivate students and utilize my creativity more frequently? Make a list of 5–10 items.

2. Looking at your list, pick out the one item that you think is the most important to replicate in your own thinking and teaching. Describe one way you could use that lesson in the coming week.

As a teacher team:

1. Discuss what elements made this environment so free for me to use my creativity. How can these elements be replicated in your own classrooms, even slightly?

2. Over the years I've found that some textbooks really don't sequence elements in the most student-friendly order for easier understanding. Teaching parts of speech might just not be the best way to introduce grammatical constructions. What has your experience been in sensing that students learn a function better if certain skills are mastered first? Have you ever questioned the "way we always do it" in reference to your subject area? Discuss this in your group.

The Creative Teacher's Bill of Rights

☐ You have the right to question matters that directly influence your ability to teach and your students' ability to learn, to voice your needs, frustrations, and questions without fear of retaliation.

☐ You have the right to the freedom necessary to choose the best strategies to meet your students' needs, to adapt prescribed lessons to be relevant for your students.

☐ You have the right to bear arms full of props, novelty items, markers, and supplementary materials to enhance your delivery.

☐ You have the right to embed the skills you want to teach in a creative, engaging manner, to present your content in meaningful chunks that will reflect real-life performance tasks.

☐ You have the right to a nurturing, supportive administration that focuses on the needs of the whole child and values creativity in both its faculty and its student body.

☐ You have the right to an open curriculum that allows for choice and adaptability in its implementation in order to provide life and freedom in your teaching.

☐ You have the right to counsel in the form of consistent, ongoing, meaningful, up-to-date professional development opportunities.

☐ You have the right to take risks and not be chastised if some of those risks seem to fail, the right to work in an environment where sharing ideas and offering help is the norm.

☐ You have the right to be treated as the professional you are and to be given the freedom, support, and backing to do your job effectively.

☐ You have the right to say *no* when asked to take on extra responsibilities that tend to drain you of your energy, time, and ability to function in a healthy, creative manner.

4

What's Going On?

With the technological advances of the past decade has come the ability to collect, collate, staple, and serve up an unprecedented amount of data. This data provides a new window through which we can now compare and evaluate the performances of students and schools across the country. What has also emerged with this access to evaluative information is a nationwide focus on assessment as the necessary guide to bettering our public school systems. No Child Left Behind (NCLB), one of the most ambitious educational bills to date, differs from its predecessors insofar as it places the threat of punitive financial repercussions on school districts failing to sufficiently meet benchmark standards. States put in place mandated tests as the measuring sticks for compliance with these federal regulations. With NCLB, "the federal government has stretched its tentacles of control into every corner of American classrooms, sweeping aside the hard-earned knowledge of researchers and teachers and confidently asserting that 'we know best'" (Yatvin, 2007, p. 26).

Some of the efforts and strategies being implemented by school districts that are frantic to pull up scores and meet state guidelines are having unintended long-term negative effects on students, teachers, and our educational system as a whole. These negative results range from a lack of funding for subjects not being tested to a decline in tolerance for answers that are "different"; from an absence of energy, joy, and creativity in classroom activities and instruction to a growing atmosphere of pressure and diminished self-confidence; from a lack of risk taking to an increase in bright teachers leaving the profession and an increasingly demoralizing environment for many teachers and students alike. As Popham (2008) puts it simply, "test scores influence students' self-perceptions, and self-perceptions influence students' lives" (p. 87).

SIDE EFFECTS OF THE MANDATED TESTING PHENOMENON

The increase in testing, and its repercussions on teachers and students, is proving detrimental. The number of tests some school districts require teachers to administer and students to prepare for and then take is digging deeply into the actual time allowed for instruction. Ironically, when studying what makes for high-scoring performance on high-stakes tests, Guthrie (2002) found that 40 percent of student success was due to reading ability, 20 percent to level of background knowledge, 15 percent to motivation, and only 10 percent to familiarity with test format (the remaining 15 percent was unaccounted for). Since many schools focus on test preparation through direct work on specific test-like items and formats,

> this focus becomes especially problematic for large numbers of struggling readers often concentrated in low-income neighborhoods. . . . The schools that reacted to pressure for higher scores on high-stakes tests by subscribing to the intensive test preparation appear to have inadvertently encouraged less literate behavior. The loss of time spent on subjects such as science, social studies, art, and music may be creating a void in the background knowledge and vocabulary acquired from learning in these areas. . . . Teachers need to be allowed and encouraged to spend the school day doing activities that contribute to the building of reading ability, not just preparing for testing. (Hedrick, 2007, p. 65)

The numbers are now showing the inefficiency in spending so much class time taking practice tests. One researcher glibly compared practicing for high-stakes tests to be about as effective as practicing for an annual physical.

In a rush for a more standardized delivery of curriculum to raise test scores, some districts have usurped the teacher's power of judgment by offering scripted lessons and requiring "fidelity to implementation" of packaged programs, textbooks,

Preparing for state tests is like practicing for a physical examination.

and manuals. Although these purchased tools are useful at various stages of student development for some students, the most harmful result of seeing them as one-size-fits-all strategies is a disenfranchisement of teachers in terms of using their professional ability to determine the most important methodology for teaching students in their classroom at any point in time. As Joanne Yatvin (2007) points out, "no text writer at a distance, regardless of knowledge or experience, can do as well as a good teacher physically, mentally, and psychologically in touch with students. In favoring scripted programs, the Department of Education implementers of

NCLB reveal that they do not understand that teaching demands contextualized planning, personalized treatment of students, and circumstantial decision making" (p. 29).

Narrowing the Curriculum

An article well worth all educators' examination is Donna McCaw's (2007) "Dangerous Intersection Ahead," in which she says, "Few would argue that the spirit of a child contains many ingredients: laughter, curiosity, love, adventure and creativity. Yet in our push for a testing-focused accountability movement, stress levels are running high and creativity may be running at an all-time low. . . . Much is lost when the myopic view of achievement is solely focused on tests and measurements. When the doing becomes more important than the being, joy and passion can be lost" (p. 33). Ironically, more and more children are being left behind since the implementation of NCLB as schools drop courses and time once designated for the arts, for play, for a traditionally broad curriculum and instead narrowly focus on test preparation and a smaller number of subjects. Michael Gieb notes that one of the outcomes of an emphasis on standardization in performance is a kind of standardized mentality, which

> doesn't prepare us for the real world in a real company. It prepares you for a world where people follow orders; where you focus on getting the right answer for the teacher, professor or boss. Every company that I work with now—and I work with many of the top companies in the world—is desperate for people who can think . . . for themselves. . . . They desire individuals who can come up with new ideas . . . integrating logic and analysis with imagination and intuition. (Quoted in McCaw, 2007, p. 35)

Stress

Like a low-grade infection, another one of the most insidious effects of all this is the high degree of stress that is filling administrators' offices, teachers' faculty lounges, and students' classrooms. Eric Jensen (1998), in *Teaching With the Brain in Mind*, points out the biological effects of stress on students' ability to learn and retain learning. Here is his list, illustrating how stress compromises the ability of both students and teachers to do the quality work in the classroom that they want to do and that the country expects them to do; I've adjusted the wording to apply to teaching as opposed to learning:

- Excess stress and threat in the school environment may be the single greatest contributor to impaired [teaching performance].
- Chronic stress impairs a [teacher's] ability to sort out what's important and what's not.

- Threats [that teachers perceive from administrators or fellow faculty members] activate defense mechanisms and behaviors that are great for survival but lousy for [teaching].
- Chronic stress makes [teachers] more susceptible to illness--more test stress means more sickness, which means poor health and missed classes, which contribute to [a lower degree of teacher] performance.

YOUR TURN

As an individual:

1. This section contains some gloomy observations. All of these effects certainly aren't affecting you, but some of them might. What is your take on the effects of state-mandated and other standardized tests on the children in your classes? On you? Write a freewrite journal entry on your experience.

2. Besides all the gloom and doom reported here, there are some good results of the nation's push toward improving student performance in every state. Make a list of as many items as you can that are positive results of this focus. Which one is true for you?

3. Look at the list of Jensen's (1998) statements on the effects of stress. Circle any that are possibly affecting you. Jensen offers two approaches for reducing stress: manage the conditions that induce stress and find personal strategies to counteract them. What have you found to be effective in dealing with stress in your life? What stress-release techniques have you heard about but have not tried yet? Try one.

As a teacher team:

1. In your journal, draw a line down a sheet to form two columns. Label the columns "Testing Effects on My Students" and "Testing Effects on Me." In each column, fill in about five examples from this section of the chapter and/or from your personal experience. Share your lists with your team.

2. Besides all the gloom and doom reported here, there are some good results of the nation's push toward improving student performance in every state. Make a list of as many items as you can that are positive results of this focus. Which one is true for you? Share this list with your team.

3. Discuss the effects of stress on teachers. Jensen (1998) offers two approaches for reducing stress: manage the conditions that induce stress and find personal strategies to counteract them. Share with your team the stress-release techniques that you have found successful. Pick one to try that you haven't yet.

THE WHOLE CHILD, THE WHOLE TEACHER

Everyone has seen the need for raising the bar on student performance across the country, and every teacher desires the best learning situation and outcomes for his or her students. The ability to find the areas of student learning that need improvement so that they might be addressed is applauded by everyone in education. But an overemphasis on any one method or strategy (in this case, testing) doesn't allow for balance and respect for the human beings affected at every level. Nothing

> will transform education if we fail to cherish—and challenge—the human heart that is the source of good teaching. . . . Here is a secret hidden in plain sight: *good teaching cannot be reduced to technique; good teaching comes from the identity and integrity of the teacher.* In every class I teach, my ability to connect with my students, and to connect them with the subject, depends less on the methods I use than on the degree to which I know and trust my selfhood—and am willing to make it available and vulnerable in the service of learning. (Palmer, 1997, ¶ 10)

It's this ability to get back to looking at education from the human perspective once more that is necessary if we are to begin a discussion on how to nurture and build our collective creativity as educators in order to meet and lead students into an unpredictable future.

NCLB's Reading First section requires "explicit, systematic instruction," meaning that any skill or body of information is divided into discrete, step-by-step lessons to be learned by rote. Instructors present the objective of each lesson, principles, process, and some examples of application. Students memorize those elements and practice by applying them in controlled situations. Practice continues until students can apply the principles or the process correctly on their own. Yet Joanne Yatvin (2007) points out that

> the problem with this type of instruction is that it does not square with what we know about how children learn. Decades of research on children's learning show that children tend to be random, concrete, piecemeal learners. Children do not start learning anything by rules and systematic steps. They experience concrete examples of phenomena, draw what they think are the principles from them, and then experiment by creating their own examples. If the created examples work, children accept their original principles; if not, they adjust them and try again. (p. 27)

Schools are systematically stripping their kindergartens and early grades of opportunities for this kind of learning and filling their precious time with rote memorization and unrealistic expectations in the name of boosting achievement scores. Although Reading First has provided many teachers with a blueprint for reading instruction, its glaring deficiencies have had a negative effect on instruction in the long run. The fact that only one member of the National Reading Panel, Ms. Yatvin, had taught reading in a classroom setting should have thrown up red flags to the rest of us. She also authored the panel's minority report in 2000.

TEACHING THE WHOLE BRAIN

When the school's emphasis is on the whole child—when there is an atmosphere of passion, safety to take risks, respect for creative efforts, energy resulting from empowerment and involvement in decision making, decrease in stress for everyone—test scores go up. One point that might be good to bring up now is the fact that "we must constantly remind ourselves that the ultimate purpose of evaluation is to enable students to evaluate themselves" (Costa, 1989, p. 2). Sometimes this singular truth gets lost in the mounds and mounds of data being collected on each child, each school test, each state assessment.

Acknowledging the needs of the whole child is acknowledging the need to teach to the whole child's brain, not just the part that we have traditionally labeled as housing left-brain preferences. In the past three and a half decades, over forty-five thousand articles and books—most of them medical and scientific—have been written on the left-brain/right-brain issue. The theory that the two brain halves control different modes of thinking is the hypothesis spearheaded by Roger Sperry, a 1981 Nobel Prize winner. As Robert Ornstein (1997) points out in *The Right Mind*, right-brain ideology crept into every corner of culture and society during this time, including "Beethoven biography, photography, drawing, cooking, auto repair, and housekeeping" (pp. 87–88). But while we have a natural tendency toward one way of thinking, the two sides of the brain work together in our everyday lives. The right focuses on the visual and processes information in an intuitive and simultaneous way, looking first at the whole picture and then at the details; the left focuses on the verbal and processes information in an analytical and sequential way, looking first at the pieces and then putting them together to get the whole (Boddy-Evans, 2009).

We know now that learning and brain processes are not as neatly categorized as first thought in Sperry's era, but a discussion of how students view the world and how their preferences tend to color their ability to learn and to solve problems is very relevant today. This is especially true because when learning or thinking creatively, a student's ability to process information is enhanced when using both hemispheres simultaneously. Many charts have been compiled to attempt to list the various characteristics that each hemisphere displays. On most such charts you will usually find the right-brain tendencies to be visual, responds to word pitch, feeling, tactile, kinesthetic, creative, subjective, intuitive, holistic, likes open-endedness, surprises, imaginative, emotionally responsive, intuitive, gets jokes, loves novelty, responds to music and art, spontaneous, prefers music/sound while studying, gestures when speaking, recalls people's faces, processes information in chunks, wants direct experience, extroverted, less punctual. Whereas the left-brain tendencies are verbal, mathematical, responds to word meaning, processes information linearly, prefers formal study setting, remembers names, likes structure, predictability, intellectual, plans ahead, speaks with few gestures, follows rules, adheres to deadlines, analytic, punctual, responds to logic, awareness of time, sequential, objective, recalls facts, introspective.

Like Gardner's (2006) multiple intelligences, the left-/right-brain preferences are only of value to educators if they are allowed to inform teachers' decisions on how learning can be more richly facilitated. Edward de Bono (1970) says that one way of teaching creatively is to use a different entry point to get to the problem or the lesson. A ready-made guide for teachers to do this is to use all of these various paths described in the right-brain characteristics in order to get to the left-brain structures, which are the basis of the school's culture—words, numbers, sequential learning, logical thinking, analytical discussions of material. No longer is one's teaching style, whether stimulated by left- or right-brain preferences, an excuse for not including strategies and activities that complement the learning styles of all students.

For many teachers, teaching more creatively might be as basic as shifting awareness and inclusion of the strategies and approaches that are outside their immediate preference as a predominately right- or left-brained educator. To do this, first look at the characteristics of a left- or right-brained teacher as described by Diane Connell:

The Teacher With a Left-Brain Preference

- generally prefers to use lecture and discussion
- incorporates sequence (outlines on board, overhead)
- likes to adhere to prepared time schedules
- gives independent work for problem solving
- assigns more research and writing
- prefers a quiet, structured classroom
- usually has a clean classroom with everything in its place

The Teacher With a Right-Brain Preference

- generally prefers to use hands-on activities over lecture
- incorporates more art, manipulatives, visuals, and music
- tends to embrace Gardner's (2006) multiple intelligences
- likes to assign more group projects and activities
- prefers a busy, active, noisy classroom
- has classroom materials and books scattered all over

Source: Connell, Diane. (2009–1996). *Left brain/right brain: Pathways to reach every learner.* Scholastic Web site. Retrieved March 2008 at http://content.scholastic.com/browse/article.jsp?id=3629#twoSides

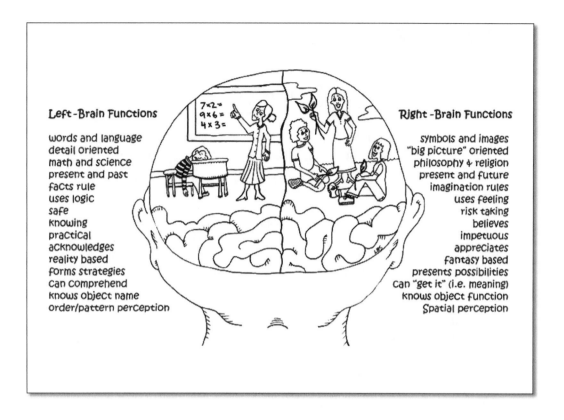

Left-Brain Functions

words and language
detail oriented
math and science
present and past
facts rule
uses logic
safe
knowing
practical
acknowledges
reality based
forms strategies
can comprehend
knows object name
order/pattern perception

Right-Brain Functions

symbols and images
"big picture" oriented
philosophy & religion
present and future
imagination rules
uses feeling
risk taking
believes
impetuous
appreciates
fantasy based
presents possibilities
can "get it" (i.e. meaning)
knows object function
spatial perception

The point of this discussion of brain preferences is that *both* sides need to be accessed, stimulated, and strengthened in teachers as well as students for education of the whole child to be effective and meaningful. The predominantly right-brained teacher can be more creative by including and balancing his or her natural approach with that of left-brained counterparts. The same principle goes for naturally left-brained teachers. No wonder that more left-brained individuals go into education. They found the classroom a comfortable environment with the emphasis on those areas of the brain that are their strengths.

School is a haven for left-brain strengths and characteristics. But the excuse "that's not how I teach, that's not my style" isn't really relevant if one's awareness is moved from what the teacher's comfort level is to what the needs of the students before her or him actually are. And I've always found it much easier to move my right-brained students to an understanding of the (mostly left-brained) skills and material to be mastered by beginning first within their comfort zones and then including strategies that complement them throughout the unit of study.

YOUR TURN

As an individual:

1. Read the descriptors for the right- and left-brained teacher once more. Circle those that seem to feel more comfortable to you. Underline those that seem very uncomfortable.

2. List three strategies or activities that you have built into your lessons in the past couple of weeks that play into the opposite brain preference. How did they turn out?

3. Make a list of strategies that are the least unnerving for you that you can incorporate into your next unit design.

4. Using the chart and list of tendencies which appears in this segment, have a discussion with your students over what they think are their preferences. Have them list the tendencies which apply to them and turn them in to you. Discuss the types of assignments students like best—group work, independent work, long term assignments, silent work, etc. Talk about the need to involve all learning styles and experiences within the class structure.

As a teacher team:

1. In your group discuss the descriptors for the right- and left-brained teacher and which apply to each group member.

2. Discuss what the main atmosphere of the school is as it applies to these descriptors. How are the traits of the opposite preference looked upon in your school? Try to give examples.

3. Make a list of strategies each of you can incorporate into your next unit designs which would be the least unnerving to try.

4. Using the list of preferences that appears in this segment, make plans to discuss with your students what they think their preferences are. Have them list those that apply to them and turn this list in to you. If your team meets again, bring in these lists and use them as the basis of a discussion about what your students say about their specific comfort zones.

5. Discuss the types of assignments students like best (group work, independent work, long-term assignments, silent work, etc.). Brainstorm new ways to involve all learning styles and experiences within the class structure.

THE NECESSITY OF TEACHER EMPOWERMENT

This subsequent lack of empowerment is resulting in many fine teachers leaving the field, depleting our most vital resources for the future. One of the main reasons teachers give for changing careers is the shrinking perception of the need to recognize teacher empowerment and professionalism as key agents of change. Manuals and programs too often are seen as more capable of solving learning problems than the teachers themselves.

Whenever a packaged program is touted as "teacher proof," teachers take another hit to their morale and feel a growing lack of respect by their administrators and the community.

Teachers who have been in the classroom for some time are aware of the reality that "even the best ideas, when they become programmatic, become reified and lose their vitality. Teachers always need to put their own stamp on any prepared materials by framing and adapting them to meet the needs of their specific students in their unique situation" (Wilhelm, 2007a, p. 50). In a nutshell, this is why programs cannot work without the expert adaptations of a reflective teacher. Teachers also are aware that, with few exceptions, "everyone on the same page on the same day" is a travesty of justice for real teaching. Sharon Draper (2001), former U.S. Teacher of the Year and author of bestselling young adult novels and professional development books, aptly summarizes this: "Teachers are the most flexible humans on the face of the earth. They know that all lesson plans are contingency plans, that their completion depends upon thousands of other factors besides the teacher and the student. The school day, filled with hundreds of children who have individual needs and requirements, is a constant ebb and flow of what we plan to do and what we actually accomplish" (p. 41). If we can't be flexible with our plans as the day progresses, we feel a growing stress and helplessness invade and fill us with discontent. If we know in our deepest hearts that we are not meeting the needs of the young people in front of us, this tension between what we know and what we feel we must do has the effect of a lessening of energy, a bleeding away, you might say, of the spirit.

Above all, as Wilhelm (2007a) points out, "the authority in the classroom is and must be the teacher. As a teacher, I don't want some outside agency or publisher creating my agenda. I am the world's only expert on my students at this point in time in my particular school and classroom. Therefore, the ultimate professional decision-making power must rest with me. But to wield this decision-making power effectively, I must deeply understand pedagogy and I must know my own students" (p. 50). This is empowerment. This is a necessary ingredient for personal creativity to thrive and flourish in the classroom.

First and foremost, teachers are artists, not mechanics or accountants. This fact gets lost in view of the forms that need filling out, the grades that need tabulating, the new teaching methods and structures imposed from above—often changing with the seasons in many districts. Yet our strongest vein in the classroom is that of artist. Matthew Kay (2008) says it well:

> If I hadn't been allowed to be an artist in the classroom, if my curriculum had been some stranger's standardized script, these girls may not have found their voices. . . . If we want to convince dynamic, young educators to choose the inner city as the place to master their craft—we've got to remember that the best are artists. They like to create. And if they aren't allowed to do so, they will

rebel—or they will leave. The chance to be an artist has convinced me to stay—"merit pay" not withstanding [*sic*]. (¶ 11)

I differ with him on one statement: "the best are artists." All are artists, albeit some of us are closet artists, some are blocked artists, and some just need nurturing to let our artistic spirits loose.

YOUR TURN

As an individual:

1. Write down your definition of teacher empowerment. Give examples of what it looks like in the classroom and what the classroom looks like when it doesn't exist for the teacher.

2. When have you felt most empowered in your life to do what you wanted to do? Explain the circumstances, the feel, the outcome, and the persons involved in this experience.

As a teacher team:

1. Write down your definition of teacher empowerment. Give examples of what it looks like in the classroom and what the classroom looks like when it doesn't exist for the teacher. Read your definitions to each other. Discuss their similarities and differences.

2. When have you felt most empowered in your life to do what you wanted to do? Share with each other the circumstances, the feel, the outcome, and the persons involved in this experience. Share how you felt about it with a partner on your team.

NEEDS OF THE 21ST CENTURY, GLARINGLY VISIBLE

Finally, there is a disconnect between what trends are occurring in public education and what is being articulated by experts as the changes necessary to meet the needs of today's world. "Over the past decade the biggest employment gains came in occupations that rely on people skills and emotional intelligence and among jobs that require imagination and creativity. . . . Trying to preserve existing jobs will prove futile—trade and technology will transform the economy whether we like it or not" (Cox, Alm, & Holmes, 2004, p. A27). The current growing understanding that the ability to provide our students with the skills to flourish in the 21st century is contingent on a refocusing of our priorities and understanding of the shift in contemporary society's educational needs.

Daniel Pink's (2005b) *A Whole New Mind* gives a stunning view of where we stand today in regard to the demands of the past and the demands of the present:

The last few decades have belonged to a certain kind of person with a certain kind of mind—computer programmers who could crank code, lawyers who could craft contracts, MBAs who could crunch numbers. But the keys to the kingdom are changing hands. The future belongs to a very different kind of person with a very different kind of mind—creators and empathizers, pattern recognizers and meaning makers. These people—artists, inventors, designers, storytellers, caregivers, consolers, big picture thinkers—will now reap society's richest rewards and share its greatest joys. (p. 1)

If we in education give these and similar calls for a different emphasis on preparation for success in tomorrow's workforce even the least bit of attention, the discussions of our curricular offerings, how we deliver them, and our primary emphasis on what we consider appropriate student performance will be expanded far beyond the simple measure of our current testing programs. The call is out and getting louder for more emphasis on creative growth—for all of us to be creative teachers so that we can transform the classrooms we currently occupy.

Let me offer an example of one such disconnect. As educators, most of us feel that we are working to prepare students for their immediate future as well as a much more distant future. We want them ready for third grade if they are in our second-grade class, for high school if they are in our middle school, for college if they are in our high school. Many times I was asked by students applying for various colleges to fill out a teacher recommendation form for them. Usually this consisted of a chart accompanied by a letter about the student's abilities and performance. Most of the charts were pretty generic, but all seemed to include the same traits. Figure 4.1 is a sample.

Please note the categories in which I am supposed to rate the student: creative, original thought; motivation; and independence, initiative are the top three. Just how often have any of us intentionally set up situations, whole activities, or strategies for the main purpose of building these patterns of behavior? And if we do, where do we ever note just how well students are growing and exhibiting these attributes for them and their parents to see? Where do these elements appear on a report card or other reporting mechanisms? Yet here they are, waiting for my judgment and serving as a possible determining factor in a student's ability to be accepted into a college. Do students even know these are attributes that colleges and universities hold in high esteem? How do we show our students that we hold these attributes in high esteem?

Students develop creativity when teachers don't simply allow for creative expression, but rather serve as role models and show them what creativity looks like. As someone who works with hundreds of teachers

Figure 4.1   Form Used by Colleges to Rate Students Seeking Admission

FORM USED BY COLLEGES TO RATE
STUDENTS SEEKING ADMISSION

Please feel free to write whatever you think is important about the applicant, including a description of academic and personal characteristics. We are particularly interested in the candidate's intellectual purpose, motivation, relative maturity, integrity, independence, originality, leadership potential, capacity for growth, special talents, and enthusiasm. We welcome information that will help us to differentiate this student from others.

Ratings

No Basis	Academic Skills and Potential	Below Average	Average	Good	Very Good	One of the Top Few Encountered in My Career
	Creative, original thought					
	Motivation					
	Independence, initiative					
	Intellectual ability					
	Academic achievement					
	Written expression of ideas					
	Effective class discussion					
	Disciplined work habits					
	Potential for growth					
	SUMMARY EVALUATION					

yearly in helping them turn students into better writers, it always comes as a surprise to many that I strongly urge them to write while their students write; share their work with their classes; be a living, breathing role model of what a writer looks like, talks like, struggles with, and feels. Who would ever hire a guitar instructor who doesn't play the guitar? Who would trust themselves to a heart surgeon who read a book about heart surgery but never actually performed an operation? Who can trust a writing teacher who doesn't write? Well, how can we produce more creative-thinking individuals if we do not attend to the work of bettering ourselves as creative teachers on a consistent basis?

YOUR TURN

As an individual:

1. Look at Figure 4.1. What is your initial reaction to the elements being scored?

2. Since we are trained to use rubrics and scoring guides for major papers and products we assign, and Figure 4.1 appears to be a rubric for high school achievement, what do you think is missing in how students are prepared to score well on this form?

3. List some of the changes you would institute in teacher preparation that would address these elements more specifically?

4. Copy this form, and distribute it to your students. Discuss how it could mean getting in or not getting in to the college of their choice. Ask them to rate themselves on this form and give evidence for their answers on the back.

As a teacher team:

1. Look at Figure 4.1. What is your initial reaction to the elements being scored? Share your thoughts with the team.

2. Since we are trained to use rubrics and scoring guides for major papers and products we assign, and Figure 4.1 appears to be a rubric for high school achievement, discuss what you think is missing in how students are prepared to score well on this form?

3. List some of the changes you would institute in teacher preparation that would address these elements more specifically?

4. Copy this form, and distribute it to your students. Discuss how it could mean getting in or not getting in to the college of their choice. Ask them to rate themselves on this form and give evidence for their answers on the back. If your team meets regularly, discuss the results of this discussion and its implications for your teaching.

DROPOUTS AND HIGH ACHIEVERS

A student rebellion against traditional and, in some cases, archaic methods of educating students is already in motion. In a report on graduation rates across the country, Swanson (2008) found that only half of the students in large urban cities were receiving diplomas and 17 cities showed even lower graduation rates—citing Detroit as graduating only a quarter, Indianapolis less than a third, and Cleveland's public schools a little more than a third. The study estimates that approximately 1.2 million students are dropping out of high school every year. This number represents a staggering future cost to the country in terms of low wages, a ballooning need for subsidies, increased crime, and a lack of human productivity. Who can deny that there is an overwhelming need for more creative approaches to how we educate our young, especially those in the neediest of situations. The old ways just aren't working. To hit this point home, consider what Jonathan Kozol has to say:

> NCLB widens the gap between the races more than any piece of educational legislation I've seen in 40 years. It denies inner-city kids the critical-thinking skills to interrogate reality. When they reach secondary school, they can't participate in class discussions. . . . NCLB's fourth-grade gains aren't learning gains, they're testing gains. That's why they don't last. The law is a distraction from things that really count. . . . Instead of at least bringing equality to segregated schools, NCLB substitutes a regimen that kills the motivation of minority children, demands the impossible of inner-city principals, and drives away the most dynamic teachers. (Quoted in Mundow, 2007, ¶ 6–7)

This problem is compounded by the fact that the achievement gap between black children and white children seems to increase considerably for the high-achieving young black students as they progress through their education: "After tracking North Carolina students in grades 3–8, [one] study found the black-white gap in math widened for students who started out achieving at the 90th percentile or higher and narrowed among students at the bottom of the distribution. Those researchers attributed the trend, however, to new state policies that put pressure on schools to reduce the numbers of students scoring at minimum levels on state tests" (Viadero, 2008, ¶ 21).

Another dangerous disconnect is the belief that seems to drive many in the accountability movement: "If you cannot measure it, it does not exist" (Block, 2002, p. 9). Block goes on to explain that

> the question of measurement ceases to serve us when we think that measurement is so essential to being that we only undertake ventures that can be measured. . . . There are many children whose capacities or accomplishments cannot be measured by a standardized test, . . . but our educational system is increasingly driven by a high-stakes testing mentality. When the test becomes the point, then teaching methods and curricula are herded into performing well on the tests. Nontest-related learning becomes secondary. [This] pushes us into a world where we only undertake what is predictable and controllable. So much for imagination and creativity. (pp. 22–23)

Experimentation is what brings about creative breakthroughs, not intellectual analysis. It is 21st-century schools that promote creativity that will tend to be outward looking, with links to schools in other countries and involvement in national competitions and arts events. Schools that are capable of being transformed from organizations that produce compliance and attendance to those that nurture attention and commitment will be lead by creative administrators and teachers who are nurtured and flourish in environments that value time given to individual and collaborative creativity. This valuing of creativity is one of the mind shifts and keys necessary to transform schools into places prepared to educate students for the demands of a not-so-distant future.

YOUR TURN

As an individual:

You've read a rather gloomy account of some of the fallout from our nation's current emphasis on a testing mentality. Now it's your turn to begin to turn the tide. Set your clock for 15 minutes.

1. Start making a list of all the possible and impossible desires you can think up for the perfect school, the perfect environment, the perfect conditions—anything you can imagine that would be teaching heaven for you and your students. There are no limits except for your creativity!

2. Keep this list. At the end of the book, I will ask you to do this same activity to see if we have succeeded in shaking loose your imagination enough to really stretch your list into something wonderful.

3. For now, put a check mark next to any items on your list that are actually within your control to bring about now.

4. Begin to move in the direction of changing anything within your immediate power. Choose your first item to work on now.

As a teacher team:

You've read a rather gloomy account of some of the fallout from our nation's current emphasis on a testing mentality. Now it's your turn to begin to turn the tide. Set your clock for 15 minutes.

1. Individually, start making a list of all the possible and impossible desires you can think up for the perfect school, the perfect environment, the perfect conditions—anything you can imagine that would be teaching heaven for you and your students. There are no limits except for your creativity!

(Continued)

(Continued)

2. Share your lists with each other. At the end of the book, I will ask you to do this same activity to see if we have succeeded in shaking loose your imaginations enough to really stretch your lists into something wonderful.

3. For now, put a check mark next to any items on your lists that are actually within your control to bring about now.

4. Begin to move in the direction of changing anything within your immediate power. Choose your first items to work on now.

PROLOGUE #5

Affirmations: One Way to Rewire You for the Creativity You'll Need for the 21st Century

Candace Pert, former research professor in the Department of Physiology and Biophysics at Georgetown University Medical Center in Washington, DC, has revolutionized our understanding of emotions as the link, in fact the glue, between mind and body. She has articulated a scientific understanding of the power of our minds and our feelings to affect both our health and our sense of well-being. On the topic of affirmations, Pert (2008) states that they "help us to learn positive thought patterns that change our reality. Thought patterns come from networks of neurons that fire together. . . . The more often a network fires together, the stronger the synaptic connections become. . . . Repetition in a relaxed, pleasant, loving state of consciousness can most efficiently promote the probability of a given thought pattern. We learn best when we are anticipating pleasure."

Below are just such affirmations that, repeated over time, can rewire the patterns of your thoughts concerning your relationship to your own creativity as well as that of others. Some have their origins in statements made by Julia Cameron (1992) in *The Artist's Way,* which was written to help unblock artists having problems utilizing their creativity. Others have a basis in affirmations written and recorded by Belleruth Naperstak from her series on accessing one's intuition more effectively. Perhaps picking a few from the list and typing them up for yourself would be a more practical way to use them. If there is one that particularly appeals to you, why not type it up and tape it on your computer or your refrigerator? These are meant as jump starts to help you shift your present mind-set to one that will help make the present look more and more like the future you can envision.

- ☐ I have everything I need within myself to allow my creativity to expand.

- ☐ Creativity is the natural order of life, and that life is energy—pure, creative energy.

- ☐ There is a creative force infusing all of life—when I allow myself to plug into this force, I increase my own energy and I energize my students and those around me.

- ☐ I am building the habit of noticing creativity around me, and I delight in the surprise it affords.

- ☐ I am ready to start looking for opportunities to spark my lessons with that creative touch that only I can give them.

- ☐ I am like a spiritual shark. I keep moving, never resting on yesterday's laurels, always beginning anew and putting more and more life into my lessons.

- ☐ I take risks and learn from my mistakes since I expect to teach with passion and enthusiasm.

5

Links Between Creativity and Research-Based Instruction

BRAIN RESEARCH: A GOLD MINE FOR CREATIVE STRATEGIES

Magnetic resonance imaging (MRI) machines can measure the sequence of thinking, the electroencephalogram (EEG) can chart the brain's electrical production, and spectrometers can measure the change in specific neurotransmitter levels. All of these, plus many other instruments, provide us with far more information about the brain than was ever available to us just 15 or 20 years ago. What should we do with all this new information? Eric Jensen (1998), in his practical and informative book *Teaching With the Brain in Mind*, suggests that we become "consumer literate," start using action research in our own classrooms to test these learning theories. We should keep notes and then take our findings to faculty meetings, our districts, our departments of education. Brain research sets the stage for us to begin laying a more relevant and effective foundation in the classroom. It also gives us a wonderful way to use our creativity to take theory and turn it into classroom practice. What more powerful use of the cross-disciplinary fertilization method is there than wedding educational pedagogy with current brain research findings?

Since so much more information about the workings of the brain is available to the general public today, what was considered private researchers' property has quickly moved into the realm of common knowledge. Cover stories in both *Time* and *Newsweek* in 2007 were dedicated to brain research. A common vocabulary and system of exchanged understandings is quickly developing among educators and the public. Most educators can agree with Carol Ann Tomlinson and Layne Kalbfleisch (1998): "Three principles from brain research: emotional safety, appropriate challenges, and self constructed meaning suggest that a one-size-fits-all approach to classroom instruction teaching is ineffective for most students and harmful to some" (p. 52). I am going to touch on just a few of the better known areas of this wide field of research to show how inviting it is to try out our own creativity in order to enhance brain research effectiveness in the classroom:

- novelty
- meaning and choice
- challenge without threat
- visualization
- emotions and bodies

NOVELTY

The brain likes novelty. It is intrigued by it, and it pays attention to it (Jensen, 1998). Anything you can do to make the learning unique, observes Marilee Sprenger (2008), may make the learning permanent. Novelty is one of the finest ways to dissolve discipline problems in a class and release the deadly stranglehold of boredom. We've all learned that the best strategy becomes old after a few implementations. The insidiousness of routine that slides into numbing boredom is death to any good attempt at engaging and capturing the attention of a class. For years I've given workshops for new teachers across Missouri. My advice is always the same: get a notebook that will be used specifically for capturing strategies during any and all inservice and professional development experiences. What new teachers need are pockets full of strategies so that they can teach the same concept in many, many different ways. I tell them to watch the presenter for good ways that he or she delivers information (group activities, variety of techniques to elicit feedback, audiovisual aids, etc.), watch and cherry-pick any and all good strategies they see.

Test your novelty ability.

Then I give them a Novelty Ability Test. Each person gets an index card and a small coin envelope containing five items. They are to empty the items on the table and then list all five of them on the index card, adding the little envelope itself as number six.

All of the teachers—no matter what age level they teach, no matter what subject matter might be their focus—then have to write down an idea of how they could use each of the items to either begin a lesson or activity or use it during the lesson. I give them a couple of ideas by showing them how they could use the little coin envelopes:

> You can use the coin envelopes to have every student write down a prediction of what will happen to a particular character in a book,

then write their names on their envelopes and place them in a fish bowl until the book is finished. Or you can use the envelopes to give differentiated assignments to students. If you have three-tiered activities for a specific skill, you can place the assignments in the children's envelopes according to their skill ability and tell them the assignments were specially chosen for each of them.

Teachers are always amazed at the great ideas that other teachers come up with and are just as amazed at the quality of their own creative ideas. My lesson is not to go find the same strange little items like the ones in the envelopes I had out at the workshop—a fake eyeball, playing dice, a lettered bead, a ticket, a little row of stickers—but to begin looking around as they shop for similar little things that could put a little novelty into an otherwise ordinary activity. My best haunts for cheap things I can buy in sets of 30 are the Target $1 rows that are usually reduced to 50 cents in a few weeks, after-Halloween sales, office supply stores, and Wal-Mart. I tell teachers in my workshops that they don't have to know exactly how to use the items, but rather just that they are curiosity pieces and that a perfect use will show up later on. This is always my experience.

YOUR TURN

As an individual:

1. Take the Novelty Ability Test yourself. How easy or difficult was it to think up ways to use the five items? Remember, this is simply an exercise to see how much of a habit you have acquired in noticing items that can be useful for providing novelty in your lessons. Anyone can improve his or her "novelty quotient" with practice.

2. Take a personal field trip through the Dollar Store, Target's $1 rows, an office supply store, a home supply store. Make a list of items you could use in a novel way during or before a lesson. Keep adding to your list during each trip out to a store.

As a teacher team:

1. Mentally go through your classroom cabinets and desk drawers, boxes, and files. Make a list of the stuff, props, and non-school-owned materials you have accumulated. What is the most unusual item on your list?

2. Compare this item as well as your list with those of your team members. Explain how you use your favorite novelty item.

MEANING AND CHOICE

These two terms began to take the lead in all my planning as the years went by. I found that giving students choices whenever possible resulted in more student ownership of the assignment, more quality in their work, and more feelings of comfort and enjoyment. As Jensen (1998) notes, we know that the brain acts differently when choice is offered. Choice changes the chemistry of the brain. When allowed to make choices, students feel more positive about the task and look forward to participating, which triggers the release of the endorphins dopamine and serotonin.

My creativity came out in not settling for a single way to do most any assignment. Instead, I was always providing my classes with an array of equally rigorous but varied choices. And "meaning"? The search for it is innate (Caine & Caine, 1994). Effective teaching recognizes that meaning is personal and unique, and that students' understandings are based on their own unique experiences. If a student ever asked me, "Why are we doing this?" I had better have a good, substantive reason to offer. Marion Diamonds and her team of researchers at the University of California at Berkeley believe that enriched environments unmistakably influence the brain's growth and learning (Diamond & Hopson, 1998). An enriched environment for children, among other things, gives them opportunities to choose many of their efforts and modify them, allows children to be active participants rather than passive observers, and presents a series of novel challenges that are neither too easy nor too difficult for at their stage of development.

Thematic units always provide meaning for students and satisfy the need to see how the things they are doing and learning fit together. The freedom to develop interesting and multigenre units is something that satisfies teachers' as well as students' hunger for meaning in education. I know that some wonderful packaged thematic units are available from publishers and professional groups, but it's the experience of creating projects themselves that energizes teachers and infects students with that same energy and excitement.

The concept of meaning is wedded to the concept of purpose. When those "repeaters" in my class (described in Chapter 3) were learning how to distinguish correct from incorrect uses of the apostrophe, it was done within the context of meaning. They had a specific purpose for learning the material—to be adequately equipped with the information in order to catch mistakes on business signs. Whenever you can create a purpose for learning that is immediate and specific, it's always easier for you and students to work through the material. When I look back, I can see that most of the assignments I created were directly linked to that basic understanding of how our brains operate and thrive.

Just like recognizing good items that can provide novelty is a habit anyone can acquire, so, too, are all teachers able to develop the habit of consistently providing choices and purposes to students. Thoroughly grounded in good research, these are opportunities to exercise your creative muscles.

Mouse/Poet Assignment: Choice and Reflections

I've noticed that students often connect the ability to have a choice in their learning with the ability to use their creativity. *Choice* should be one of

My students can do that!

those words that teachers write on the top of their hands so they can remember its importance when they create the lessons and assignments they will be bringing with them into the classroom. Nothing offers students more opportunities for buy-in than being offered a choice in how they spend their mental energies. Choice doesn't need to be the offering of totally different activities; choice can be built into any structure. Below is a prompt I gave students that satisfied the biographical research requirement in the curriculum and provided every student plenty of room for creative input and choice. Although I felt it was a pretty straightforward prompt, my students considered it wide open and filled with possibilities for choice and imagination.

The Mouse and the Poet Project

PROMPT: You are a mouse who lives with a poet for a period of time in the poet's life that is important because of its relation to his or her poetry. You will explain both your role in the poet's writing as well as facts from the poet's life, exerpts from poems (whole poems if not too long). Basic facts should all be biographically true: time period, setting, situation, poems, people . . . but your involvement of course is left to your imagination.

REQUIREMENTS:

  **all materials should be typed in 12 pt. with poems in italics . . . font should be uniform throughout
  **illustrations must be found connecting to text throughout the book . . . and consistent in design
  **sheets may be glued, taped to book but as NEATLY as possible
  **generous margins need to be maintained throughout (see sample page)
  **title page, clean 1st page, dedication page should be present before text begins
  **story line, true facts, poems, illustrations should all flow well together

---

One of the final segments of every complex task I assign is an accompanying reflection sheet. This is always the best way to take the temperature of the assignment, the student, the whole experience. At first, students try to tell me what they think I want to hear from them, but as time goes by, and they realize I am really looking for honest feedback, these papers become far more valuable and essential. John Dewey once wrote something to the effect that we don't learn from experience but rather we learn from our reflection upon that experience. I take this to heart. Sometimes

I have students tell me what kind of effort they put into this paper or project—a gauge for them as well as for me. They realize that their work is not jeopardized by the truthful acknowledgment that they might have waited until the last minute or that they were only using a couple of their cylinders when producing it. I tell them it is not reasonable for them to spend total focus and time on every assignment, but when they do spend all their energy and focus and effort, I want to know it.

One young lady writing about this mouse/poet project had this to say:

> The best part about this assignment was the amount of liberty we had to be creative. I felt that I learned a lot about T. S. Eliot without having to research and write a boring biography. Biographies also don't allow for much reading of the actual poetry, but this project definitely did. . . . This made me find and read poems that I normally wouldn't have read and then really try to figure them out. I am proud that I could do it.

Another girl responded:

> First of all I have to say that this alternative assessment has certainly been the most fun project I've ever had to do. . . . I learned so much about my poet and what I wrote was only half of what I learned. I found out I can start a project ahead of time and end up with something pretty good. The easiest part was the research, the hardest was deciding what information to use and picking the pictures because they had to coincide with the story, so I drew them and they weren't all that good. I liked this project and it helped me use my imagination a lot more than usual. It was fun to write.

This student also contributed positive feedback:

> I liked this project. Not only do you have to use your research and writing skills, but you also have to use creativity so it won't sound like a biography. . . . I'm proud of myself because I didn't put it off until the last minute, I've gotten so much better at not procrastinating. I basically learned everything I wrote about this poet. I haven't ever really studied poetry so I had a lot to learn. . . . Now I want to know more.

Not everyone was happy with the assignment, though, as this student explains:

> I did not like this project. I do think my book was the best thing that I've done all year though. It was very time consuming and I had to re-write my story line 2 or 3 times before I actually liked what I wrote. I had a very hard time with this project. When I glued my pictures in, the ink from them got on the other page. I was very upset. My poet, Rita Dove, is a very interesting person and it was fun to learn about her. I learned that I do better on things when I enjoy what I'm doing. The most difficult was thinking of a story and incorporating facts, the easiest was the pictures. I just hope I get a good grade.

Let me stop here to talk about the origin of this sweet little project. As I began firming up my assignments into performance tasks, I also started looking for real-world products that my students could replicate. My mantra became "My students can do that!" I judged every possible idea that flashed through my mind against whether that statement applied to it. With this as the benchmark, I developed projects in which students wrote, designed, and edited whole teacher's guides over novels, used individualized education plan forms from the special education department to write up reports on Holden Caulfield, did "literary" archeological digs, created their own restaurant menus after looking at the descriptive language in many that I had brought in, changed short stories into movie scripts, annotated art gallery exhibits, produced magazines and newspapers.

Like most English teachers, I haunt book stores as frequently as I can. Often I have no particular book in mind; "I'm just looking." On one such trip, I stumbled upon a great little book, *The Mouse of Amherst*, written by Elizabeth Spires and illustrated by Claire A. Nivola (2001). This 64-page book about Emily Dickinson is told from the point of view of a mouse named Emmaline. When I saw this book with poems artfully tucked into the narrative and delightfully accentuated with black ink drawings, I tried out my mantra and came up with a definite *yes*—my students could indeed do this!

Another random act of fate coincided with this book's discovery. As head of the communication arts department that consisted of more than 20 teachers, one of my duties was ordering the yearly supplies. That meant I did comparative shopping for everything from Post-It notes and pencils to supplementary novels, films, and teacher's guides. Along with checking out all the catalogs that piled up on my desk throughout the year, I usually would go through the Dover Publications catalog because of its low cost and wide variety of book selections. I came across a number of blank books that had gorgeous covers from works of famous artists. Now, although I might come off sounding like I've lived a charmed life as a teacher for my entire career, I am a flawed creature. One of my glaring flaws is my propensity for jumping too soon at seemingly great ideas. I thought these books would make ideal journals for our freshmen, especially since they were only a dollar apiece. The only problem was that, as usual, I didn't really check the dimensions carefully enough. These books measured $5.5 \times 4 \times 0.2$ inches. When they showed up in August, I was amazed. These weren't what I had anticipated. This is when *The Mouse of Amherst* bubbled to the surface, and I thought these little journals would be the perfect vehicles for my mouse/poet project in the spring.

The reason I am taking up your time explaining the background of this assignment is that this set of circumstances incorporates many of the elements of creative thinking that I explained in earlier chapters: randomness (the availability of 125 little blank books), cross-disciplinary fertilization of ideas not usually combined (*The Mouse of Amherst* as the model for a class assignment), surprise (confronting my initial mistake), and lateral thinking (waiting for an idea to surface that would turn a mistake into an asset).

YOUR TURN

As an individual:

1. This coming week, as you plan what you are going to assign your students to do for a particular lesson, make up a comparable set of assignments. Or if not too difficult, make up three and have them do a "You Pick Two." I've found you can get more work out of children when they have a semblance of choice available to them.

2. What are your common practices concerning asking students to reflect on their work? Jot down when and under what circumstances you ask students for their opinions on what they are doing, how well, and so on.

3. Do you ever ask your students how you are doing? What you could change to make an assignment better? What to keep? Write down what you could possibly learn from doing this with your students.

4. I made a mistake in ordering these little books but ended up using them in a productive, creative way. When have your mistakes turned into real opportunities? Jot down a couple of your mistakes gone good.

5. "My students can do that!" can be a battle cry for authentic tasks, performance projects, real-life experiences, and definitely engaging activities for students. Make a list of possible "my students can do that" activities that could match up with your curriculum. Keep this list, adding to it as time goes by.

As a teacher team:

1. This coming week, as you plan what you are going to assign your students to do for a particular lesson, make up a comparable set of assignments. Or if not too difficult, make up three and have them do a "You Pick Two." I've found you can get more work out of children when they have a semblance of choice available to them.

2. Discuss your common practices for asking students to reflect on their work. Explain when and under what circumstances each of you asks students for their opinions on what they are doing, how well, and so on.

3. Do any of you ask your students how you are doing? What you could change to make an assignment better? What to keep? Discuss what you could possibly learn from doing this with your students.

4. I made a mistake in ordering those little books but ended up using them in a productive, creative way. When have your mistakes turned into real opportunities? Jot down a couple of your mistakes gone good, and share them with your team

5. "My students can do that!" can be a battle cry for authentic tasks, performance projects, real-life experiences, and definitely engaging activities for students. Make a list of possible "my students can do that" activities that could match up with your curriculum. Write down the ideas that everyone on your team comes up with. Keep this list, adding to it as time goes by.

CHALLENGE WITHOUT THREAT

Challenge can only work in a classroom where there is an atmosphere of safety to try something new, to take a risk, to go out on that proverbial limb. In fact, the impact of threat or high stress can alter and impair learning and even kill brain cells (Kotulak, 1997). In this world of testing, where getting the right answer seems so important, where elementary schools need to prepare for children who break down under the pressure of standardized tests by providing a "crying room," in this toxic atmosphere it is difficult to convince teachers or students to think big, take a leap, and perhaps crash. It is difficult to explain that this is what learning is all about while staring in the face of realities that speak the opposite. But this is our job, and I walk into classrooms again and again where this is happening.

One rule of thumb I show new teachers how to use when trying to balance challenge and threat is to have easy activities if the content is unusually difficult and difficult, complex activities when the content is pretty easy. If both content and assignments are hard, the students lose heart and give up. If both content and assignments are too easy, students quickly get bored and lose interest or respect for the material.

I would like to share an example that a young teacher wrote up to give her students after reading the book *Forged by Fire,* by Sharon Draper (1998). This is a very high-interest, low–reading level book that contains gripping accounts of abuse, death, drugs, and survival through love. I used it as a book club choice while serving as a literacy coach at Vashon High School, an inner-city St. Louis school with an all-minority student population. When my class was finished with these books, I gave them to a young teacher, Charlene Cofer, who wrote six prompts for her students to choose from using the RAFT (role-audience-format-technique) prompt writing template. Here are two of them:

1. You are a social worker assigned to Gerald's case after Aunt Queen dies. Your supervisor asks you to find out whether Monique and Jordan can provide a good home for Gerald and Angel. Write a report on your findings. Your final, typed copy must contain some background on child abuse and parents in prison. Your report must also include support and details from the book. Finally, conclude your report with your professional opinion as a social worker.

2. You are a fire department investigator studying the fire in Chapter 1. Write a report that details the causes and effects of the fire. The report should include statistics on how many fires are started accidentally by children, statistics on how many fires happen when children are home alone, and information taken from the book about the circumstances of the fire in Gerald's apartment. Finally, make some conclusions and state your opinion as an investigator. Should anyone be charged with a crime in connection with this fire? What could be done to prevent fires like this in the future?

Writing prompts like these that give students a role, an audience, a format, a purpose for researching a question, and a connection to both the book and real life is using your creativity for the best of all possible outcomes.

YOUR TURN

As an individual or as a teacher team:

1. Pick a section of content you are planning to cover in the near future. Write up a prompt that would contain the same elements of the two prompts above.

2. Discuss how these prompts differ from or are similar to the ones students usually are given.

3. Try the prompt with your students.

VISUALIZATION

The human brain can normally register over 36,000 images per hour, and the eyes can take in 30 million bits of information per second. Yet most of what the brain learns is nonconscious, and studies done on the impact of posters, pictures, drawings, symbols suggest an even larger impact than originally believed (Jensen, 1998). With this in mind, consider the fact that some statistics place the number of visual learners at 67–70 percent. Others state that children who live in poverty could actually be closer to 80 percent. In her article "Increase Your Brain Power," Donna Walker Tileston (2003) writes that "at least 87 percent of learners need visuals. Contextual learning is essential as we work with students from poverty" (¶ 19). The fact remains that even if a conservative number—65 percent of the population—consists of visual learners, when teachers lecture they are reaching less than half of the class. "Students need learning strategies that accommodate their learning styles. Many of these learning strategies help not only the visual learner but also make the classroom activities more engaging and therefore better learned by all" (Vakos, 2008, ¶ 6). This fact alone should prompt teachers to rethink much of how they deliver instruction, directions, content, behavioral expectations—everything that falls under the umbrella of teacher-to-student communication.

I say this from experience. When I stopped to really question just how much I was tapping into this visual lens that my students were seeing through, I began to see so many ways I could improve. At first I had to consciously remind myself to find visual props or pictures, or to use students to act out the procedures and class rules I wanted them to follow, or to have them draw little sketches next to their vocabulary words. After awhile of seeing what great results I was getting from just these small changes in my teaching methods, it became second nature to me to make sure I complemented my words with visuals. While reading the chapters that follow this one, keep an eye out for how much visual representation plays a key role in suggested activities. I consider visualization not just a strong brain-friendly tool to use, but a creativity power tool that boosts my teaching with energy and life.

YOUR TURN

As an individual or as a teacher team:

Since so much in this book will have an overlay of "visualization in the classroom," I am taking this opportunity to have you look at how visualization can affect your own world. We preach that a little sketch or splash of color can shift the brain's response for our students, so why not for us as well? This activity involves stickers and your plan book.

1. Find and buy (usually at local teacher supply stores or online) stickers that represent "hands on," "writing activities," "reading activities," and so on. The stickers shown here are my favorites because they are easily understandable and very tiny. Any that make sense to you will do just fine as long as they represent something you want to strengthen in your lessons.

2. With stickers in hand, go over a week of your lesson plans and place the stickers where they show evidence of your intentions to specifically have students do what they designate. Use a little hand where students will be involved in hands-on work, use a little pencil where they will use writing as a thinking tool during your lesson, and so on. This will give you a visual insight into just how much you are or aren't embedding the kinds of strategies you want to.

3. Staple to the front of your lesson plan book sets of stickers that you have picked to represent those areas you want to include more often in your class day. Then as you plan your activities, place a sticker by those activities, strategies, exercises that directly relate to the skill you are trying to strengthen. This very act will not only make your efforts more visible to you but will make you *want* to use the stickers and so nudge you to think up ways to insert these activities!

EMOTIONS AND BODIES

From brain research we know now that when we get emotional about a task we are involved in learning. Brain research has confirmed that emotions are linked to learning by assisting us in recall of memories that are stored in our central nervous system. . . . Emotions aid in memory retention (learning) of [a] situation as being good or bad. Decreasing threat ("driving our fear," mistrust, anxiety and competition) through cooperation, providing safe places, and providing a motivational climate for positive emotions ensure that learning will be retained. (Lackney, n.d., ¶ 13)

This kind of atmosphere is necessary if active learning is to take place. Active learning, according to David Brown and Curtis Ellison (1991), is not merely a set of activities, but rather an attitude on the part of both students and faculty that makes learning effective: "The objective of Active Learning is to stimulate lifetime habits of thinking to stimulate students to think about HOW as well as WHAT they are learning and to increasingly take responsibility for their own education" (p. 40).

The following three images first came from workshops I attended years ago. I have seen the same statistics represented elsewhere since then, so the data seems to be fairly consistent with current research on active learning. I simply love them. I seldom put together a packet of handouts for a workshop or presentation that doesn't have one of these close to the beginning. Everything a teacher needs to know about why we should move from a traditional delivery system to a more active, constructive approach is right here. After all, "learning engages the entire physiology. Teachers can't address just the intellect" (Caine & Caine, 1991, p. 80). Teachers who complain about a lack of student involvement, or frustration over how little their students remember when the tests come around, need to check out the relationship between passive experiences and more active ones.

The first image, the oldest of the three, illustrates the results of research conducted in the 1960s by Edgar Dale, who is often cited as the father of modern media in education. According to Dale, the least effective method of instruction (the top of the cone) involves learning from information presented through verbal symbols, that is, listening to spoken words. The most effective method (the bottom of the cone) involves direct, purposeful learning experiences, such as hands-on or field experiences.

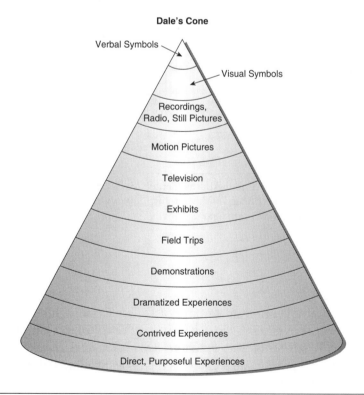

Dale's Cone

Verbal Symbols
Visual Symbols
Recordings, Radio, Still Pictures
Motion Pictures
Television
Exhibits
Field Trips
Demonstrations
Dramatized Experiences
Contrived Experiences
Direct, Purposeful Experiences

Source: Abilene Christian University Adams Center for Teaching Excellence. (2000). *Why use active learning?* Retrieved March 2009 at http://www.acu.edu/cte/activelearning/whyuseal.htm. Reprinted with permission.

The next image, which represents the results of research conducted by National Training Laboratories in Bethel, Maine, gives the approximate retention rates that can be expected from various types of learning experiences. Lecture (the top of the pyramid) achieves an average retention rate of only 5 percent. On the opposite end, the "teach others/immediate use" method achieves an average retention rate of 90 percent.

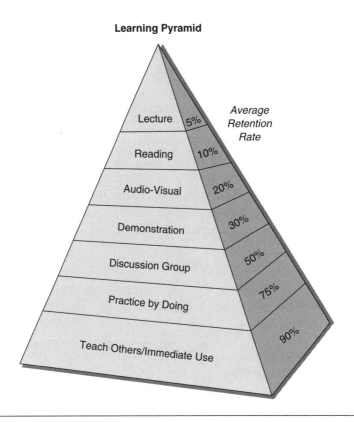

Source: Abilene Christian University Adams Center for Teaching Excellence. (2000). *Why use active learning?* Retrieved March 2009 at http://www.acu.edu/cte/activelearning/whyuseal.htm. Reprinted with permission.

The next figure is another version of Dale's Cone, which incorporates the information above and includes more explanation, making it easier for me to use with students and teachers alike. This chart was created by Bruce Hyland using the Dale's Cone as his base. Students always find this information fascinating.

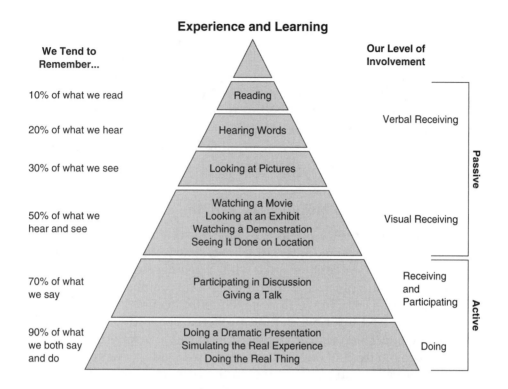

Additions by Bruce Hyland.

Much is written today about the need for education of the whole child—mind, body, emotions—the whole little person. The strongest pathway for memory is through the emotions (Sprenger, 2008). Yet many classrooms seem like places where emotions are frowned upon and considered rather dangerous to ignite. They can be. But creative teachers need to be able to excite students' emotions and use them to engage students in memorable learning experiences. Look at the lower sections on the last of the three figures. Anyone who is "doing" is bound to be using his or her body and emotional ability to get the job done. No wonder the percentage of what we tend to remember is so high! If students remember 90 percent of what they both say and do, doesn't it seem only reasonable to build many opportunities for these experiences into your planning? And built in on a regular basis, not just if you have time at the end of the unit?

Another number that seems sadly in contradiction to the material in this Experience and Learning figure is the fact that over 80 percent of class time is usually filled with *teacher talk*. And it's not just that "eighty percent of the talking in schools is done by teachers. When children do talk, they are usually restricted to providing short answers to the questions teachers ask" (Calkins, 1991, p. 100). Nothing is more passive for students than to be subjected to this all day. Jensen (1998) adds that if you want creativity from students, it works to get them out of a stressed state with a walk, music, humor, or storytelling. In other words, honor the whole child—body and mind—if you want high results and a happier classroom.

In the description of the Fortune Telling Activity that follows, be aware of the fact that although it may not be visibly apparent that an emotional load is embedded in this introductory attempt at building in prior knowledge, it definitely is. Simply by having students at the front of the class, out of their desks, role-playing, you are allowing for a powerful impact on how they will perceive the material and act during the rest of the unit.

So Far From Fluff: An Introductory Activity

An administrator leery of "fluff"—time-wasting activities not directly aligned to curriculum standards, guidelines, state test preparation—might have his or her blood pressure spike while opening the door to my classroom as I begin the process of introducing John Steinbeck's *Of Mice and Men* to students. There, in the front of the room in chairs facing the class, students sit dressed up in wigs, pink feathered boa, old hats, vests, with neon orange and green signs hanging around their necks. And where am I? I'm standing in front of one of these costumed students with what looks like a crystal ball, telling his fortune. In the corner of the room, a movie camera captures the action. The rest of the students are busily filling in character charts of these individual psychic readings that I am giving.

Right now, the administrator would hear me ask the one female student in the row of chairs if she is indeed Curley's wife. Our improv exchange would go something like this:

Me: You are married to Curley, aren't you?

Curley's Wife: Yes.

Me: You look lovely in pink feathers, you know.

Curley's Wife: Thank you.

Me: Let me look into this crystal ball . . . hmmm . . . I'm beginning to see something . . . yes, why, you want to be in the movies, don't you!

Curley's Wife: Yes, I do.

Me: Of course, I can see you clearly now . . . your dream is to be famous and in the movies and wear pretty clothes and have everyone take your picture, am I right?

Curley's Wife: It sure is!

Me: Class, write that down. Curley's wife's dream is to be a famous movie star. You do have the makings of a beauty queen, my dear. Now let me look in this crystal ball once more . . . oh, my . . . yes, I'm beginning to see something that you need to look out for . . . something you definitely shouldn't do. Yes, here it is . . . *don't go in the barn!* Repeat after me . . . *don't go in the barn.*

Curley's Wife: Don't go in the barn.

Me: Now promise me you'll listen to what I've just told you. It's very important!

Curley's Wife: I will. I mean, I won't go in the barn.

Me: Thank you for coming here today. It is a pleasure to meet you.

In like fashion, I would introduce each character of significance in the book, give a little background information, and have the students write down on their charts something that the character should be sure not to do and what the character's dream is. What I am embedding into my students' minds is prepackaged prior knowledge. "The brain's susceptibility to paying attention is very much influenced by priming. We are more likely to see something if we are told to look for it or prompted on its location" (Jensen, 1998, p. 43). They have an idea about what each character is like, what moti-

Give them roles for maximum engagement!

vates their actions, as well as a hint of the conflicts each will experience in the novel. Never after doing this activity has it failed to happen that when we get to Chapter 5, when Curley's wife enters the barn where she will meet her death at Lennie's hands—someone inadvertently calls out, "Oh no, she's going into the barn!"

Those students sitting in wigs and holding props in the front of the room aren't just any students. They are the ones I am pretty sure are the least likely to follow along with the novel, the ones whose attention drifts away the soonest, the ones I most need to involve in the book. I ask, beg, cajole them into sitting up there; promise extra credit; tell them they wouldn't have to say much; tell them they'd be filmed and get to see themselves in our class movie. Most grudgingly agree and drag themselves to the front of the class. Why these students? Because they will follow their character throughout the book to see just what happens to him or her. They assume responsibility for that character automatically. When a test comes around and students are trying to keep the characters straight, they will turn to one of these students and ask, "You're Curley, aren't you?" This is the visual image that students use to identify one character from another.

So, this "fluff" activity provides visual images, hints at a series of possible conflicts to look for, sets up the internal motivations that will influence behavior, gives the weakest students a reason to engage in the text. Not bad for an activity that is highly entertaining and student friendly!

Fortune Telling Chart

Lennie	**Curley**
Don't _____	Don't _____
_____	_____
You Dream _____	You Dream _____
_____	_____
Curley's Wife	**Candy**
Don't _____	Don't _____
_____	_____
You Dream _____	You Dream _____
_____	_____

George
Don't _____
_____
You Dream _____
_____

input

YOUR TURN

As an individual:

Improv activities are great for igniting student interest, emotion, curiosity, and motivation. Often we keep these types of exercises for the end of units—as reviews of material, as celebrations after the "hard work" is over. Yet setting these up at the beginning of a unit can sometimes have a greater impact on how that unit will go.

1. Mentally look over the various units you cover during the year. Pick out at least two that could be enriched with an improv activity to introduce the subject matter.

2. Jot down to your idea notebook these two specific units and ideas for celebrating their beginnings with action.

As a teacher team:

1. Discuss the improv activity I used to introduce the novel. How could it be adapted to one of your lessons or units?

2. Talk about the reticence some teachers might feel at the thought of role-playing with their students. Consider what advice you would give such teachers to help them get started using one of these techniques with students.

3. In pairs, role-play that conversation between a teacher who feels uncomfortable using this sort of strategy and one who enjoys it.

Letter From Arthur Costa

Dear Fellow Teacher,

We are often exhorted and admonished to be more creative, innovative, and inventive. In the day-to-day life of the classroom, however, as we try to implement mandates from an external authority, prepare students for tests that seem insignificant to them, and conform to accountability for making annual yearly progress, we have little inclination to draw on students' creative potential. In such barren school environments, some teachers understandably grow depressed. Teachers' vivid imagination, altruism, and intellectual prowess soon succumb to the humdrum routines of unruly students, irrelevant curriculum, impersonal surroundings, and equally disinterested coworkers. In such circumstances, the likelihood that teachers would value the development of students' creativity and imagination is marginal.

Slumbering under this pall, however, are innate creative forces with which all human beings come well endowed. We simply have to know how to liberate them! As Kevin Elkenberry says, "You are creative. Your creativity may be in a deep sleep, but it is there. All you have to do is wake it up and put it to use." This valuable, readable book, *Transformers: Creative Teachers for the 21st Century*, offers strategies that can stir your creative juices and, in turn, help students become more creative thinkers in their future lives.

Seven Habits for Highly Creative Teachers

To exercise and draw forth those creative resources within you and to create classroom conditions for students to maximize their creative potential, teachers might draw on certain *habits of mind* (Costa & Kallick, 2008) in their classroom:

Habit 1. Creative teachers listen in order to understand student's ideas. They

- challenge students with relevant problems and then listen to, explore, and build on their responses;
- use wait time, giving students ample opportunity to think and compose responses;
- clarify when they do not understand a student's idea; and
- remain nonjudgmental about students' responses.

Habit II. Creative teachers are flexible thinkers. They

- teach toward multiple and simultaneous outcomes;
- practice style flexibility as they value the diversity within a group, enabling individuals to recognize the wholeness and distinctness of each other's ways of experiencing and making meaning;
- change their minds based on additional information and data or reasoning that contradict their beliefs;
- are able to shift, at will, through multiple perceptual positions, knowing when it is appropriate to take a bird's-eye view and do big-picture thinking (this is known as *macrocentric*, similar to looking down from a balcony at ourselves and our interactions with others, and is useful for discerning themes and patterns from assortments of information); and

- know when a situation requires detailed precision, taking the *microcentric* worm's-eye view, examining the individual, minute parts that make up the whole.

Habit III: Creative teachers are problem solvers. They

- can approach problems from a new angle, drawing on a repertoire of alternative, novel problem-solving strategies;
- are often intuitive, holistic, and conceptual since to solve problems with incomplete information, they need to perceive general patterns and jump across gaps in their knowledge; and
- tolerate confusion and ambiguity, and are willing to let go of a problem, trusting their subconscious to continue creative and productive work on it.

Habit IV: Creative teachers are empathic. They

- can perceive a situation from their own point of view (*egocentrism*); and
- can perceive a situation through another person's orientation (*allocentrism*).

Habit V: Creative teachers find humor. They

- deliberately create situations that are funny, intending to cause others to laugh;
- avoid sarcasm and instead use humor to entertain, delight, and surprise others; and
- recognize, create, and evaluate whimsical ideas and situations, and therefore can laugh at themselves.

Habit VI: Creative teachers are metacognitive. They

- are aware of the kind of thinking they are engaged in;
- can describe how they engage in this type of thinking;
- evaluate whether the way they are thinking is effective; and
- plan how they will manage and modify their thinking the next time the same type of thinking is needed.

Habit VII: Creative teachers are responsible risk takers. They

- are adventuresome, intuitive, and unafraid of failure, viewing "failures" as learning opportunities;
- know the significance of and are inclined to approach tasks with clarity of outcomes, a strategic plan, and necessary data; and
- draw from past experiences, envision success, and create alternatives for accomplishment.

So, fellow educators, wake up that imagination of yours! Even under trying conditions that may not evoke your most creative callings, the act of teaching does provide innumerable opportunities to employ and model your ingenuity.

Sincerely,
Arthur L. Costa

6

Transformational Journey

From the Inside Out

We know that information becomes knowledge only when students use it in meaningful ways, not when dispensed and parroted back. The heart and intellect must be aligned if genuine transformation is to occur. This holds true not only for students, but for teachers as well. I've dealt with some young teachers who get exasperated with me as I begin to talk about the need to build community in their classrooms before they can legitimately demand responsible behavior. I tell them that taking time to reach students, getting to know just what makes them kings and queens on Saturday and Sunday, will facilitate classroom management issues in the long run. These teachers say they know all that; they learned it in their classes. But when I observe them, watch how they relate to students formally and informally, I see that their book learning hasn't translated into action. The heart and intellect haven't been aligned; no real transformation of relationships, teaching readiness, and effectiveness has been achieved. One of my suggestions to help move book knowledge into heart knowledge is to take on the quest for the "Saturday/Sunday Kings and Queens."

THE SATURDAY/SUNDAY KINGS AND QUEENS

You know how something you read tends to stick with you and pop up again months or even years later? Well, that's the effect that *The Geranium on the Window Sill Just Died, but Teacher You Went Right On*, by Albert Cullum (1971), has had on me. It's a little book of strangely intriguing pictures with little one- to two-sentence captions on the adjoining pages. The caption that made the most lasting impression on me is this: "I was good at everything—honest, everything!—until I started being here with you. I was good at laughing, playing dead, being king! Yeah, I was good at everything! But now I'm only good at everything on Saturday and Sundays" (p. 38). Brain research findings all point to the need for meaning, for the ability to relate new information to prior knowledge. All say that the student's question, "How does this relate to me?" needs answering again and again. If a teacher can locate and play to a child's internal seat of meaning, create a relationship that subconsciously says to the child, "I know who you are and I like what I see," then the game of motivating, engaging, capturing the student's interest is half won.

We need to find out who our students are on Saturday and Sunday to more easily connect with them so that we can then more easily teach them. And where does creativity come in? It comes into the picture in terms of how we find out who they are and then what we do with that information. For example, Lupe Fiasco, a hip-hop artist, might not be my weekend music of choice, but I am aware of him and especially his song "Kick, Push," which is about skateboarding. This is a little golden nugget in my bag of potential connections to student interests. With it I can offer a cool song to a skateboarding student's amazement and evident pleasure, and use that Saturday/Sunday knowledge later as a hook for a lesson or assignment. Say we are investigating censorship before reading *Fahrenheit 451*, by Ray Bradbury. Each student decides on an area in which he or she feels censored, justly or unjustly, as a teenager. They are told to come in with "proof" such as pictures, quotes, articles. Since signs prohibiting skateboarding are everywhere in many communities, my skateboarder is urged to take pictures of places he or she can't skateboard and then find articles or public transcripts of discussions at city hall about his topic. In physics, there is ample opportunity to consider the dynamics of the jumps, the speed, the actual construction needs of the board itself. Geography classes could choose a sport or recreational hobby and track its growth across the country or make a brochure of favorite cities to visit and locations of places where this hobby is most accessible. Any content area can be made meaningful with an overlay of Saturday/Sunday interests.

Discover the Saturday & Sunday Kings and Queens.

A few years ago, MIT Professor Henry Jenkins (2004) visited a sixth-grade classroom and told the students that he often speaks with the people who develop video games. He asked the students what they would like to ask these people if given the chance, at which point "the hands shot up. The kids asked . . . about the influence of game violence, the impact of technological developments, how and why games tell stories, the nature of interactive entertainment, and the economic motives shaping the games industry. . . . The students spoke with confidence and passion; they made compelling arguments; they supported their positions. The astonished teachers told me that the most articulate kids here had not opened their mouths all term" (¶ 1). This is why we dip our minds into the worlds that fascinate our students. Through these worlds we lead students into the educational arena to sharpen their higher-order thinking skills. Does it really matter that much what breed of animals these gladiators pit themselves against? Isn't it the process that counts?

As the days and years go by, we learn more and more about our students' interests. We would never have considered investigating these interests had we not been teachers and had we not asked. I learned about rap from my inner-city students. I had the privilege of sitting in on a meeting of the Vashon High School chapter of the Hip-Hop Congress while they were preparing for the convention that would be held in St. Louis that weekend. They were holding a rap competition to determine their chapter's entries. I watched and listened to young black men ages 15–18 pit themselves against each other with only words for weapons, words that slipped and slid over rhymes and beats, that demonstrated quick wit, manipulation of language, a richness of layers and connotations. When a particularly good metaphor was used, the young all-male audience would react with appreciation as genuine as any members of an upper-level college seminar studying the wordplay of England's most celebrated poets.

No one could ever try to convince me that the inner-city high school student in our large cities is incapable of understanding or appreciating the literary legacy we teachers of English love so well. The question isn't whether they are able to learn the content but rather whether their teachers are prepared and able to present the material in a way that makes sense to these students, makes constructing meaning possible, makes the bridges strong and safe enough for them to move from the known to the unknown with assurance and confidence. One book that I've found to help teachers do just that—move students from the known, in this case hip-hop, to the unknown, especially traditional poetry—is Alan Sitomer, a former California Teacher of the Year, and Michael Cirelli's (2004) *Hip-Hop Poetry and the Classics for the Classroom*. I use this book to connect our classic curriculum to hip-hop poetry through standards-based language arts instruction.

Years earlier, I had learned about hunting from my rural students. Not the hunting you see on television on Saturdays, where men in expensive outfits and gear whisper into microphones about getting the trophy animal on game preserves, but hunting on family land that goes back generations and is a source of livelihood, respect, and escape. I was taught about hunting for food and learned how to cook that food myself. I felt firsthand how starved our spirits are for those walks on the land, through the woods, and how most people have no idea what is missing from their lives that is causing an internal hunger to rage. A book I suggest that all teachers read is *Last Child in the Woods: Saving Our Children From Nature-Deficit Disorder,* by Richard Louv (2006). Boys and girls now live a "denatured childhood"; they've come to think of nature as more of an abstraction than a reality. Louv links children's alienation from nature to attention-deficit hyperactivity disorder, stress, depression, and anxiety disorders, not to mention childhood obesity. He gives a strong case for nature's ability to teach kids science, nurture their creativity, and keep them healthy physically, emotionally, and psychologically.

YOUR TURN

As an individual:

Often we discover our students' passions and interests naturally throughout the course of the school year. Make this a priority issue as early as you can.

1. List three ways you get to know your students when the school year begins.

2. Skip a line or two between each example.

3. Go back to your list, and write down how you consciously use this information later in the year. If you can't think of any way, then write down how you could possibly use this information in the future.

As a teacher team:

Often we discover our students' passions and interests naturally throughout the course of the school year. Make this a priority issue as early as you can.

1. List three ways you get to know your students when the school year begins.

2. Skip a line or two between each example.

3. Share what you have listed with your group.

4. Go back to your list, and write down how you consciously use this information later in the year. If you can't think of any way, then write down how you could possibly use this information in the future.

5. Add to your list any of your group members' ideas that you could use.

YOU, THE SATURDAY/SUNDAY KING OR QUEEN

Of course, the other side of the coin is what ignites your interests and passions on Saturday and Sunday. There is a middle ground between sharing too much of your personal life with students and sharing nothing at all. Part of the art of teaching is learning just where that authentic center lane exists and using it to advantage. Students are fascinated by the thought that you even have a life outside of the classroom. Letting them in on your own Saturday/Sunday passions can be one of the strongest methods of allowing them to relate to you and learn from you that life is made up of more than textbooks and book reports. We all know what can happen if teachers go too far off the center and bring too much into the classroom—disaster. But we also know how rich a contribution our own lives can make in widening students' horizons of future possibilities.

What are your passions? Your loves? Sometimes you need to pour them over your students like bucketloads of raw sunshine. These are gifts that need distributing. The rural teacher who loves ballet or Chinese history can open students' minds and hearts to a world they may never know existed otherwise. The young man who has always been passionate about baseball can bring in his old baseball card collection to enthrall a group of fourth graders who have been bitten by the same delicious baseball bug a generation later. We are "exposers"—like the darkrooms of yesterday, we expose our very selves to the film of the classroom and make indelible impressions on young minds. It's part of the job. Wise men and women know instinctively that the curriculum of the classroom will always first and foremost be the teacher.

YOUR TURN

As an individual:

1. List three of your passions, interests.

2. Skip a line or two between each example.

3. Go back to your list, and write down how you consciously use this information to connect with students. If you can't think of any way, then write down how you could possibly use this information in the future.

As a teacher team:

1. List three of your passions, interests.

2. Skip a line or two between each example.

3. Share these with your group.

4. Go back to your list, and write down how you consciously use this information to connect with students. If you can't think of any way, then write down how you could possibly use this information in the future.

5. Add to your list any of your group members' ideas that you could use.

TRANSFORMATIONAL STAGES

Transformation is within but is accelerated by our outside environment. Yes, we are responsible for our own interior development, but this can be slowed down or speeded up by where we teach, with whom, and the sustainable environment in which we find ourselves. So for purposes of your own growth, I suggest finding like-minded persons with whom to share your enthusiasm, your successes, your questions, your thoughts. Avoid those people who have made peace with the status quo and given up any desire to be agents of change. These people inadvertently spill an oil slick of poison over anyone's enthusiasm because they've shut down that part of themselves that once had vision, hope, belief in themselves and others. Some of these teachers are still capable of being inspired into action, but some aren't.

Age has nothing to do with this. I've met young teachers who have shut down inside and allowed negativity to be their most dominant personality trait. I've met teachers still in the classroom after 35 years who can hold a class of students in their hands and motivate them to greatness far beyond what those children ever conceived possible for themselves. Age, gender, race, personality, location—none of these make any difference in determining which teachers can transform others and which cannot. We all have the potential, and at some point we all decide which of these two groups of teachers we will join.

Because transformation is an "inside job," let me go to the interior rivers of our common psyche for a moment and examine our journey. One of my most influential mentors has been Joseph Campbell. Years ago I bought all of his lectures and interviews that were on tape and had him whispering in my ears every summer when I had time to walk, to exercise more regularly. At first, he was just filling my head with interesting but unrelated facts about mythology, foreign systems of thought, historical trivia. At some point, though, everything began to hang together and form a tapestry of insight and understanding. I was getting grounded in a worldview I had never considered before. I was getting educated. As I look back, I can see that I was able to achieve new insight and understanding because I was patient, I was not concerned about how many times it took me to repeat tapes until understanding began to dawn on me, I had no one telling me I was a fast or slow learner. No one was grading my accumulation of facts or forcing me to be assessed prematurely. No pushing, no judging, no punitive repercussions . . . just continued curiosity and broad new pattern making going on in my head. So if you want to expand your capacity for being a creative-minded adult, I suggest embracing a patient attitude and preparing to just enjoy the journey for its own sake.

The fact is that a real change in how we see things—how we perceive the world and ourselves—is never quick, never solely constructed with intellectual facts. Real shifts in understanding take patience and the melding of emotion, mind, body, and time. We each may need to hear the same things said over and over again before any light bulb goes off and we find ourselves awake. As teachers we plant seeds of this transformation in our students' minds but may not be around when those little light bulbs go on. Ours is a career built on faith that what we do will eventually take root and flourish. So we slide back and forth from seeing ourselves in the midst of transformation and seeing ourselves as the agents of just such transformation in those whom we teach.

OUR HERO'S JOURNEY: MOVING TOWARD OWNERSHIP

> *The hero is a champion not of things become, but of things becoming: the dragon to be slain by him or her is precisely the monster of the STA-TUS QUO: "Hold fast the keeper of the past!" The hero's task has always been to bring the new life to a dying culture.*

—Campbell (quoted in Brown & Moffett, p. ix)

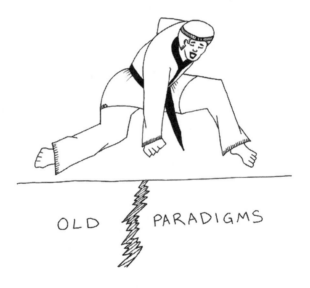

The stage of the hero's journey that I would like to focus on is the first one—loss of innocence—especially since so many teachers are leaving the classroom before they move much further on their journey in education than this first level. Teachers stay in a blocked stage of false innocence as long as they believe that individuals or forces outside themselves can provide easy solutions to the complex and chaotic problems confronting them. These teachers wish for the good old days. They are nostalgic for the past . . . if only things were like they used to be. These people believe there are silver bullets that will fix the students, the administration, the curriculum . . . if only we could find the best ones. They rely on outside experts to fix their situation. They assume that if they only care about kids all will be well. They fail to acknowledge the changing character of growing knowledge and strategies that is directly tied to student achievement. In an upcoming chapter, Linda Henke will explain how, as a superintendent, she addressed the culture that develops when a school is stuck in just this stage.

Some of the "if only" phrases heard most often from teachers can be found in John Brown and Cerylle Moffett's (1999) *The Hero's Journey: How Educators Can Transform Schools and Improve Learning*:

- If only the kids had good homes.
- If only we didn't have to deal with such diversity.
- If only parents could read to their children at home.
- If only kids respected authority (or each other).
- If only the district, school board, or state would stop bugging us.
- If only we didn't have to cover the curriculum and teach to the test.

The first stage of innocence is not restricted to first-, second-, third-year teachers. Some teachers who have spent many years in the classroom have never moved past this phase and have their own litanies of "if only" statements. Many of them yearn for a past in education that was never really there at all. The thoughts of those who feel that moving toward a new level of personal creativity would take too much effort might sound something like this:

- Why don't kids just sit up straight and listen to my lectures?
- We never had all these projects and crazy activities, so why should they?
- I know my teaching style; the kids need to adjust to me if they want to learn.
- I don't get paid enough to spend so much time on preparation—that's what manuals are for.
- If students would behave better, I'd start using some of those creative activities.
- My students wouldn't know how to handle choice or group work; they'd get out of control. They are happier with worksheets and seat work.

When one finally awakens to the reality of how things really are, that it's up to you and that no one has the definitive answer to solving your challenges, it is at this point that a panic often sets in. Teachers feel overwhelmed and seem unable to join the dream of what they wanted to be and do as a teacher with the reality of the difficulty of the job, the weight of the responsibilities, the lack of time and sleep and understanding from those who aren't "toiling in the field" as they are. It's important for someone to tell them that they shouldn't confuse this awakening with a sign that they're in the wrong business; it is in fact a sign, but one that they are ready to roll up their sleeves because they are indeed in the right business. Only by dropping the innocent, false hope for a distant past or a magic hidden answer outside of themselves can one move forward into the present and future. No true change or transformation will occur within a system if its members cling to the outworn notion that some external expert or set of experts can ever save them or if they feel the persons above them have all the answers. In *The Living Company*, the metaphors that Arie de Geus (2002) employs to analyze corporate management could well be applied to educational institutions: "The essence of learning is the ability to manage change by changing yourself" (p. 20). For those who have moved past the stage of naïve, false innocence, developing and unleashing your personal creativity is the first step to dealing with the changes that are now present.

What could we expect if we were to meet up with a "transformed" teacher? Brown and Moffett (1999) give these characteristics:

- approaches change fearlessly
- knows that his or her moral core is a shield
- has the courage to say *no*
- believes that "we teach who we are"
- feels that strength comes from resiliency
- views learning as one's life blood
- believes that one act of courage can change the world

YOUR TURN

As an individual:

1. Transformation is seen at the ability to change oneself and eventually others. It's been said that in the past one hundred years, unbelievable change has occurred in every aspect of our lives with the exception of one area—our schools. Spend 10–15 minutes freewriting your thoughts about this statement.

2. What point do you think I am trying to make about change in my description of my experience with Joseph Campbell's taped lectures and interviews? How does this relate to what goes on in schools or what is expected of schools today?

3. How often have you heard any of the previously listed statements signaling that a teacher is stuck in a stage of false innocence? In your opinion, what have been some of the results of such statements on themselves, on others?

4. What would happen in your building if no one felt there were any valid outside excuses or outside answers available to help them solve their immediate problems? What would the faculty lounge conversations sound like?

As a teacher team:

1. Transformation is seen at the ability to change oneself and eventually others. It's been said that in the past one hundred years, unbelievable change has occurred in every aspect of our lives with the exception of one area—our schools. Spend 10–15 minutes freewriting your thoughts about this statement.

2. Discuss what point you think I am trying to make about change in my description of my experience with Joseph Campbell's taped lectures and interviews. How does this relate to what goes on in schools or what is expected of schools today?

3. How often have any of you heard any of the previously mentioned statements signaling that a teacher is stuck in a stage of false innocence? Share your opinions on what have been some of the results of such statements.

4. If no one in your building felt there were any valid outside excuses or outside answers available to help them solve their immediate problems, what would the faculty lounge conversations sound like? Try an improv faculty lounge conversation with your group.

YOUR QUESTIONS: THE MAIN TOOL OF TRANSFORMERS

Whether it's forming the essential questions that will direct the planning of a unit's materials, strategies, and activities so as to more readily facilitate understanding or it's coming to a realization that the questions that dominate the class discussions are far more important than the answers that are generated; whether it's a mind-set that sees tests as opportunities to probe for student theories, misunderstandings, and have them delve more deeply into the many repercussions of what has been studied or it's your own personal questioning of what you are doing daily in the classroom, why a lesson was successful, why it fell short, what you can do to change the dynamics of a class's behavior: questions are the life blood of a thinking, growing person living an engaged, rich life—especially a teacher's life.

One of the fundamental underpinnings of Wiggins and McTighe's (2005) *Understanding by Design* is the necessity of asking and stimulating probing questions to uncover the meaning and understanding beneath the often glib presentation of facts found in textbooks. When teachers and students discover the life and energy created in a classroom dominated by respect for questions that don't have easy one-answer responses, dominated by performance tasks devised to investigate possibilities and test the validity of everything and anything—when this discovery dawns on teachers and students, the world of education goes from black and white to color, just like that original version of *The Wizard of Oz* when Dorothy went from Kansas to glorious Technicolor Oz.

It's the questions that change the mental patterns for both the young and old. Evidence of thinking in our students is exhibited not by them repeating answers they have heard from us but by them developing questions about the material that have not been generated by the teacher or the textbook. If we acknowledge and reward good questions, we will build much stronger thinking patterns in our students.

Transformation comes more from pursuing profound questions than seeking practical answers. Ironically, when dealing with questions of vision, identity, our desires for a healthy school environment that prepares students for their futures, it is the conversation that is the action. The struggle with the complex realities is the solution, a faith in the dialogue itself rather than a search for the right answer, the right new program, the right packaged formula of reform.

Consider all of the committees you have ever been on, the discussions about how to handle or improve the current situations that are of interest and consequence to the smooth running of your institution. Some questions will, by their very nature, limit the flow of ideas and suggestions. Others will enrich and expand this initial stage of problem solving or idea gathering. A thoughtful examination of the repercussions of the very questions we ask would move us light years ahead in developing creative, dynamic solutions. With the help of Peter Block, let's take a look at what dynamics are in play when we begin with *how* questions. Block (2002) discusses these issues in far more depth and clarity in his book *The Answer to How Is Yes* than I ever could. What I am attempting to do here is offer a brief overview to provoke your consideration of common questions we hear and voice all the time.

- **How do you do it?** This question infers that others know and we don't, that the right answer is just around the corner if only we are told the correct methodology. It skips the more meaningful question of whether this is even worth doing in the first place.
- **How long will it take?** This question forces us into considering only those actions that are qualified by their speed. If this is a criterion, then dialogue and whole-group input is seen as wasting time. No transformation comes quickly, but we continually hope for ways to prove that it might.
- **How much does it cost?** This places a price tag on initial brainstorming ideas. If cost is an overriding issue, then we automatically throw out many ideas that hit on our real values. Many important issues aren't even discussed. As Block (2002) notes, this question "puts the economist at the head of the table" (p. 19). We only have to look at the health care industry to see what damage this priority can do to values.
- **How do you get those people to change?** Any time this question surfaces, it is a wish to control others. We imply by this question that we have the answers and know what's best for everyone. If this is frequently heard at meetings, then a point to make here is that

"people resist coercion much more strenuously than they resist change" (Block, 2002, p. 21). People are always more likely to change from someone setting an example than by demanding that they change. It's example that transforms.

- **How do we measure it?** This states that if you can't measure it, it does not exist. This question moves us into a state of considering only those elements that are predictable and controllable—not novel, imaginative, creative, fresh. When measurement is given too important a place in the educational equation, then everything is tilted to fall in line with producing measurable results. Everything else is reduced to secondary importance. Also, this question needs to be examined for purpose. Is it for control and oversight? For learning? For those being tested? For a third party?

- **How have others done it successfully?** The idea behind this question is that we must place ourselves in the role of imitators rather than real leaders and innovators. We would rather not take any risks. Seldom does another school's experience lend itself to whole-package replication. The variables are too wide and deep. What another's experience and success can do for us is give us hope that we, too, can make strides. The same goes for another's lessons, units, ideas. Unless you tweak them to fit your circumstances, the potential for success diminishes.

YOUR TURN

As an individual:

1. Questions are the life blood of a thinking, growing person living an engaged, rich life—especially a teacher's life. With this in mind, make a list of 25 questions on *anything*. They aren't going to be answered, just asked.

2. At some appropriate time in your teaching, make an audio recording of a class lesson. Listen for questions. List as many as you can. Mark them *student questions* and *teacher questions*.

3. Examine the quality and scope of an average set of questions in your class. What can you do to embellish, reward, acknowledge student questions?

4. Write down your thoughts on Block's (2002) explanation of *how* questions. Next time you are in a committee going through a problem-solving experience, see how many of these tend to surface.

As a teacher team:

1. Questions are the life blood of a thinking, growing person living an engaged, rich life—especially a teacher's life. With this in mind, make a list of 25 questions on *anything*. They aren't going to be answered, just asked. Share any that you wish to share with your team.

(Continued)

(Continued)

2. At some appropriate time in your teaching, make an audio recording of a class lesson. Listen for questions. List as many as you can. Mark them *student questions* and *teacher questions*. Discuss these with your team.

3. Examine the quality and scope of an average set of questions in your class. What can you do to embellish, reward, acknowledge student questions? Share your results with your team at a follow-up meeting.

4. With your team, discuss your thoughts on Block's (2002) explanation of *how* questions. Next time you are in a committee going through a problem-solving experience, see how many of these tend to surface. Predict which ones are most frequent in your experience.

CREATIVE THINKING VERSUS CRITICAL THINKING

We can't invite a discussion on how we elicit questions or entertain questions without looking at how we deal with information in and of itself. Without considering how our thinking patterns work and which ones we find that we depend on to best navigate our way through life, we really don't have the tools to alter or use them consciously. Just as we favor the right or left hemisphere of the brain as the lens through which we perceive the world around us, so too do we favor a critical or creative method of thinking to deal with that world. Just as we are far more effective if we utilize both sides of the brain, so too are we more effective thinkers if we employ both types of thinking strategies when confronting our daily realities. This section aims to shed light on both vertical and lateral thinking modes.

Edward de Bono, nominated for the Nobel Prize in Economics in 2005, is regarded by many as the leading authority in the field of creative thinking, innovation, and the direct teaching of thinking as a skill. de Bono's (1970) *Lateral Thinking: Creativity Step by Step* is a great resource for those of you really interested in exploring ways to develop creative thinking among various groups of individuals. The very term *lateral thinking,* as opposed to vertical thinking, takes a giant leap into a clearer explanation of the function of creativity. According to de Bono, vertical thinking is logical and sequential judgment used at every stage. Most of us habitually apply vertical thinking to the majority of issues we think about.

Lateral or creative thinking is concerned with generating ideas, whereas vertical or critical thinking is concerned with finding the right idea. Vertical thinking throws out any information that isn't "right" as it progresses; lateral thinking welcomes all information and isn't concerned about "rightness" until the very end. Vertical thinking is analytical, while creative thinking is provocative—able to open or provoke a new line of thought. With vertical thinking one moves step by step in a logical order toward a reasonable solution, but with lateral thinking the steps don't have to be sequential; one can jump ahead to a new point and fill in the steps later. Also important is that vertical thinking is by nature judgmental and selective, using the negative to block certain thinking pathways, while lateral thinking makes no judgments and accepts all ideas and, in fact, plays with ideas without any seeming purpose or direction until an insight appears or doesn't appear. Lateral thinking finds no problem in going down wrong or alternate paths along the way, whereas vertical thinking excludes what is considered irrelevant. As de Bono (1970) explains, though, both types of thinking are necessary: "Vertical thinking is immensely useful but one needs to enhance its usefulness by adding creativity and tempering its rigidity" (p. 7). I imagine you can look at these two patterns as deductive and inductive in their approaches to information.

A concrete example of both methods of thinking is how my husband and I go shopping. He, the epitome of the vertical thinker, has a list and chooses his route both to and through the stores in quest of the precise items on that list. He never "wastes" time looking at other items along the way, never considers changing his mind. I, the perfect example of his opposite, might have a list but look at the store aisles as gold mines of possibility and am open to any changes in my proposed gift or food list and want to go down all the aisles, just looking. He thinks I waste time, and I think he wastes opportunities for better purchases. We compromise and together get the job done satisfactorily, but it took some getting used to on both sides.

When it comes to the classroom, it was always very easy for me to buy items to use as novelties, props, or prompts without having the slightest idea how or when I would use them. My motto has always been "If you can get 30 of anything cheap, do it and think of how to use them later." My cabinets were always filled with magnificent sets of 30s waiting for their mission in life to evolve. I was always aware that they were in the cabinet and always ended up using them at precisely the right point in my teaching. I had an unbounded faith that my mind would match up the items with a specific need sooner or later. That is truly an exercise in lateral thinking.

Creative, lateral thinking is not generally a natural phenomenon. Our brains are built to develop patterns and sustain them. If something seems to be working, or even if it isn't working, we seldom feel the inclination to look for another method of doing it. Our brains don't have a mechanism for updating or changing the patterns of behavior or thinking that we have developed. It takes creative, lateral thinking to break down existing patterns in order to liberate information and consider new ideas (de Bono, 1970).

If a teacher has been teaching grammar for years through worksheets, diagramming, following the Warriner's series of textbooks from the first chapter through to the end, and then using Scantron tests to assess accuracy, he or she will find it very difficult and unnecessary to change that procedure for another method. It takes a great deal of effort and internal resolve to change the belief system in this method and try what seems like a radically new way of approaching grammar. Usually this same vertical-thinking teacher finds it difficult to accept the research that says children don't need to learn formal grammar before writing whole papers, that children don't need to be drilled on writing sentences before they can be allowed to write lengthy papers, that worksheets don't really allow for carry-over into student writing. Why? Because these don't seem logical and time efficient.

Another example is the difficulty some teachers and administrators have in seeing processes such as those for writing or learning as recursive rather than linear. Sometimes skipping a phase, or doubling back to repeat a phase, is important and necessary for good writing or learning to develop. Teachers trying to keep the entire class on the same step of the process tend to use it artificially and miss its power and validity. Many of us remember Madeleine Hunter's seven point direct instruction model: objectives, standards, anticipatory set, teaching (input, modeling, check for understanding), guided practice/monitoring, closure, and independent practice. This was and is a wonderful construct for good, effective teaching. But even though Hunter tried very hard to explain that this was only a guide, that variations could and should be made to fit the needs of the situation, many administrators began carving each step in stone and carrying them around to each observation and evaluation.

I once taught in a building where the evaluating administrator had codified each step into specific substeps that needed to be adhered to with religious rigor. Under "checking for understanding," all teachers were to walk up and down the aisles to check each child's work. One of this administrator's evaluations was with a speech teacher who had her students sitting in a circle. The teacher's evaluation showed she was penalized because she had not gotten up to walk around the circle during the "checking for understanding" segment of the lesson. Instead, she had asked each student to verbally redefine areas of the material for the group. The need to sequence and stick to a linear progression is so strong in some people's thinking habits that veering off course seems tantamount to inviting failure. Much misunderstanding of each other's viewpoints and motives in discussion of curriculum, discipline, and other areas of school procedures begins with how we see and adhere to our specific method of thinking.

YOUR TURN

As an individual:

1. In your notebook, describe the difference between vertical (critical) thinking and lateral (creative) thinking. Try giving an example of each to fit your explanations.

2. Now go back and reread this section to see if there is anything you could or should add to your descriptions that would make them more understandable to others.

3. Go over how you usually urge your students to think through problems and challenges. Do you allow for time to investigate other options? To make wrong guesses? To try out different ideas? Can you point to times when you encouraged your students to take a more lateral approach to how they attacked assignments? Write down how these two methods of thinking do or could play out in your teaching.

4. Brainstorming sessions are the prime times to utilize creative thinking modes. Next time you use brainstorming with your students, help them practice using this "other" method of thinking. Prepare a lesson on lateral thinking for your students.

5. Write down in your notebook a comment about the examples I gave for how vertical thinking can affect one's attitude toward change and procedures. Then examine how you think when confronted with change and standardized procedures.

As a teacher team:

1. In your notebooks, describe the difference between vertical (critical) thinking and lateral (creative) thinking. Try giving an example of each to fit your explanations. Discuss your examples with each other.

2. Now go back and reread this section to see if there is anything you could or should add to your descriptions that would make them more understandable to others.

3. Go over how you usually urge your students to think through problems and challenges. Do you allow for time to investigate other options? To make wrong guesses? To try out different ideas? Can you point to times when you encouraged your students to take a more lateral approach to how they attacked assignments? Write down how these two methods of thinking do or could play out in your teaching.

4. Brainstorming sessions are the prime times to utilize creative thinking modes. Next time you use brainstorming with your students, help them practice using this "other" method of thinking. With your team, prepare a lesson on lateral thinking for your students.

5. Write down in your notebooks a comment about the examples I gave for how vertical thinking can affect one's attitude toward change and procedures. Then discuss how you think when confronted with change and standardized procedure.

THINKING IN METAPHOR

Metaphor is our most potent key to allowing the right hemisphere of the brain to communicate with the left. There is no long-lasting creative thinking without sharpening the use of metaphor. We can utilize our own creativity quite effectively by simply helping our students understand complex information and processes through the metaphors we offer them. Chances are, if you think about it, you already are a dynamic metaphor-making machine day in and day out. As soon as you see those blank stares, those glazed-over eyes that signal a total lack of understanding, you go into "metaphor mode" automatically:

"Well, think about this as a . . . ."

"Pretend that . . . is a . . . ."

I lump similes under the big-daddy term of metaphor here for practical purposes. The point is, this is one of our basic teacher tools for building understanding, one we expand and sharpen consciously to improve student comprehension. This is an area in which we can use our creativity to great advantage and satisfaction.

Matthew Kay (2008) gives an example of how he uses a metaphor for the abstract concept of our "ideas" that exemplifies the power of metaphor as the medium for understanding in the classroom:

On the first full day of every year, . . . I put a big rubber ball under my shirt and pretend to give laborious birth to it. We name this child "my idea." I pass it around nervously, and when someone drops it, I snatch it up and curl into the fetal position. They laugh. I eventually get over my shock and learn to trust again, slowly passing it, then throwing it around the room for everyone to touch. There are two morals: first, you can't protect your idea forever, and second, our ideas grow when, by dialogue and debate, others are allowed to get their fingerprints on them. (¶ 7)

Such metaphors grab students' attention and cement the allusive abstract points the teacher tries to convey. I've been working on a metaphor system that could demystify the reading process for struggling adolescent/preadolescent readers. I feel that every learning process already exists in a child's experience. If we can tease it out and show them the metaphor, they can more easily embrace the techniques and processes we are trying to instill as mental models and patterns. Here's my metaphor for reading:

Welcome to the Party!

Intro: Pretend you are new to the school and have been invited to a party. Let's see how this experience is like reading a new book.

Then I go through the main tenets of good reading strategies in terms of going to a party. For example, text structure would be the purpose of the party, the size, whether it's formal or informal. Prior knowledge would be having a friend who knows the background of the people attending the party, what most will wear, the who's who of cool people. I go through all the strategies, making my metaphor more and more concrete and vivid. Other reading strategies I cover in this metaphorical structure are visualization, questioning, finding key information, making inferences and predictions, making meaning, and summarizing.

YOUR TURN

As an individual or as a teacher team:

1. Examine the various stages of reading techniques as represented in the party metaphor. Which ones seem a good fit? Do any seem too much of a stretch? Could you suggest a better idea for any of the segments?

2. How could you set up a demonstration of these steps in your class? Could you have students act it out, with a microphone overlay voicing what the main character is thinking? Could students make posters of each step to hang up and use as your working metaphor? (This is the beauty of a great metaphor—students grab it and go back to it again and again. Building your own classroom metaphors for various behaviors creates a sense of class identity and community unique to your room.)

MORE POWERFUL METAPHORS

I read an article by Rosemary Faucette (1997) that provides the best metaphor not only for the writing process but for all creative processes while allowing students to experience the various stages firsthand. Titled "Using Play-Doh to Teach the Writing Process," it is one of those jewels that is definitely a keeper for almost any grade level. The gist of the article is a comparison between a writer and a sculptor. Faucette goes through each step of the writing process until students have constructed a final piece—in this case, a pencil holder. It's such a great hands-on kinesthetic activity that delightfully explains an abstract process in colorful, concrete terms. While the students work with the Play-Doh, the teacher reads and explains each step of the process, continually comparing the process of a sculptor to that of a writer.

I won't go through the entire exercise, but I do want to talk about a couple of profound points Faucette (1997) makes that are fundamental understandings of the creative process and remove a couple of our most common mental blocks to using creativity more effectively. One point is the major difference between the creator and the critic residing within each of us. The prewriting, presculpting stage is the time when "you are getting ideas and putting them together in new ways, preparing for the final production. During this stage only your creator is at work. Your critic is asleep. For some of you, your critic wants to come out and judge, judge, judge. Tell your critic politely to be quiet" (p. 3). With this brief admonition, we are teaching our students how and when to use their lateral, creative thinking abilities and to tell their vertical, critical inclinations to wait and be patient. I had my students name their critic and sit him or her in the corner until it was time for the critic to join the conversation about the object we were creating. I also use this simple explanation when talking to members of writing guild chapters on how we all too often spoil a creative undertaking by allowing our critic to show its disapproval much too early in the process. At each such presentation, I see eyes light up with recognition of how they've been sabotaging their own projects by allowing their critical thinking to kick in prematurely.

Another of Faucette's (1997) important points is the unending potential for ideas that we all have, yet hardly ever access. After students mold their first version of a pencil holder, I tell them to "mush" it up and start on a completely new idea. We do the mushing up three times. This drives some students crazy, but in the long run proves the fact that, yes indeed, there are new and different ideas in their heads, and if they only stop at their first idea, it's very probable that they will miss one of their best ideas. In fact, often it isn't our first idea that is our best, yet we seldom set up structures that demand students think past that first effort.

This activity is a good way to set some of the classroom metaphors for the year, especially if you take pictures of children working through each stage and, after having them enlarged, made into posters to hang around the room. I've used this activity with adults and children of every age. It makes a perfect entry point for a discussion of creative thinking and how to generate ideas.

YOUR TURN

As an individual or as a teacher team:

This section deals with metaphor as a thinking device. In it I call teachers dynamic metaphor-making machines. To see just how true this is in your own teaching, decide on a day to take an inventory of your metaphor-making behavior. As you teach, listen to yourself. Using those metacognition skills of yours, keep your ears open for every time you use a metaphor to explain a concept or textual question to students. On a page of your notebook, keep a tally or record of as many as you can recall.

FRAMES, NARRATIVES, SCRIPTS: HOW WE THINK

Why so much on metaphor in a chapter about transformation? Because there can be no substantive change in our action until there is change in our thinking. We don't change our thinking until we are first aware of how we think and what we think. This uncovering of our own thinking is the groundwork, the preparation of the field for the planting of a new crop of ideas and subsequent action. (Notice how I start loading on the metaphors myself as I begin talking about abstracts. We all do this!)

In Chapter 1 of Michael Michalko's (2006) interesting book *Thinkertoys: A Handbook of Creative-Thinking Techniques*, he writes, "To be creative, you have to believe and act as if you are creative" (p. 2). The place where all transformation begins is right there within yourself, not in collecting more lessons, more self-help books, more research-based strategies compiled by the finest minds today—no, it all happens within your mind. Michalko gives an anecdote about a CEO of a large publishing house who felt his editorial and marketing departments lacked creativity. He hired a team of psychologists to spend the year finding out just what made the difference between creative employees and less creative ones. They discovered only one difference between the two groups: the creative people believed they were creative and the less creative believed they were not. So it seems we tend to act on our thoughts, especially our thoughts about ourselves.

George Lakoff, a distinguished professor of cognitive science and linguistics at the University of California, Berkeley, and senior fellow at the Rockridge Institute, is another person who writes about the importance of how our thoughts dictate our beliefs and how those thoughts are formed within our minds. He is one thinker and writer that those of us intent on improving education should read and listen to very carefully. Although most of his recent emphasis has been on relating embedded thought patterns to the world of politics—*Moral Politics: How Liberals and Conservatives Think* (2002), *The Political Mind: Why You Can't Understand 21st-Century American Politics With an 18th-Century Brain* (2008), and others—his basic explanation of how the brain takes in and forms thoughts should be of vital interest to educators entrusted with shaping young minds. If we are intent on teaching our students to problem solve for problems that don't exist yet, it is necessary to take a close look at just how the brain reasons.

One point is becoming clearer and clearer the more we become knowledgeable about the science of the mind: René Descartes' ideas on the separation of the mind and the body were not the only mistakes he made. His whole 18th-century view that reason is "conscious, literal, logical, universal, unemotional, disembodied, and serves self-interests" (Lakoff, 2008, p. 2) just isn't the case. In fact, science can now show us that 98 percent of our thinking—of what our brains do—happens without any awareness on our part at all. Also, instead of emotion getting in the way of reason, we now know that emotion is required if we are to reason at all. Apply that to our teaching—to our ideas on what a well-disciplined classroom looks and feels like. Apply that to how much of the content is delivered across the country today.

Lakoff (2008) explains that frames, the cognitive structures that we think with, make up the bulk of our thoughts. These frames have narratives—even scripts—and appropriate emotions that are expected to go with specific events. A frame has roles, predictable scenarios, relationships that we impose on reality to try to make sense of it. Examples of such frames that Lakoff uses are a restaurant (hostesses, cooks, waiters, tables, chairs, menus, checks, food, etc.) and a hospital (doctors, nurses, sign-in persons, patients, visitors, X-ray machines, surgery rooms, waiting rooms, beds, etc.). We expect things to appear in reality as they appear in the frames we have formed. Is there little surprise that the frame of school that many people hold in their minds forces them to resist change and restructuring? Although the majority of people polled agree that schools need to be transformed to fit the needs of today's society, that creativity should be taught and encouraged, when it comes time to make real changes, those unconscious frames of what really should be "school" rise up and negate all reasons why change should occur.

This look at internal frames that influence and in fact compose our thinking is a look at how we learn organically as opposed to artificially. Watch young children, from preschool through elementary grades, while at play. They act out the frames that are developing into their grasp of reality. Children play in little kitchens, with dump trucks and matchbox cars. They build buildings with Legos, with blocks. They play with dolls, whether traditional baby dolls, action figures, or Barbies. And all the while, children provide the narratives, which tell stories that have morals. They explain how one should or shouldn't live one's life. They outline the children's sense of reality that will pretty much stay fixed unless consciously examined and questioned later on. Here's where important learning is going on and could be worth listening to.

I am very interested in how we naturally learn, and I tend to think we could get more done and faster if we stopped imposing learning outside of its more effective time and place. This drive toward having kindergartners spend more and more time on academic learning complete with tests, grades, and crushed self-esteem, as opposed to developing those frames and narratives for broader thinking structures, doesn't seem healthy nor do I think it will yield long-term productivity.

I've mentioned more than once that the best assignments at any level always come about when I gave students a role, a purpose, a format. These are frames within which I ask them to work. Because this is how we think, the products, the writing, the thinking is always of better quality than if I didn't couch the work within a frame. And more important, when I structure activities within a frame, we are free to examine why we think the way we do and peel the unconscious nature away from these frames, look at them, and decide whether we want to continue embracing them as they appear. Our stereotypes and prejudices exist in the unconscious worlds of these narratives, scripts, and frames that we aren't even aware are dominating our thoughts. What could be more vital to our job as educators than helping students recognize and take control of their own thinking processes and thus their own ability to make meaningful decisions?

Transforming our thinking might be accomplished more readily if we take a hard look at the frames we embrace. One of those frames embodies how we perceive creativity and how we see ourselves as creative human beings. Digging out this frame from our unconscious, shaking it up, and redefining it as it applies to ourselves as teachers is paramount to our transformation.

YOUR TURN

As an individual or as a teacher team:

Michalko (2006) believes that "the worth of the ideas you create will depend in large part upon the way you define your problems" (p. 2) and he describes a problem as "an opportunity in work clothes" (p. 22). Here is his Tick-Tock exercise for reframing negative thoughts into more positive ones:

1. Divide a piece of your notebook paper into two columns. Label them *Tick* and *Tock*.

2. In the Tick column, write down any and all negative thoughts that keep you from being more creative in your classroom.

3. Quietly examine your list of negatives. Check to see who you are blaming, how you are twisting or blowing things out of proportion.

4. In the Tock column, substitute an objective, positive thought for each thought in the other column as if you were the most creative thinker in your school.

5. If you are working as a team, share a couple of your negatives/positives with each other or ask each other for help in developing really strong Tock entries.

The Administrator's Creativity Checklist

The following list is derived from Wayne Morris's (2006) *Creativity: Its Place in Education*.

☐ I make it clear to my faculty that creativity is of high value to me.

☐ I have added creativity to appear on teachers' performance reviews.

☐ I help teachers understand my vision of creativity by providing professional development opportunities and time for discussion to dispel false myths of what creativity really looks like in the classroom.

☐ I have put a system in place to consistently recognize and reward creative efforts and processes.

☐ I am building an expectation in my staff to infuse creativity in their lessons and planning strategies.

☐ I provide resources for teachers to participate in creative endeavors with their students.

☐ I urge my staff to go outside the school to tap the creativity of the larger community.

☐ I provide and welcome suggestions on how to make the environment more conducive to creative thinking.

☐ I demand that my team of administrators verbally encourage rather than dampen the creative risk-taking efforts of faculty members.

☐ I realize that mistakes will be made and express this to my faculty along with my determination to be supportive.

☐ I will model this dedication to creative thinking and acting in my own career.

7

The Administrator's Role in Providing a Creative Environment

If one man has the last word on creativity and the optimal conditions for creativity to grow and flourish, I think many would agree that Mihaly Csikszentmihalyi is indeed that man. While researching and working to draw together all the ways to help teachers activate and expand their own creativity, I was haunted by the following sentence that Csikszentmihalyi (1997) had written: "It is easier to enhance creativity by changing conditions in the environment than by trying to make people think more creatively" (p. 1).

The following section is an example of how one superintendent broke ranks with the traditional mind-set of what schools should look like and act like and began her journey to change conditions in the environment in order to jumpstart the creativity of her teachers, administrators, and students. Linda Henke, superintendent of Maplewood Richmond Heights School District, in Missouri, draws a picture of administrator leadership, vision, and patience that is sorely in need of replication across our country if we are serious about moving the educational system into the 21st century.

Metaphor and School Transformation

Linda Henke

> *Without heart and spirit nourished by cultural ways, schools become learning factories devoid of soul and passion.*
>
> —Kent Peterson and Terry Deal (2002, p. 7)

Eight years ago I accepted the superintendency of Maplewood Richmond Heights (MRH), a small urban district nestled next to St. Louis, Missouri. As an assistant superintendent in a neighboring district for ten years, I had watched MRH flounder from one crisis to another. It seemed that in spite of serving only one thousand students, the district consistently suffered all of the crises of large urban school districts. In 2000, when the superintendency opened for the fourth time in five years, I decided to test my theories about school culture and systems thinking in what appeared to be a broken system. I applied, and the next thing I knew I was moving from an upscale suburban district with a great reputation to a district that couldn't seem to get it together.

AN INFORMAL ETHNOGRAPHIC STUDY

Because my new assistant superintendent and I were hired in January and didn't officially start work at MRH until July, we approached the district for six months as an ethnographic study. During several evenings and on Saturdays we set up shop in a nearby coffee house and invited any staff member who wished to talk to us about the district to join us. We promised a free cup of coffee, a listening ear, and complete confidentiality. Over the course of those six months, we had individual conversations with almost 40 staff members, all of the MRH board members, the mayors and city managers of the two towns served by the district, and individuals identified by my new Board of Education as important to the life of the community. We also talked with close to a dozen graduates and students of the district.

What became clear in those conversations was a school culture rooted in negative images of the students, the staff, the school itself, and the broader community. Maplewood, one of the towns we served, was identified by several of the speakers as "Maplehood." One teacher commented, "For most of the county we are considered the unwashed hordes from the south." The myth of the victim played itself out in many of our conversations, evidenced by statements such as this: "We do the best we can with the students we have." Others commented that resources weren't available to meet the intense needs of many of their students—over half of whom lived in poverty. One of the city managers described the district as an albatross that hung around the city's neck.

SCHOOL CULTURE

Discussing the impact of school culture in determining what people pay attention to, Peterson and Deal (2002) comment, "A school's culture sharpens the focus of daily behavior and increases attention to what is important and valued" (p. 10). Culture, they note, "is manifested in people's patterns of behavior, mental maps, and social norms" and perhaps is best defined as "the way we do things around here" (p. 9). The negative mental maps of MRH held by those involved in the work of the schools shaped the teaching and learning, the interactions of individuals and groups, and the sense of self-worth of the adults and children in the district.

Prevalent Beliefs at Maplewood Richmond Heights in 2000

- The children who come to us have so many problems that we cannot expect to produce the same results as other schools.
- These students need the basics: drill and practice is the best way to help them.
- Teachers and administrators have different goals and can work together only with union monitoring and formal agreements.
- This district is not a place where you build a career.
- Schools within the district must fight each other for community respect.
- Parents are the enemy.
- Resources can be pulled away at any moment. It is every teacher for him- or herself.
- Improvement efforts are primarily about fulfilling state mandates rather than about real change. Wait a while and the initiative will be gone.
- I do the best I can in my classroom—what goes on in the rest of the district is not my responsibility.

As I reflected on the interviews and the initial months of work, I was struck by a culture that was often toxic—for the children and for the adults who worked there. A full third of the high school students were diagnosed as needing special education, and the school teetered on the verge of being labeled academically deficient by the state. The teachers association was in continual conflict with the school board and the administration, and staff turnover was over 25 percent. Fifty percent of the students who could attend the school chose not to—instead choosing private schools, parochial schools, or home schooling.

A school's culture emerges in part from the metaphors that shape attitudes and behaviors. Lakoff and Johnson's (1980) seminal work on metaphors defines them as "experiencing one concept in terms of another" (p. 5). The brain abstracts experiences into concepts and then connects these with other concepts to build understanding. Metaphors frequently emerge from historical experiences that become part of the unconscious daily life in an organization. The ability to link schooling to other images suggests that metaphors have potentially powerful implications for influencing school life, and exploring the linked concepts might support school reform by influencing attendant behaviors, attitudes, and beliefs. At MRH, in the absence of any other coherent vision, the metaphor of the factory dominated the lives of teachers and learners alike.

SCHOOL AS FACTORY

The impact of the machine metaphor has been well documented in social, scientific, and political thinking for centuries. The world of the early 20th century existed in a mechanical universe shaped by Isaac Newton, and the factory emerged as the prized organizational tool as the century began. Perhaps no other organization took on the metaphor of the factory as fully as did American schools. Strong echoes of factory theory advanced by Max Weber and others still infuse much of schooling in the United States. Centralized decision making, specialization, a view of productivity as time spent on work, and assembly lines all became embedded in our mental model of school. Woodbury (1991) notes that "the factory saw workers and parts as interchangeable, and early behaviorists saw the children as empty vessels to be filled" (¶ 13).

Of course, the problem with this view of children, learning, and schools has been argued fiercely by progressive educators for decades. Children are not products, and teachers are not machines. The factory metaphor minimizes human potential, creativity, interaction, and innovation. Yet, interestingly, schools that serve the neediest students frequently are the ones that most closely adhere to the view of school as factory. The dehumanizing of teachers who work in such settings is seen in materials described as "teacher-proof" and in policies and procedures that minimize the ability of teachers to deal with individual students' unique perspectives as well as ways and rates of learning. Students who do not succeed in such mechanistic settings are seen simply as seconds off the assembly line—and from schools are passed too often to prisons, the other institution that adopted wholeheartedly the factory metaphor.

In almost every community in the United States, elements of the factory metaphor remain embedded in schools. In places where poverty, lack of leadership, or other social issues sap a district's energy, schools too often hyperbolize the factory metaphor and frame the work of schools in ways that narrow the possibilities for children and adults to thrive. The additional hammer of accountability, which has become such a force since the passage of No Child Left Behind, also magnifies the issues and thwarts creativity and innovation in addressing school reform. This seemed to be true for MRH—a district that had been spiraling downward for many years.

THE SEARCH FOR NEW METAPHORS

Schon (1993) advocates that new and better solutions can often emerge from supplying an alternative framing metaphor. The use of an alternative metaphor to revitalize the school culture in MRH was intriguing to administrators and the Board of Education. We saw metaphor as offering a compact and rich package that could provoke an organization's thinking about its purpose and approaches in new and nuanced ways. In *Myth, Metaphor, and Leadership*, Cherry and Spiegel (2006) identify the following purposes for reframing by way of metaphor:

- Encourage people to think differently about themselves, their organization, and their relationship with the organization.
- Help people problem solve creatively and proactively.

- Identify a prevailing and outdated institutional myth and develop a new proactive story for your organization.
- Discourage the influence of resisters to change.
- Lead creative thinking and problem solving by example.
- Assess, reinforce, and perpetuate spiritual values within your organization. (p. 101)

We began to search consciously for metaphors that would counter the self-limiting image of the factory. Certainly, we recognized that simply identifying fresh metaphors would not resolve all of the serious issues facing the district, but the idea of inventing a new "story," a new way of talking about teaching and learning, seemed intriguing. And clearly, we needed to find alternatives to help teachers focus on positive images of themselves and their learners as well as on the primacy of student learning work as central to their teaching. We wanted metaphors that would lead us in exploring the active, constructivist approaches to teaching and learning that we felt would help children and adults thrive in a respectful and nurturing environment.

The Expedition

Our metaphor work started with the middle school, perhaps the most problematic of all of the district's schools. The pattern of enrollment was clear—MRH was hemorrhaging at the seventh and eighth grade. Students would continue through our elementary schools, and then families would move from the district before their students began in the middle school. This first metaphor was perhaps the easiest. A well-known national program focused teachers and children on expeditionary learning, and one of its key slogans was "We are crew, not passengers."

We began our work with the national organization and commenced with the study of what life in school would be like if we thought of education as an expedition. Expeditions meant that teachers and students left the confines of the classroom often, and this was certainly not easy in the early days. On one of the first expeditions, to a nearby science center, the police were called to break up a fight. On an early overnight trip, most of the teachers returned refusing to speak to each other. I have to admit that in the first few years, as we put students and teachers on the bus to visit a site where they would study, I'd be praying under my breath that everyone would come back safe and sound.

Christy Moore, a science teacher at the middle school, has been with MRH for seven years. She admits that in the early days it was sometimes a nightmare: "We were unsure what we were doing, and this approach forced a degree of collaboration among teachers that was really unusual. At first we thought of expeditions as something we did in addition to 'real school.'" But years of experience have changed that: "When we leave the school building, it's as though the school layer comes off. Students see teachers in a different light. We become more human and in some ways more vulnerable. This helps build relationships—which is perhaps the most critical part of what we do with teenagers. We eat, brush our teeth together, and we are changed because of the closeness."

Christy notes that at first the expeditions seemed exhausting and complicated, but now students leave the classroom several times for each unit of study. "There were so many resources we were overlooking," she says, "and now we are much more interdisciplinary in the way we think about our work. I plan my units with the social studies, English, and math teachers so we get the most out of our units. We are not isolated in our own rooms."

Christy also recognizes that relationships with both teachers and children are transformed because of the expeditions. Because the adults are working so closely together, they problem solve together. She describes one situation: "In the past when students misbehaved, we sent them to the office. Over time we realized we were relinquishing important control. Now we do much more reteaching about appropriate behavior than ever before. I think about my teaching from the Dog Whisperer's perspective. I think about how I need to change my behaviors to help students succeed—very different from how I used to approach students."

In the past three years, discipline referrals have dropped by 75 percent. Christy attributes a good part of this to the focus on learning as expedition. She notes that even the difficult tasks they take on (clearing brush at a nearby park as part of service learning, the eight-mile hike as part of an extended stay in the mountains of Tennessee) give students cause to celebrate their accomplishments. "It's like boot camp in some ways," she notes. "Kids love to accomplish something important. And kids have so much now that they want to read and write and talk about. This learning is real."

The Studio

The second metaphor to evolve was at the Early Childhood Center, serving students in preschool, kindergarten, and first grade. The elementary school's principal and teachers began to study the work in Reggio Emilia, Italy—considered by many to offer the finest early childhood programs in the world. A grant allowed the staff to work with a skilled group of university professors to explore the unique philosophy of the Italian program. At the heart of Reggio Emilia's work is the atelier: the studio, where students learn to express themselves with a wide range of media. And so the early childhood staff members began to examine what life was like in a school that resembled a studio.

JoAnn Ford, a preschool teacher who has worked in MRH for over 20 years, had just returned from a trip to Italy to see the schools she had been reading about when I asked her to take some time to visit with me to discuss how the metaphor of studio had influenced her practice. JoAnn comments that she thinks everyday of a Piaget quote: "If you teach a child something, you have stolen forever his opportunity to discover it." She goes on to explain,

When I operate my classroom with this in mind, I relinquish a lot of control. Today I see that my students are really doing important thinking. My classroom has become a studio which is something like a think tank of three-, four-, and five-year-olds. When we had the earthquake earlier in the year, my students developed hypotheses of what had happened. One child thought that dinosaurs underground were shaking the earth. Students expressed their understandings of the earthquake with drawing, with blocks, in lots of different ways.

JoAnn's enthusiastic description of her classroom highlights the value placed on students' construction of understanding. In the studio, students have become active participants in shaping the conversation. They have also learned to use a broad range of media to express their learning. JoAnn discusses the evolving role of documentation panels, which record examples of students' work, excerpts from their conversations, and photographs of them working: "At first we were very hesitant about developing documentation panels. We asked, 'Who is this for?' It began, I think, for most of us as window dressing. Now we realize documentation is not simply display. Now students, teachers, and parents all use the panels to talk about what we have learned and what we are learning now."

JoAnn is quick to note that changes in practice took years; only the superficial changed overnight. The key point of leverage for her and for her colleagues was sustained opportunities to discuss, explore, and think about alternatives with an expert in the area as a coach: "Regular collaborative time has really changed our practice. Now our best and our worst come to the table. We trust each other."

As JoAnn and her colleagues waded into a new metaphor, she found herself questioning "some of the things we do because we've always done them. . . . I sat up in bed one night and said to my husband, 'Where do adults walk in straight lines without talking? Why do we take so much pleasure putting kids in lines? If we really are a studio, would people need to move in straight lines? And does an entire class always have to move? Wouldn't smaller groups be moving to find what they needed?'"

And so the study of the studio evolves, supported by expert coaches who help teachers frame questions, examine their practice, and help students express their learning in a broad range of media.

The Museum

The metaphor for the elementary school emerged from an *Education Leadership* article by Peg Koetsch, Linda D'Acquisto, Allyn Kurin, Sonja Juffer, and Linda Goldberg (2002) about students producing museum exhibits. I sent a copy of the article to the elementary principal and asked her to discuss the piece with her staff. Koetsch et al. outlines the experience of a school where students created displays of their learning for other students and the community. A number of MRH teachers were interested in exploring the metaphor, so we arranged for Linda D'Acquisto to begin working with a small team of volunteers. The results of the first museum opening were infectious. Parents, teachers, and children all had something to talk about, and parents came to the opening at their children's insistence. It was the biggest parent event we had ever held. Clearly, we were on to something.

Within two years, the entire school was involved in producing exhibits as part of inquiry education incorporating science and social studies. When the district passed a bond issue that allowed MRH to build a new elementary school, we approached the design with the idea of a museum in mind so that every grade level would have an exhibit area. As visitors enter the foyer today, they are greeted with a sign that welcomes them to MRH Elementary School and Museum. A brochure announces the exhibits that are available for viewing and how to secure a personalized tour with a docent.

Dan Lyons has been a teacher in the district for 10 years and currently serves as the elementary gifted teacher and chair of the Museum Board of Directors, a group of students who deal with the operation of the museum. Dan was in the original group that experimented with museum exhibits and now supports students and teachers in learning in this way. He notes that both students and teachers in the museum school think much differently about their work than when he first started at MRH: "Thinking about our school as a museum opened up so many ideas of what is possible. We used to teach the American Revolution as a series of facts. Now we do an object study, a visit to a local museum, and a perspective wall. More and more, we are feeling comfortable going where students are interested in the topic. We're no longer driven by the textbook. Students' questions become very important, not just a nuisance."

This kind of teaching, Dan acknowledges, requires teachers to be both skillful and collaborative: "When you aren't following a textbook, you have to get very clear about what you want children to learn." He also emphasizes that this work has become much more social for both teachers and students: "You can't be successful at the elementary school and stay in your classroom. You are expected to be planning with your team and helping your students learn from the exhibits other grade levels are producing."

The work at MRH Elementary strikes Dan as more authentic now that it is guided by the museum metaphor:

> Kids are much more aware of "other" because they are constantly thinking about how well we are communicating with our audience. Do we need graphics or charts or an experience to help little kids understand our exhibit? What about our grandparents? And the conversations have deepened. The openings give children opportunities to have rich conversations with adults. Parents, grandparents, aunts—they all come to openings because the kids are excited to tell them about what they have learned. Kids really like being experts.

Kathy Stroud, who has just completed her first year as principal at MRH Elementary, agrees with Dan: "Parents come to exhibit openings because their kids are excited." But what intrigues Kathy even more is how the idea of museum is changing teacher practices beyond preparing exhibits: "I see students and teachers taking a much longer view of their work than I have in other places. They are not thinking about bits and pieces of knowledge—they look for patterns and connections. Classroom walls are covered with questions students are investigating and things they are discovering."

Finding new metaphors for how we think of school

The elementary school staff continues to work with Linda D'Acquisto, each year peeling back more layers of the museum metaphor and exploring the implications for their work.

The Apprenticeship

At the high school, the principal and teachers have begun to explore focusing on students as apprentices. While this is the least developed of the metaphors thus far, three major changes in the school are attributable to it.

First, we recognized that students need to have teachers who are themselves experts. This meant promoting both content area expertise and real-world experience for our teachers. The principal now encourages teachers to select "an area of scholarship," and the district supports additional coursework, seminars, and travel to help teachers become experts. We encourage science teachers to become involved in actual scientific research. One of them has traveled to the Galapagos Islands as part of a research team; another works with the local scientific community and has been able to secure internships for her students. Students are actively participating in a study of migratory birds on our campus as a result of another teacher's experience. We encourage English teachers to write and publish and social studies teachers to become experts in a particular era or region of the world. This acknowledgment and support of expertise stands in stark contrast to the world of the factory, where teachers too often are viewed as interchangeable parts.

Second, the high school curriculum focuses much more on authenticity of work than in the past. In all courses, performance events at the end of each unit of study now require students to apply their learning in a real-world setting. And the specific curriculum offerings have also begun to change. We have a new environmental sustainability curriculum whereby students research topics such as alternative energy sources for the school district and report their recommendations to the Board of Education. A conference writing program requires students to attend regular individualized writing conferences with their teacher throughout the year to ensure that their writing is improving. New courses in Web design and videography are taught by individuals who first worked in the business world and can thus show students how to apply their new skills.

Patrick McEvoy, the principal at the high school for the past 10 years, has big plans for the apprenticeship metaphor. He would like all of the students to complete a real-world apprenticeship in an area of interest during their high school career. He has already begun to work with a teacher team to explore this possibility. And he has learned from the other schools in the district: "One thing I noticed was that in all the other schools in the district, displays of student work are very important. So I got to thinking that [this] should be true in a school that focuses on apprenticeship as well. The students need to think of their learning as their work. They need to be proud of it. So we implemented the academic wall of fame."

The high school's wall of fame takes up a major part of a hallway on the main floor, and all teachers in the school display some of the best work from every course that they teach in a given quarter. The display includes a picture of the student who created the work and the rubric that was used to evaluate the piece. Students take a good deal of pride in the wall of fame and frequently encourage visitors to take a stroll down the hall to see the kind of work that is done by students at the school.

REFRAMING BELIEFS AT MRH

The use of metaphors to fuel school transformation is in many ways directly counter to the current thinking on school reform, with its intense emphasis on accountability. In MRH, however, we have found that over time we have shifted important attitudes and practices as a result of our reframing of the work that we do. Current widespread beliefs, as illustrated by the previous comments from teachers in the district, include the following:

- MRH is a place where creativity and innovation are valued.
- Collaboration is critical to our work in the district.
- Our students thrive in environments that support them in building their understandings through active, social learning.
- The learning work that our students produce is important to us: we display it, analyze it, and celebrate it.
- MRH hires and supports high-quality teachers who assume important leadership roles in the district.
- Parents are an important part of our success.
- Genuine change takes a long time and requires both outside experts and our own best thinking to take root.

Over the past eight years, teachers have become much more satisfied and no longer see the district as a short career stop. Teacher turnover has dropped to around 12 percent, which is less than half of what it used to be. Our elementary school museum program features prominently in Linda D'Acquisto's (2006) recent book, *Learning on Display*. We have attracted back a full 50 percent of the parents who had fled the district earlier. Tests scores are up, and so is college attendance. While we know we still have much to learn and improve, our students are now learning to apply their skills and build their understandings in rich environments that celebrate their voices and their contributions to our learning community.

YOUR TURN

As an individual:

1. Dr. Henke uses metaphor as the tool to redefine what school means. For 10 minutes, freewrite about your thoughts on the three metaphors she uses at the various grade levels within her district.

2. What other metaphors might she have used that would work to change the image of the factory model school? Come up with one for the grade level you are currently teaching, and develop what it would look like in action.

3. In Maplewood Richmond Heights, what behaviors were altered among the students and teachers by implementing this change in the conditions of the environment?

4. Give a copy of this chapter to the administrator in your school or district that you feel has the most creativity-friendly tendencies.

As a teacher team:

1. Dr. Henke uses metaphor as the tool to redefine what school means. For 10 minutes, freewrite about your thoughts on the three metaphors she uses at the various grade levels within her district. Discuss with your team what you wrote.

2. What other metaphors might she have used that would work to change the image of the factory model school? Come up with one for the grade level you are currently teaching, and develop what this would look like in action. Share your ideas with your team.

3. Discuss with your team the behaviors that were altered among the Maplewood Richmond Heights students and teachers by implementing this change in the conditions of the environment.

4. Give a copy of this chapter to the administrator in your school or district that your team feels has the most creativity-friendly tendencies. Follow up later with that administrator by discussing what might be feasible for your school to try; offer the suggestions your group came up with in Question 2.

Leslie Wilson's Thinking Patterns That Help Create New Ideas

- Explore new ideas and learn to become flexible in your thinking.
- Practice visualization—learn how to create concept maps, illustrative schema, and sketch ideas out.
- Explore other fields looking for new theories and ideas that can be synthesized and adapted.
- Keep a record of your explorations. Keep an "Idea Journal."
- Learn to think in possibilities—diverge, be expansive in your thinking. Generate lots of ideas, then refine them.
- Practice trying to look at things holistically and try to get the big picture.
- Learn to focus in on parts of a problem, then come back out to the big picture.
- Don't get in a rut. Force yourself to try new things. Experiment with new strategies and play with ideas imaginatively.
- Think of yourself as an "idea artist" or an "idea vendor."
- Combine ideas. Let ideas and thoughts ferment and percolate, "sleep on it," and then revisit the issue or problem.
- Take time to imagine new ideas and possibilities. Practice daydreaming and visionizing.
- Look for ideas and inspiration in ordinary places. Scan books, magazines, articles, advertisements and photos for new ideas.
- Ask family members, friends, co-workers and even strangers for a fresh perspective.
- Brainstorm and free associate frequently.

Source: Wilson, L. O. (2005). *Thinking patterns that help create new ideas.* Retrieved February 23, 2009, from https://www.uwsp.edu/education/lwilson/creativ/thinking.htm. Used with permission.

8

What Can We Do to Strengthen Our Creative Muscles?

FOR OURSELVES—THE GIFT OF SURPRISE

Everyone who writes about enhancing creativity at some point will speak of the need to reawaken the sense of awe, surprise, curiosity, and wonder that we all owned as small children. We need to take hold of this attitude and habit of mind with both hands for any serious creativity to become our mode of operation. Happily, this is quite within our ability no matter what our age, our position, our present condition. Just knowing your goal is half the journey toward attainment, right? And the cultivation of curiosity and surprise is the best antidote to routine and the best remedy for that most pernicious of all evils of the classroom: *boring*. Without awe, your teaching becomes dull, boringly predictable, and routine. So what do we do to nudge that curiosity into life again?

Try actively seeking out one surprise each day. Keep a notebook, and each day record one thing that actually surprised you. Talk and, even better, listen to students during passing periods or before school—students you wouldn't normally contact. Try to surprise one class, one student, or one fellow teacher each day. Do or say something unexpected, break the normal classroom routine with a fresh beginning or ending. Aim to surprise someone or some group daily. After teaching the same content for years and expecting the same answers to questions, it's really a necessity to

Prescription for Creativity:
Surprise your class once a day.

keep alert for different ways to approach the material and elicit new ideas and responses. When a student surprises you with what he or she says or has written, make it a big deal. When you give an assignment and tell students that you want to be surprised, it's an invitation for them to think creatively; it's a signal that you don't have a specific single right answer in mind. Whenever I assigned projects, I made it clear that I wanted students to aim for something I hadn't seen before. So it was always a real goal of theirs to try to fill me with the pure enjoyment of surprise.

Let me give you an example. For years I taught Hawthorne's *The Scarlet Letter*. Now, this is a book with long sentences punctuated liberally with dashes—a book in which the two main characters don't even speak to each other until Chapter 16. In other words, a very slow-paced and difficult book for today's fast-paced, digitally infused teenagers to grasp, much less enjoy. Although it was always a challenging book for teacher and student alike to work through, my students always ended up enjoying it. Why? Because of the postreading activities and projects they did. One that especially grabbed my young readers was the Right-Brained Project, which students prepared entirely outside of class to create the substance for our end-of-book celebration.

I explained to them the theories concerning the differences between right- and left-brain dominance. Most students found themselves very comfortably in the left-brain camp. These were my honors juniors who excelled in math, science, social studies, and language arts. I told them the aim of this assignment was to strengthen and illuminate some of their right-brain tendencies that seldom got the opportunity to shine. They were to produce something that exemplified their most creative abilities or that was a leap of faith into an area of skill or art that they had never explored before. They were to exemplify the essence of the book in any manner they chose. I said, "Surprise me! In the past I have gotten the most remarkable projects. Surely your class can bring in even more amazing ones."

And bring in amazing projects they certainly did. One girl wrote a musical piece that portrayed each of the four main characters, and she performed it on her clarinet with her friend playing a flute. This girl had the same assignment a few years later for admission to the Julliard School of Music—taking a work of literature and composing a musical piece to interpret it. Another girl was interested in making something with stained glass and even took an afterschool class to make her version of the scarlet letter, which glowed when lit from behind. I got sweatshirts that lit up with tiny Christmas lights in the shape of an A. I got homemade cakes made by boys dabbling in the culinary arts. One boy tried his luck at needlepoint. I had whole Puritan costumes made and modeled. One of my favorite projects arrived at the classroom door just as a student was ready to present. It was her little four-year-old sister dressed up in scarlet and gold to represent little Pearl, "the living symbol" of the scarlet letter. I was so awed. The whole class was. Even now, years later, I still have lace bookmarks with quotes from the book sewn into them, dolls in proper Puritan garb, black-and-white blown-up pictures of students enacting important scenes, journals, earrings—all assorted evidence from classrooms of years ago gracing my bookcases, all successful evidence of attempts at surprise.

A note here for the skeptics in the crowd who wonder what this activity had to do with meeting the standards, preparing for state tests, involving students in rigorous problem-solving practice. Although the atmosphere in my classroom on Scarlet Letter Day was always jubilant and lively, these products of varying quality and workmanship were the result of high-level problem solving—the difficult work of innovation, of trying to out-surprise the last year's class with their efforts. This was an exercise in jumping into the untried world of new experiences and performances. Stretching at its finest, you might call it. I had each student write up the "History of the Project" to accompany his or her presentation. This way, all the false starts, the roadblocks, the frustrations got a chance to be heard along with the end product. As a child, I always had wonderful ideas when assigned projects but found that the end products never lived up to my expectations. I told my students that. I wanted them to try the wonderful ideas anyway and let the History of the Project paper pick up the slack for the possible misshapen results. With such right-brained projects, the students' delight in their newly discovered creativity and the opportunity to experience freedom of expression was palpable.

Then there's the art of following up on curiosity. We all experience being curious about something we've read, heard, seen, thought about, but we seldom do anything about it. It's in the follow-up that the art of feeding curiosity lies. When someone mentions something in another field of learning that you don't know much about, get used to visiting one of the online wizards of curiosity, Google or Wikipedia, to see what they have to say. At no time in history has it been easier to "look it up" than it is today. Build this habit into your students. When their curiosity perks up, tell them to hit the keys and let us all know what they find out. What you value is what they will value. If you value following up on wisps of questions and curiosity, so will they. If you begin to actually start implementing these suggestions, in the words of Mihaly Csikszentmihalyi (1997), "you should feel a stirring of possibilities under the accustomed surface of daily experiences. It is the gathering of creative energy, the rebirth of curiosity that has been atrophied since childhood" (p. 348). Another by-product of stimulating our curiosity and relearning how to enjoy our creative energy is "to keep concentration focused . . . [by which] we not only avoid depression" (p. 348) but also avoid the experience of burn-out, which has the potential of making our teaching careers torturous and often, for some, short-lived.

YOUR TURN

As an individual:

1. In this section the two main suggestions are in reference to surprise and following up on curiosity. Choose one of these, and write it on the top of your lesson plan page for the week. Also write it on a Post-It note, and attach it to the top of your computer.

(Continued)

(Continued)

2. Keep a log of your attempts to do focus on either of these topics. Give yourself a couple of weeks of effort before making any judgment on its validity as a creativity stimulator.

3. At the end of a couple of weeks, use your log to freewrite about what you tried, what happened, how it felt, whether you feel you should continue. If you decide not to continue, do the same process with the other topic.

As a teacher team:

Experience tells us that it is always easier to develop or change habits if we have friends trying to do the same thing as we are. So for this activity, pair up.

1. In this section the two main suggestions are in reference to surprise and following up on curiosity. Decide as a pair on one of these topics, and write it on the top of your lesson plan pages for the week. Also write it on a Post-It note, and attach it to the top of your computers.

2. Keep a log of your attempts to focus on either of these topics. Give yourself a couple of weeks of effort before making any judgment on its validity as a creativity stimulator.

3. At the end of a couple of weeks, use your log to write a letter to your partner about what you tried, what happened, how it felt, whether you feel you should continue. Exchange letters, and reply back to each other.

4. If you decide not to continue, do the same process with the other topic.

MINDFULNESS, AWARENESS, AND ALL THAT GOOD STUFF

Creativity is both our birthright and our ever-present source of energy and meaning. The more we tap into our well of creativity, the more we are our authentic selves and radiate a joy in living. The first step to a richer interior life, and to a more creative life, is to nurture a state of awareness, mindfulness, a sensitivity to what your senses are taking in from your surroundings. This results in a quieting of the furiously paced loops of thought for a while and an awakening to what is going on in the present moment. This is not simply a mental attention but rather, as Dorothea Dooling says, "an attention which relates and mobilizes the sensitive intelligence of the body, the affective intelligence of the feeling, and the ordering intelligence of the mind toward a more total openness to what is . . . and the real life, the living energy, which it contains" (1987).

Personally, I always seem to follow a moment of self-awareness with an automatic response of gratitude. So grateful to be the one here and now in this classroom with these human beings teasing out for them an understanding about how the world works—teaching. I've spent so many of my teaching years grateful for my role and always hoping for more grace and effectiveness in its playing out, trusting that the ocean of techniques, tools, strategies I've been swimming in year after year will serve up the precise ones I'll need to handle these students at this time with this material. Another attribute of personal creativity is definitely a trust in the competency of the unconscious to provide the resources necessary at the moment—an unabashed trust in yourself, your inner self.

So how to do this? I have an admonition I give to the young teachers I see in the new teacher's assistance program required by our state for certification. Not many clap, or nod their heads in agreement, or give me the body language that shows they are with me on this point. But I share this with them anyway: whenever you are in a classroom with a group of students, they deserve the full attention, the mindfulness of disposition, the state of awareness that says, "I am yours now, your teacher for your needs, your security. My mind is wholly focused on you now, nothing else is important." In practice, this means no sitting at the computer while students are in your class. No giving them "seatwork" and then working on your grades, your e-mails, or your planning for the next lesson. If they are doing seatwork, then you are walking the rows, checking for comprehension. You are available for the shy students to finally voice their confusion, available for the students with little confidence to have you stand next to them while they tentatively work on the problem, write the next line, hoping for your approval. This discipline, being wholly present to your students, is rewarded again and again by the subtle understanding that students get about your generosity of attention, the intensity of your desire for them to be successful. This isn't lost on them. This idea is better said by photographer David Ulrich (2002):

> The fundamental task of creativity, therefore, is to be fully present—in this moment, and with all that it contains. . . . Attention is a gift that we are capable of giving at any moment. We know or strongly suspect that people (including ourselves), animals, plants, and all living things thrive when given our real attention. To bestow this care in our [teaching] . . . is the only sure means toward the richness of a true quality of relationship and engagement. (pp. 26–27)

I find that it is in this state of attentiveness that our energy expands, amplifies, and touches others, fostering their own energy levels to rise and respond. This is the mystery of the alive classroom and a concrete step toward increasing your creative abilities. As some of you have surmised, this "mindfulness" has been not only the root or key principle of all Eastern approaches to a more resonant life, but also the core message of American philosophers such as Thoreau, Emerson, and Whitman. It is also found in most of the Native American wisdom as well. In his introduction to *Wherever You Go There You Are*, Jon Kabat-Zinn (2005) defines mindfulness as

> paying attention in a particular way: on purpose, in the present moment, non-judgmentally. This kind of attention nurtures greater awareness, clarity, and acceptance of present-moment reality. It wakes us up to the fact that our lives unfold only in moments. If we are not fully present for many of those moments, we may not only miss what is most valuable in our lives but also fail to realize the richness and the depth of our possibilities for growth and transformation. (p. 4)

Consider what creative power is available to the teacher who pays attention to his or her class in this particular way. Practicing this mindfulness will result in a spilling over of sensitivity in most every area of your teaching life that needs your focus. The following list of such areas that will be positively affected comes from *Understanding the Common Essential Learnings* (Saskatchewan Education, n.d.).* In becoming a more attentive teacher, you will find that you begin to

- analyze your own thinking processes and classroom practices and provide reasons for what you do;
- be open-minded, encouraging students to follow their own thinking and not simply repeat what you have said;
- change your own positions when the evidence warrants, being willing to admit a mistake;
- consistently provide opportunities for students to select activities and assignments from a range of appropriate choices;
- exhibit genuine interest, curiosity and commitment to learning;
- undertake the organization and preparation required to achieve learning goals; seek imaginative, appropriate and ethical solutions to problems;
- become more visibly sensitive to others' feelings, level of knowledge and degree of sophistication;
- show sensitivity to the physical elements which contribute to a stimulating learning environment through the physical arrangements and displays you provide or facilitate; and
- allow for student participation in rule setting and decision making related to all aspects of learning, including assessment and evaluation.

---

*This list was adapted from *Dimensions of Thinking: A Framework for Curriculum and Instruction* (p. 31), by Robert J. Marzano, Ronald S. Brandt, Carolyn Sue Hughes, Beau Fly Jones, Barbara Z. Presseisen, Stuart C. Rankin, Charles Suhor. Alexandria, VA: ASCD. © 1988 by ASCD. Used with permission. Learn more about ASCD at www.ascd.org.

YOUR TURN

As an individual:

1. The first part of this section is a call for awareness, or mindfulness. The suggestion I give young teachers is to train themselves to stay away from the computer while students are in their classes. Of course, this does not apply to when the computer is being used for class activities or lessons. Debate with yourself about this issue. One side will give the pros and the other the cons. Try to get at what you really feel about this suggestion. Practicality? Importance? Possible to do? Reasonable request? Talk it out.

2. Circle 10–15 words from the suggestions about what you should do to be a more attentive teacher. Write a couple of sentences using some of those words (adding other words as well, of course) to finish this stem: *If I want to genuinely try to improve my self-awareness in the classroom, I will* . . . .

As a teacher team:

1. The first part of this section is a call for awareness, or mindfulness. The suggestion I give young teachers is to train themselves to stay away from the computer while students are in their classes. Of course, this does not apply to when the computer is being used for class activities or lessons. You and a partner are going to debate this issue. One person will give the pros and the other the cons. Try to get at what you really feel about this suggestion. Practicality? Importance? Possible to do? Reasonable request? Begin by first jotting down all the points you can think of to make your point, and then go at it with your partner.

2. Circle 10–15 words from the suggestions about what you should do to be a more attentive teacher. Write a couple of sentences using some of those words (adding other words as well, of course) to finish this stem: *If I want to genuinely try to improve my self-awareness in the classroom, I will* . . . . Read your sentences to each other. Compare how many of the same words were used by each member of the group.

BEGIN WITH FOSTERING CREATIVE COURAGE

"We must replace fear and chauvinism, hate, timidity and apathy, which flow in our nation's spinal column, with courage, sensitivity, perseverance and, I even dare say, 'love.' And by 'love' I mean that condition in the human spirit so profound it encourages us to develop courage. It is said that courage is the most important of all the virtues, because without courage you can't practice any other virtue with consistency" (Angelou, 1997, p. 132). David Ulrich begins his section on the three principles of creativity with this quote from Maya Angelou. Hopefully he will be flattered that I do the same. As teachers, there is a different kind of courage necessary to own and wear to school every day than others experience in their occupations. The daily discipline of this courage is what shapes us as educators, keeps us from burning out well before our time, and saves us from sinking into a mentality of pessimism and despair.

Ironically, this courage reveals itself in a consistent attitude of joyful expectation. You know you will be gloriously surprised by the sparks of intelligence and curiosity your students exhibit. You know that kindness will be repaid with kindness by even the most unruly of your charges. You know that trying new approaches, learning new methods is your own personal access to the youth potion of your career. You have learned that you leave your personal fears, disappointments, angers outside the door as the bell rings. You are on stage, you might say, and this act demands total unselfishness of demeanor and exudes an atmosphere of hope, enjoyment, and vision. This courage is the construction of your school face, the classroom persona that becomes real and genuine and natural to you as you constantly practice its discipline. We say that doctors have a "practice." This is ours, our classroom practice, that which frees up our ability to unleash our creativity with generosity and finesse.

Don't confuse what I am describing as joyful courage with a Pollyanna attitude. It takes less energy to slide into negativity than to continue an upbeat manner throughout the school year. This is not the naïve, innocent exuberance of the untried and the untested. Rather, it is the courage of the veteran whose eyes are wide open to the flaws and inconsistencies of the institution we call education. I always found February to be the crabbiest month for most teachers. I made it a point to put more pizzazz into my lessons and consciously try to keep from dipping into the poisoned well of complaining or becoming short-tempered that whole month.

Sometimes our efforts are mistaken for an inability to acknowledge the harsh realities that surround us. I was accused of this a few years ago. I was serving as a literacy coach at Vashon High School in the heart of inner-city St. Louis. I made it a habit to always be in the halls during passing periods to greet students I was working with or just make eye contact and smile at everyone who passed my way. Everyone usually smiled back and eventually greeted me by name as the year went on. One day, I walked by one of the custodians and said, "Good morning."

He stopped me and said, in effect, "You always seem so happy. I guess you don't realize just how bad some of our lives are, how bad most of us have it, do you? I guess nothing happens to you like it does to us."

I was stunned.

It wasn't until a few hours later that I figured out how to answer. I made sure I found the man, and said to him, "I sure do know how bad the circumstances are for you and those who attend this school. I am appalled by the stories I hear daily from students and teachers alike. But that doesn't mean I don't see it as my job to try and bring a smile to their faces, to slide their minds from their immediate problems to something else that might give them hope and a chance for a better tomorrow. I don't think it does any good to try to let everyone around me know just what I'm struggling with right now either. But here goes: I was just informed that I have a pretty good chance of having MS and am scared to death what this might mean to my husband's and my future. I just found out my married second son is sterile and will never be able to father a child. And I'm tired, so terribly tired from leaving my home at 4 a.m. and driving over 175 miles one way to get here before the first bell rings at 7:15. That's my baggage today, and I usually keep it locked in the car as I enter the building, but I'm sharing it with you because of what you said this morning." We talked a little longer, and it was as if north and south met at a crossroads and got an inkling of each other's point of view. He never passed me in the hall after this without giving me the warmest of smiles.

LET'S LOOK AT FEAR FOR A MOMENT

Of course there isn't courage without the existence of fear. Standing in front of a classroom of students is sometimes one of the most exposing, fear-initiating circumstances that an adult can imagine. It is surely not for the faint of heart. Day after day, we set ourselves up for ridicule, obvious failure of one sort or another, stressful confrontation. How we handle the initial fear of putting ourselves in such a position is at the heart of our development as a person, a teacher, in transition to greatness. I'm tapping David Ulrich (2002) one last time for insight into the creative force that fear can offer us:

> What we fear the most is the very thing that we are called to confront and work with. Where we find fear, where we feel the most inadequate, is where the energy resides, where great potential hides, waiting to emerge into the full light of day. Once we begin, and move vigorously in the direction of our aims, a joyful moment comes when the fear and resistance move into the background and become part of our experience, but not the dominant feature. Our bliss then often emerges from behind this dark, smoky wall of fear. (p. 13)

According to M. J. Ryan (2006), author of *This Year I Will . . .*, there are three modes of existence that we all experience: comfort (doing things the way we always have), stress (a challenge seems too overwhelming, impossible), and stretching (feels a bit awkward, a little like wearing a new pair of shoes for the first time). It is in the stretching mode that change, mental growth, and creativity begin. There is always a tinge of fear in anything that smacks of change. By consciously exposing ourselves to tiny, not-too-threatening

Unless you move out of your comfort zone, you aren't learning anything.

acts of change in our daily lives, we exercise our mental muscles, and one study even shows that "continuously stretching ourselves [mentally] will even help us lose weight" (Rae-Dupree, 2008, ¶ 11). How's that for an interesting motive to work at challenging ourselves?

Speaking of fear, Ryan (2006) also explains that "whenever we initiate a change, even a positive one, we activate fear in our emotional brain. If the fear is big enough, the fight-to-flight response will go off and we'll run from what we're trying to do. The small steps in *kaizen* don't set off fight or flight, but rather keep us in the thinking brain, where we have access to our creativity and playfulness" (pp. 77–78). *Kaizen* is a Japanese term for continuous improvement. It is the philosophical basis that many Japanese companies use to improve the quality of their performance. The main idea is to make a tiny shift, a tiny improvement every day. What an interesting idea this would be to utilize in one's classroom. Today I will find a better way to distribute graded papers, or to take roll, or to ask questions, or to listen to student responses. Even if it were the *kaizen* tiny change of the week, the rewards could be astonishing: your emotional system won't rebel at the thought of change, your brain becomes more alive and active, you'll see the improvements magnified over time—and don't forget, you might even lose weight!

RESPECTING THE NEED TO MAKE TIME FOR YOURSELF

To smooth out the stress or fear, the creative spirit needs time to itself, not multitasking time shared with a thousand other demands. Time is a basic requirement for the growth and development of the human psyche. Everything in our culture and lifestyle makes this more and more difficult to attain. In today's fast-paced world, when teachers continually have additional obligations added to their loads with little seldom taken away, the ability to carve out time to think, to reflect, is a Herculean effort. But carve it out you must. How else can you ever get past the efforts of simply putting food on the table, laundry back into drawers, children to practice or lessons, and grades submitted to the office in time if you don't? And as Csikszentmihalyi, one of the most knowledgeable men on the topic of creativity and personal happiness aptly says, "survival to a certain extent depends on finding pleasure in those things that are necessary for survival. But when you begin to enjoy things that go beyond survival, then there's more of a chance to transform yourself" (quoted in Debold, 2002, ¶ 22). So making time for yourself is making time for personal transformation.

What do you do with the time once you find it? You develop your practice. A practice is a consistently repeated activity that frees your mind to wander away, play with ideas, listen to your senses, leave space between your ears for thoughts to form and amaze you with their vitality and originality. For some, a practice might be taking 30 or 40 minutes in the morning before the day formally begins and writing three pages in a notebook.

Three pages on nothing but whatever pops into your mind—freewriting. This writing is for no other purpose than to dip below your mind's surface for a short period of time and see what's rumbling around. After many years of writing such "morning pages," this has become more like a sacred practice for me. In her classic *The Artist's Way*, Julia Cameron (1992) advises this practice for anyone who feels creatively blocked. I suggest this practice for people who feel that they are losing control of their lives and need some way to feel that they are more than pawns, rather that they are the ones calling the shots and anticipating what life will toss to them next. Of course, I am what you would call a morning person, so it isn't really a burden for me to get up 40 minutes early each day.

FIND YOUR PRACTICE

For those not so awake in the early hours, I suggest a couple of other practices. Walking seems to have been the practice of choice for centuries, chosen by thinkers, writers, artists. It serves two purposes in today's busy world: it gives us a chance to exercise and walk the stress out of our muscles, and it allows us to open up the creative pathways of our brains. If you have a baby that is stroller age or a dog, you have a third built-in reason for choosing walking as your practice. I suggest you leave your cell phone at home while attending to your practice. Then for some there's yoga. I love my yoga classes, but I need to have something I can do daily on my own timeline. The fundamental quality in a good practice is that it is a repetitive activity that subtly serves to calm down the left brain's need for attention and allows the right brain total freedom to work undistracted. Women used to satisfy this need for creative thinking time when they would mend clothes, knit, do the wash by hand, wash the dishes at a leisurely pace while daydreaming out the kitchen window. Many of our modern conveniences have served to strip us of time to reflect, daydream, listen.

Besides a daily practice, you also need a special block of time on your own each week to fill your interior well. Julia Cameron (1992) calls this your *artist's date*. I never knew what to call it when I was a young mother of four under the age of five and a teacher as well, but I knew I needed a couple of hours a week to myself that was unencumbered by guilt. This is not easy to pull off, but it's seriously necessary for your whole mind and body's sanity. Sometimes I went to the park, sometimes I went to the museum, but most of the time I would take off for the mall and just walk around filling my head with colors, people watching, going through store aisles on no particular mission to find anything at all. I would sit at a café or restaurant and sip coffee or soup with an open notebook at my fingertips.

Two hours on your own may seem an eternity when you begin listing all the work that needs to be done at home, yet this personal practice is work that needs to be done as well—it's time you need to prioritize and respect. I came to a realization early in my married life that all the housework would still be there and would get done when it needed to be done.

YOUR TURN

As an individual:

1. After Maya Angelou's beautiful quote, I state that "as teachers, there is a different kind of courage necessary to own and wear to school every day than others experience in their occupations." Draw a backbone and a set of ribs on a piece of paper. On the ribs, jot down a list of the ways that you are asked to own and wear courage in your career. Be as specific as possible because it's really in the specifics, not the generalizations, that courage is required.

2. Now draw a star next to as many of the instances down the backbone when you succeeded in showing courage. Congratulate yourself for developing a strong backbone instead of merely a wishbone!

3. Plan how you can best start and sustain a daily practice like the ones I describe in this section. What preparations will you need in order to begin? What tools? Set a day, and mark your calendar when you have decided to begin.

4. Give yourself at least a three- to four-week trial period before judging whether this is or isn't working for you. It takes that long for habits to kick in and begin to take effect. Be brave and just do it!

5. Consider trying out the *kaizen* approach. Challenge yourself to change one tiny habit at a time in your daily routine—just to experience that moment of confusion when "the brain begins organizing the new input, ultimately creating new synaptic connections" (Rae-Dupree, 2008, ¶ 16).

As a teacher team:

1. After Maya Angelou's beautiful quote, I state that "as teachers, there is a different kind of courage necessary to own and wear to school every day than others experience in their occupations." On chart paper, draw a backbone and a set of ribs. On the ribs, jot down a list of the ways that each of you are asked to own and wear courage in your career. Be as specific as possible because it's really in the specifics, not the generalizations, that courage is required.

2. Now draw a star next to as many of the instances on your list when a member of your group has succeeded in showing courage. Congratulate each other for developing strong backbones instead of merely wishbones!

3. Each member should now take time to write up a plan to best start and sustain a daily practice like the ones I describe in this section. What preparations will you need in order to begin? What tools? Set a day, and mark your calendars when you have decided to begin. Discuss what each of you has chosen as your practice.

4. Give yourselves at least a three- to four-week trial period before judging whether this is or isn't working for you. It takes that long for habits to kick in and begin to take effect. Be brave and just do it!

5. Decide on a method to support each other in your efforts and to celebrate each other's attempts and consistency.

6. Consider trying out the *kaizen* approach. Challenge yourself to change one tiny habit at a time in your daily routine—just to experience that moment of confusion when "the brain begins organizing the new input, ultimately creating new synaptic connections" (Rae-Dupree, 2008, ¶ 16). Together, make lists of tiny changes that you could use as *kaizen* exercises.

HOW TO HELP YOUR FELLOW TEACHERS

Albert Cullum—*A Touch of Greatness*

A Touch of Greatness, by Catherine Gund and Leslie Sullivan, premiered nationally on *Independent Lens*, the Emmy Award–winning PBS series, on January 11, 2005. In this film's marketing description, Albert Cullum is described as an educator who believed in the classroom as a place where joy, excitement, and productivity are inextricably linked. The film affirms that mystery, magic, and grandeur can create an atmosphere for effective learning that traditional lesson plans can never match. Cullum taught fifth grade in a New York public school in the 1950s and 1960s. The film was put together from movie clips from that era, which he had Robert Downey Sr. take of his students as they acted out Shakespeare's plays, operated on bleeding nouns in the "grammar hospital," conducted marches on a pretend city hall, slid down the Mississippi on a river made from a roll of paper spread over a map of the United States that covered the whole concrete playground. Cullum's students moved through the western expansion of the United States over that chalk-drawn map. They voted during mock elections while standing on the state they were representing. Their knowledge of the states was far more than mere rote memory.

Cullum reminds us that "we must remember how children learn rather than how we teach. Through movement, through emotions, through activities, through projects—all the basics fit in. And they're learning without realizing they're learning" (quoted in Gund & Sullivan, 2005). I personally love his working philosophy on testing: "My approach to introducing [the classics] to them is telling the story. . . . And they weren't tested. No one was ever tested how much they remembered about a play. Drilling extra hard is not going to help them remember it. Helping them get emotionally involved is going to help them pass this—any test any state gives. You don't forget it. You have to have faith that the children are going to internalize." Cullum is a man who was definitely ahead of his times. But really, how would he be considered today? Would he be chastised because he isn't following the prescribed curriculum? Because he takes too long on his units and isn't drilling for the New York state tests? Because he uses material usually reserved for the upper-level honors students? Who knows?

And how was he received and accepted at the time by his peers? How do fellow teachers and the community treat the more obviously creative among them? In reality, we treat them pretty shabbily. The most creative among us are looked on with suspicion and with a deeper fear that if they are recognized as successful, then that will put an unbearable burden on the rest of us to change, to be forced to move from our comfort zones and stretch. Sometimes some of us see creative teachers as such a threat to our own way of handling a class that we go out of our way to sabotage their efforts, to belittle their successes, to dampen the enthusiasm of their students by planting doubts in their heads about the efficacy and appropriateness of these teachers' methods. We can be heard commenting on how "noisy their classes are," implying that there is a lack discipline (the main virtue of the strict teacher's classroom). We can be heard questioning "whether those students can be learning anything if they are enjoying themselves so much."

Tommie Lindsey—Against All Odds

Let me give you a couple more current examples. The first is Tommie Lindsey. He is the subject of another documentary film, *Accidental Hero: Room 408* (DeBono & Rosen, 2001). As a forensics teacher and coach at James Logan High School, in Union City, California, Lindsey has led his multiracial, low-income students to state and national recognition. Of his students, 99 percent are accepted into four-year colleges. As an African American coach in the predominantly all-white world of forensics, he has excelled to the level of being named the National Forensics Council's Coach of the Year, and in one year alone had brought 78 qualifiers to the state competition. He takes anyone who walks in his door. When his team members are unable to buy the appropriate clothes to wear in competition, he takes them shopping and outfits them himself. He has been one of Oprah Winfrey's $100,000 Use Your Life Award winners.

And what was his reception at home, in his own school, his own district? For years, no one recognized Lindsey's efforts, his state and national successes, his students' amazing accomplishments. He won the nation's top recognition (the previously mentioned Coach of the Year award) and received not even a nod from the school board or administration. It wasn't until after he attended board meeting after board meeting complaining about the lack of recognition for his students that his state winners were finally invited to perform their entry pieces for the faculty.

Recognition never need be added to the school budget; it's free. It's one of the only gifts that has such a tremendous impact on those who are its givers as well as its recipients. And yet we tend to be so stingy with our praise, our vocalized admiration, our gracious recognition of each other's life's work. Even though it's free.

Behind *The Freedom Writers Diary*

Last of all, I present Erin Gruwell, the subject of the 2007 movie *The Freedom Writers*. This American film starring Hilary Swank, Scott Glenn, Imelda Staunton, and Patrick Dempsey is based on the book *The Freedom Writers Diary: How a Teacher and 150 Teens Used Writing to Change Themselves and the World Around Them* (The Freedom Writers, 1999), which was written by Gruwell's students who had previously been labeled "unteachable and at risk." By having them read books such as *Anne Frank: The Diary of a Young Girl* and *Zlata's Diary: A Child's Life in Sarajevo*, Gruwell led her students to see their own lives mirrored in the books and to find ways to change their attitudes toward themselves and their futures. Her students wrote of their own experiences over the four years they were in Gruwell's classes. Like Tommie Lindsey's students, all of Gruwell's graduated from high school, with the majority moving on to college. The book is powerful and real. Too real for some school districts to handle because of the authentic voice, diction, and anecdotes that her students reveal.

In the chapter titled "Sophomore Year Fall 1995," Gruwell gives one of many insights into the way she was received and treated by the faculty:

> Ever since I started student teaching at Wilson High, it seemed like some teachers had it in for me. According to them, I was too enthusiastic, too preppy, and my teaching style was too unorthodox. . . . When I was assigned to teach freshmen with below-par reading skills, the head of the English department challenged me, saying, "Let's see what you can do with these kids, hotshot!" Hotshot? If she only knew how nervous and overwhelmed I really was as a first-year teacher. She never even took the time to get to know me—and yet she was labeling me. Just like the students I defended, I was being stereotyped. Teachers called me a prima donna because I wore suits; I made the other teachers "look bad" because I took my students on field trips. . . . At that moment, I understood why almost half of new teachers leave the profession within the first few years. (p. 47)

I once sat beside Erin Gruwell at dinner before and after she gave a keynote to our state language arts conference, and I suggested that Tommie Lindsey be a keynote speaker for an upcoming conference after attending his 2006 National Staff Development Council workshop in Nashville. I have used Cullum's (1971) book *The Geranium on the Window Sill Just Died, but Teacher You Went Right On* for many years with new teachers during workshops. These are real people to me, not just the objects of documentaries and Hollywood films. They also represent extreme examples of the creative teacher—the superstars—that sometimes intimidate us if they are in the room next door or down the hall from us. But more often than not, these are the people who inspire us to be more ourselves, help us reach a potential we didn't dare think we had, inspire us to rethink our own relationships with our students.

If Cullum, Lindsey, and Gruwell were asked to name their charisma, their inner light, I think they might all come up with the word *invitation*. The overriding commonality in all three of these teachers is their desire to bring out the best in their students, to invite them to become who they are meant to be. And isn't that ours also? They use the methods that arise from their personalities, and so must we. They conquer daily the fear of inviting another teacher or administrator's raised eyebrows with their unconventional approaches. Yet we live in a time when the entire country is begging for a change in approach to education. The conventional approaches of the past century aren't working. If we all take small but consistent steps out of the box that is the factory model of educating our students, the effects would be tremendous.

So instead of seeing these beacons of creative teaching as intimidating and as aberrations of good educational practice, why not let them know we appreciate the light they shed on our own efforts? Let them know we want to take up their invitation to try new approaches and strategies. Befriend, include, support, and help them instead of spreading disapproval. When young new teachers tentatively try some of the strategies they learned in college or at inservice workshops, support them. Don't give them that old "we don't do those kinds of things with our students, not in this school" response. We need to be nicer to each other to allow our own and others' creativity to flourish and enliven all of our efforts. I guess that's what I'm trying to say in this section—we need to be nicer to ourselves and to each other.

YOUR TURN

As an individual:

1. How does the faculty in your school treat innovators and creative teachers?

2. How does your faculty respond to the new ideas that young teachers bring with them to their classrooms?

3. What steps could be consciously taken to give feedback and recognition to teachers who go out of their way to involve their classes or who use creative approaches to lessons? Choose one of the steps you have identified and do it.

As a teacher team:

1. Discuss with each other how the faculty in your school treats innovators and creative teachers.

2. Discuss with each other how your faculty responds to the new ideas that young teachers bring with them to the classroom.

3. Discuss with each other what steps could be consciously taken to give feedback and recognition to teachers who go out of their way to involve their classes or who use creative approaches to lessons. Choose one of the steps you have identified and do it. Then discuss the results with your team.

Our Tiny Digital Natives

My husband and I have a combined total of nine grandchildren, whose ages are one and a half, three, four, five (two at this age), nine, thirteen, sixteen, and eighteen. It's the group of little guys I want to focus on. Any of you who have children, grandchildren, or other relatives in this range of preschoolers and have walked down toy aisles trying to pick out Christmas presents will understand what I'm about to say. From little one-and-a-half-year-old Maggie on up, they are already seasoned button pushers and screen watchers. Maggie got a pink scooter. Her fingers pressed everything on the handlebars and the stem until she found the two buttons: one played music and set off lights, and the other began talking to her. In the hands of the three-, four-, and five-year-olds were Leapsters, the Nintendo DS, and Wii controls. All of these are highly sophisticated mixes of interactive multisensory learning games or action games with instant feedback and various levels of challenge, and all require mental and physical dexterity.

These are today's youngest digital natives, born into an environment of computerized stimulation the likes of which we adults—digital immigrants—could never have imagined at their age. If you experienced none of this over the holidays because of a lack of little ones in your life, I urge you to take a trip to Wal-Mart or Target and check out just what toys are like these days. Of course, these grandchildren of mine all have their share of Legos, action figures, puzzles, books, and board games, but it's the electronic/digital aisles I'd like you to investigate.

Last year I asked my daughter to list what her three-year-old son could do on a computer. Her list included these skills: turn on the computer, adjust the volume and screen size, go to his own site, follow links to various commercial Web sites, close down windows, play games, use either a mouse or a touchpad to move the cursor, insert CDs, move from various programs and scenes on a CD. He can read icons but not words. His ability to navigate a computer isn't tested or given any value in our school's readiness assessments. These are nonexistent skills on current forms and radar. Yet these are part of the basis for the 21st-century skills that children will need to function in tomorrow's digital environment. As these young digital natives move through our classrooms, many move through technologically barren rooms and mind-sets in stark contrast to the richness of what they experience at home.

From a standard classroom observation form I was given to use in my work as a consultant, I made a list of what today's digital toys offer by way of effective teaching strategies that we are all urged to integrate into our instruction. The form highlighted important areas with questions such as these: Was differentiated instruction observed? Did feedback drive instruction? Did students appear to understand the learning objective? Was the instructional activity aligned to the learning objectives? Half of the form consistently asked for the level of student engagement, whether in relation to instructional delivery methods or specific strategies employed by the teacher. The rest of the form covered the classroom environment, physical and instructional, as well as the level of electronic technology being used. All of these areas would receive a mark of E for extensive if applied to the toys that children today are exposed to before even walking through our school doors. It is our task as digital immigrants in an unfamiliar land of technology to learn the native language and habits as soon and as well as we can. It should be our delight to allow our digital native students the opportunity to take our hands and help us along the way. Let us be lead into the 21st century by these little charges of ours and share our unique expertise with each other.

9

Technology and the Creative Classroom

No book with the words *creativity* or *21st century* in the title would be seen as legitimate or comprehensive without a helpful and insightful treatment of technology's place in and impact on education. This is not an easy chapter to write given the wide disparity of access and comfort levels that exist among faculties and districts across the country. John Ross, who received his PhD in instructional design and technology from Virginia Tech, coauthored the textbook *Technology Integration for Meaningful Classroom Use: A Standards-Based Approach* (with Katherine Cennamo and Peggy Ertmer, 2009), and is currently serving as a senior research and development specialist for Edvantia, has taken on this challenge. John offers teachers a look at technology's possibilities for more effective teaching, for an outlet of creativity for teachers and students alike, no matter what their current environment or situation. He does this without getting too "techy" on us and losing us along the way.

Swimming in a Technological Environment
John Ross

In the past day or so, how often have you used technology? And, yes, pens and pencils, garden tools, pots and pans, and the like can be considered technologies, but I want you to consider digital technologies—those that rely on some kind of computing power. Maybe you did some shopping, watched a video, or read the news online. You could have sent an e-mail or two to friends and family or left them a message on their Facebook wall. If you drove to the grocery store, the computerized components in your car probably made your trip a little safer after you used the computers that allowed you to scan your own groceries at the checkout. Using my cell phone, I'm able to go online and read reviews of a restaurant, make a reservation, map directions from my current location, and take a picture of my friends when we have dinner there that night—all on something that fits in my pocket.

Digital technologies pervade our lives. Sometimes to the point that we don't even think about them being there. And yet, though many of us can search a complex database (such as when booking flight and hotel arrangements online), manipulate real-world data and insert it into a document (by creating an itinerary of your travel arrangements), and communicate that information to interested parties across the globe (when you send your itinerary to your parents as an attachment to an e-mail so they know where you're going on vacation), many of us don't use these powerful tools in the one place that could really promote creativity—in the classroom.

Creativity and innovation are receiving renewed emphasis in the field of educational technology. As a teacher in the 21st century, it's hard to imagine not using technology to support your teaching, but how does it support creativity? How can you use technology to promote student creativity? This chapter provides some examples. In the final section, you'll learn about some ways you can use technology to become a more creative teacher.

CONNECTING TECHNOLOGY AND CREATIVITY: NATIONAL TRENDS

Arguably one of the most influential educational technology organizations is the International Society for Technology in Education (ISTE), and it may perhaps best be known for the National Educational Technology Standards (NETS) that it developed for students, teachers, and administrators. Originally released in 1998, ISTE's NETS-S (for students; updated in 2007) identified skills and knowledge students should master and demonstrate related to the digital technologies that were becoming popular in the nation's schools and classrooms. Most states adopted or adapted these standards to guide student learning about technology. The original ISTE NETS-S focused on helping students master these new tools. In reviewing the original standards, you'll find that four out of the six standards emphasized learning basic skills and concepts about different technology tools. These standards, and the NETS-T (for teachers) that followed in 2000 (and were updated in 2008), were very tool focused.

In the past decade, educators have shifted from emphasizing learning *about* technologies to learning *with* technologies. To meet the needs of students who have spent their entire lives surrounded by digital technologies, ISTE began tackling the job of revising the standards in 2006. Modeling strategies for solving this complex problem on a global scale, ISTE used information and communication technologies (ICT) to gather information from educators, business leaders, and policy makers from across the United States as well as many other nations. Through virtual town forums, online surveys, and many in-person meetings, ISTE identified the new set of technology-related skills and knowledge students need in the 21st century. Leading the new set of NETS-S is creativity and innovation.

At the release of the "refreshed" NETS-S at the National Education Computing Conference, NETS project director Lajeane Thomas emphasized that the order of the new standards is not coincidental. Creativity and innovation are the skills that were identified throughout the yearlong process as being the most crucial for students in the 21st century. In a later Webcast with Lajeane Thomas and ISTE's CEO Don Knezek, I questioned them about why creativity and innovation held this prominent position (Appalachia Regional Comprehensive Center, 2005–2006). Echoing sentiments voiced by Thomas Friedman (2005) in his popular book *The World Is Flat,* Lajeane discussed the role that creativity and innovation have played in making America the global leader. She also noted that creativity and innovation give students an opportunity to apply all of the other standards. And while technology operations and concepts remain, in the final position, the other new standards focus on a variety of learning skills and digital citizenship. No longer is there such an emphasis on tools in the standards.

ISTE spent the next year refreshing the NETS-T through a similar process, obtaining input from educators across the globe. Like the NETS-S, the NETS-T begin with an emphasis on creativity. The first NETS-T is "Facilitate and Inspire Student Learning and Creativity" and notes that "teachers use their knowledge of subject matter, teaching and learning, and technology to facilitate experiences that advance student learning, creativity, and innovation in both face-to-face and virtual environments" (ISTE, 2008, p. 1).

The Partnership for 21st Century Skills is an organization whose members include leaders of business and industry in addition to education and technology. Originally founded in part with funds from the U.S. Department of Education, the partnership has representatives from organizations such as Apple, AT&T, Dell, Ford, Hewlett-Packard, Microsoft, and Verizon as well as many education associations and service providers. The partnership has also established a growing network of state education agencies that use its work to influence policy and practice from the state house to the classroom. With input from business and industry leaders as well as policy makers and education leaders from across the nation, there should be little surprise that the partnership's framework includes creativity and innovation as vital to the success of students in the 21st century (Partnership for 21st Century Skills, 2007b).

Both ISTE and the Partnership for 21st Century Skills cite the influence of the work of Sir Ken Robinson, an internationally recognized expert in the field of creativity. His book *Out of Our Minds: Learning to Be*

Creative (2001) is an engaging discussion on creativity, its relationship to intelligence, and it is a diplomatic treatise on the failings of many education systems (and those that survive them) to equate intelligence with academic ability. That limited conception of intelligence can prevent many people from finding pursuits for exhibiting their intelligences and creative ability. One of Robinson's concepts that most resonated with me is that many people ask a conventional question about intelligence: "How intelligent are you?" I agree with Robinson that there are many forms of intellectual capacity and, therefore, opportunities for being creative since creativity is inextricably linked to intelligence. I saw this day in and day out with my own students.

I taught music, so one would think that my classes were filled with creative students who spent their time in my class flexing and building their creative muscles. While this may have been an overarching goal for my classes, much of my work was spent helping students build foundational skills so they were better prepared to be creative when the opportunity arose, whether in the concert hall or the practice room. Of course, some of my students were very musically gifted and quite capable of truly expressing their creativity. For others, though, despite their enthusiasm, reaching the point of creative self-expression was a difficult challenge.

I often tell the story of one of my most talented students to emphasize this point. I play saxophone, as did this young student, but he possessed creative potential far beyond what I had exhibited at the same age. We started playing duets during lunch, and then after school, and we often practiced together just for the sheer joy of pushing each other's musical limits. He was a highly intuitive musician and it was easy to communicate musically with him while playing duets, which is a rare relationship that many musicians struggle to find when performing with others. He was a popular soloist in our jazz and concert bands. Through his music he found confidence, and he was much liked and respected by his peers. He was voted band president, and in that role he represented the largest student group at school-based councils led by the principal and routinely met and interacted with parent booster groups. In both settings, he was decisive and eloquent—the model of a great student leader. During his senior year, I was completely taken aback to discover from his math teacher that he was in danger of failing math and not graduating. She described him as uncommunicative and unresponsive in class. To add to my horror, failing math would have prevented him from accepting one of the several music scholarships he had been promised upon graduation.

This is clearly the story of a student with a very strong musical intelligence. Not so much in math. He understood that math was important, but it was something he definitely struggled with, so much so that he became completely withdrawn. Luckily, between his math teacher, his parents, and me, we got him through math and on to college, where he excelled. Back in his element, he became drum major for his college marching band and was a popular clinician for high school drum majors across the region. He was one of the few students in the history of his university that held the drum major position for three consecutive years.

Robinson (2001) expands on the misguided conventional question of how intelligent someone might be by suggesting that a more accurate question may be, "How are you intelligent?" With creativity being a function of intelligence, and in homage to Robinson, I'd like to reframe that question and instead of asking the conventional question "Are you creative?" we might begin to work with our students to answer the question "How are you creative?"

Digital tools are helpful for allowing more students to access the curriculum and thereby providing the opportunity for them to find how they might be intelligent and creative, but these tools also play an important role when it comes to demonstrating student learning. And this is where student creativity can really be highlighted and nurtured. Creativity requires the creation of something, and relying on instruction and assessment methods that require students to recall factual information by writing short responses, matching, or selecting an answer from a list doesn't support student creativity.

The digital tools that are commonly available, such as basic productivity software that is associated with application suites like Microsoft Office, provide teachers with multiple opportunities to promote student creativity that draw on individual student talents and preferences. With word-processing software, students can create stories and reports with images, graphs, or tables and links to external resources that can be formatted to look like professionally produced books, newspapers, and Web sites. Spreadsheets and databases provide students the opportunity to manipulate and explore data, to report it in various formats such as bar graphs or pie charts, and to use that information to propose and verify creative solutions to ill-structured, complex problems. Presentation software easily supports text, images, and links to Web sites as well as audio and video files so students can engage in digital storytelling or create presentations that either augment aural reports or can be posted online and shared with others.

There are many more examples, and we'll review a few of them next, but hopefully you'll come to realize, as I have, that digital media has the capacity to not only help every child access the curriculum, but also provide flexible means to support and promote creativity as they acquire and demonstrate their own learning. Digital tools are helpful for supporting your students' varied learning preferences. And ultimately, since digital media can help students access your curriculum, through the learning preferences that they have they may be better able to discover *how* they are creative.

YOUR TURN

As an individual:

1. If you do not already have them, obtain copies of the new NETS-S and NETS-T documents from ISTE. They can be viewed and downloaded at no cost from the ISTE Web site (www.iste.org). Or if your district or state has technology standards for students and/or teachers, obtain a copy of those. Depending on when they were written, they may not emphasize creativity and innovation to the same degree as the new ISTE standards.

2. Review the language of the first standard and associated substandards in the NETS-S, or review your local technology standards for students. Consider technology-based methods that you might already use in your instruction to address the student standards that relate to creativity and innovation. What technologies are readily available to support your instruction that you might need to learn more about? What might completed student work look like when meeting this standard?

3. Review the language of the first standard and associated substandards in the NETS-T, or review your local technology standards for teachers. How do you model these behaviors when using technology with your students? How do you use technology to support student creativity and innovation? What help might you need to better address this standard in order to promote student creativity with technology?

As a teacher team:

1. If you do not already have them, obtain copies of the new NETS-S and NETS-T standards from ISTE. They can be viewed and downloaded at no cost from the ISTE Web site (www.iste.org). Or if your district or state has technology standards for students and/or teachers, obtain a copy of those. Depending on when they were written, they may not emphasize creativity and innovation to the same degree as the new ISTE standards.

2. In small groups, or grade-level or content teams, review the language of the first standard and associated substandards in the NETS-S or review your local technology standards for students. Share technology-based methods that you already use in your instruction to address the student standards that relate to creativity and innovation. Make a quick list of the technologies that are used to support that instruction. Briefly describe what completed student work looks like when meeting this standard. Each member of the team can be a resource to the rest of the team. Have individuals identify activities or technologies they'd like to learn more about from any member of the team and determine next steps for sharing, whether through one-on-one discussions or presentations at staff meetings or inservice days.

3. Use the same procedure to review the language of the first standard and associated substandards in the NETS-T or review your local technology standards for teachers. Describe what it might look like to model these behaviors when using technology with students. What do members of the group need to know to better address this standard in order to promote student creativity with technology? Consider these needs in your next steps for sharing, as described earlier.

PROMOTING STUDENT CREATIVITY WITH TECHNOLOGY

Let's look at five ways that digital technologies can promote student creativity in your classroom. These are not teaching strategies that you are going to be able to implement step by step. Instead, they are general capacities of digital technologies within which you can apply many of the strategies you find in this book and elsewhere.

Increase Engagement With the Curriculum by Incorporating Complex, Real-World Problems

If you had gone through school with me, you would have heard me constantly asking my teachers, "How will I ever use this?" While you might not have wanted me in your class, this is a natural reaction from students. It's hard for students to understand the relevance of different content and instructional activities when they are required to perform at the lowest levels of cognition—recalling factual information, filling in blanks, completing photocopied worksheets, answering odd questions at the end of the chapter. I would like to say this is exaggerated, but I am unfortunately reminded that the most popular piece of technology used in schools I visit is the photocopier. In too many schools, I see "death by handout." Students are not engaged, not interested; sometimes they're not even awake. Would you be?

This sounds like a pedagogical problem and not a technological one, but it is often the case that many of these schools have adequate technology readily available that makes engaging pedagogies possible. Almost every classroom I visit has at least one computer in it, often four or five. Every school I visit has at least one computer lab, usually several labs depending on the size of the school. And yet, far too often, the computer in the classroom is turned off or sitting under a pile of papers, the computer lab is unoccupied or—even worse—locked, and so few schools want to even tackle the use of cell phones in schools. To me, inside those technologies are the answers to the question I used to ask.

Digital technologies have the capacity to link the verbal and conceptual knowledge students must and should learn to relevant problems found in the real world, whether that world is down the hall or halfway across the country (or beyond!). Yes, you can do this with text, but not to the same degree. Much of the reason for the acknowledged "flattening" of our world is due to the rise in popularity and increase of power of ICT (like cell phones) and increased use of the Internet. In a globally connected classroom, you have unlimited access to real-world problems that require creative solutions.

In addition to identifying problems and collecting information about them, digital tools allow students to apply new skills and knowledge to propose solutions or possibly solve a relevant problem. Real-world problems are often complex and ill structured, meaning they may not have one clear answer or solution. Students can graph data, run simulations, or determine that they need more data. Their solutions may be incomplete but can still demonstrate the skills and knowledge required by your curriculum. As students develop foundational skills, they will be able to come up with more sophisticated and original solutions—solutions that may not be creative just to themselves, but on a larger scale.

Provide Access to Information and Tools That Professionals Use to Create High-Quality Work

Even at the earliest grades, students are able to access digital tools that are similar to or even the same as those used by professionals. Third graders using presentation software, like Microsoft PowerPoint, to create their own digital stories are using the same software found in board rooms and lecture halls everywhere. Students using word-processing software, like AppleWorks or Microsoft Word, have access to the same tools and functionality that generate the documents that support entire industries. And when students turn to Internet search engines, like Google or Yahoo!, they are using the same tools and finding the same information that you and I do.

Another aspect of using digital tools is that students can create products that look professional, or at least of high quality. And they can do this in a range of media, not just text. For students for whom the physical act of writing is a barrier, digital tools offer a range of options for supporting and expressing themselves. Students with limited writing skills, perhaps English language learners or even those with poor penmanship, can create documents that look like those created by everyone else in class. Depending on the instructional goal of the activity, they can check their spelling and grammar, use various formatting for text and layout, and incorporate images or other elements that support their position. In this type of activity, not only can students focus on the generation of an artifact that demonstrates what they have learned, but the tool may actually allow them greater opportunity to express their creativity.

Besides text-based documents, there are digital tools available to students on many school computers that are similar to or even the same as those used by professional musicians, mathematicians, graphic artists, photographers, scientists, and filmmakers, just to name a few. Students can compose their own music with sequencers and notation software, perform the music using digital MIDI-compatible instruments (MIDI stands for Musical Instrument Digital Interface), and then record and share their performance using digital recording equipment and audio editing software. My students did. In some schools, you will find these same hardware and software found in music studios where professionals write and record.

Many computers come equipped with drawing tools or image-editing software that can produce the same results that students see in magazines, galleries, and online. Students can take pictures with digital cameras, or even cell phones, and use software to modify them in an infinite number of ways. Students can learn and demonstrate concepts related to drawing through a range of digital tools, including hardware drawing pads and styluses, that build on and expand foundational drawing practices completed with paper and pen, pencil, or paint. These tools may also be more forgiving than traditional drawing and painting tools and can allow students to experiment more easily and quickly with colors, textures, and techniques, enabling them to find the exact creative expression they desire.

Digital video has also been made easier, and student videos can be found on school Web pages, broadcast over school networks, and even found on YouTube and other video Web sites. Young students can use iMovie or Windows Movie Maker to record discussions about their favorite books and share these videos with parents to show what they are learning. This same activity teaches them about concepts related to composition, storytelling, and filmmaking. Students can create digital personal histories that incorporate interviews with relatives and images of family heirlooms that can be shared as part of a class presentation or Web page. These histories can go beyond the sharing of factual information and include reflection and insight about each student's personality and dreams for the future. More advanced software, such as Apple's Final Cut, can be found in many high schools and can create the same professional-quality edits and effects seen on television, in music videos, and at movie theaters, and provide students untapped potential for expressing their own thoughts and ideas.

The range of probes and sensors that connect to desktop, laptop, or handheld computers allows students to engage in scientific inquiry much like scientists in the field. These sensors can measure, record, and report data related to motion, light, sound, pressure, temperature, and on and on. Building on the real-world problem idea mentioned earlier, students can use these sensors to gather data that can help them determine possible and sometimes very creative solutions to problems facing their communities. They can consider finding solutions to combat changes in water quality based on decreased precipitation. They can investigate the environmental impact of new construction of homes and roads in their neighborhood and present their solutions to their classmates, their parents, or even the community.

In addition to these tools, students can now more easily access the same data that professionals do and even contribute data to professional communities. A popular example is the GLOBE Program, which allows students to collect and share environmental data from their own environment. They can also access data from other locations around the globe to better understand different natural phenomena and their impact on people and places. Students can also access information in the form of images from art galleries, primary source documents from the Library of Congress's American Historical Collections, and tables and graphs from news services—all of which can be incorporated into student projects across the curriculum.

By accessing the same information that professionals have access to, students strengthen their foundational knowledge in a domain and are better able to judge whether an act or artifact is creative or derivative. By using the same tools that professionals use, students are better able to understand how these tools develop the products that support the industries and endeavors they might pursue. When accessing this information and using these tools, students become better prepared to stretch routine thought and tool use to the realm of creative use.

Scaffold Learning

Digital technologies provide a range of supports for learners as they master new skills and knowledge and engage in more complex thinking and learning (National Research Council, 2000). Various digital technologies allow students to explore different possibilities, developing and manipulating scenarios, and challenging ideas and outcomes that once might have seemed impossible. A scaffold, much like a ladder, allows students to get to a place they could not otherwise get to on their own. While several of the technologies discussed so far can scaffold learning, following are descriptions of a few additional forms that are especially relevant.

Technologies such as calculators, spreadsheets, and databases can provide scaffolds to promote learning in science, math, and even social sciences. These tools allow students to collect or access data, sometimes large amounts of data, and present it in different formats that make it easier for them to understand. Students can change the value of variables in spreadsheets to see the interaction and impact these changes may have, such as by changing the ratio of predators to prey. Population data can easily be graphed to show trends and patterns over time.

Data visualization tools make it easy for students to manipulate data. InspireData from Inspiration Software is one such tool. Students can gather data through surveys or observation and then quickly run visual analyses of the data. Students can compare data through several common data formats (Venn diagrams, scatter plots, bar graphs, and others) as well as viewing changes in data over time using an animated time series. Representing data in different ways is one method that can allow students to understand complex patterns and thereby begin to test assumptions and make conclusions.

Modeling software, including both two- and three-dimensional models, allows students to better understand complex concepts related to algebra, geometry, and trigonometry. Tools such as Geometer's Sketchpad allow students to create and manipulate any number of geometric shapes, which they can then interact with. Changing any part of the shape provides real-time updates to the changes in measurements, relationships, and variables associated with the drawing. When used to support real-world problem solving, modeling software can help students investigate solutions related to a range of problems that apply math, such as architecture. Modeling tools such as Google's free SketchUp software allows students to design and furnish virtual rooms or buildings, even incorporating models of commercially available products paired with costs so students can determine the most appropriate design under different budget constraints.

Simulations also provide supports to help students address complex problems. There are simulations online that help students better understand natural phenomena, such as weather systems, and complex tools and technologies, such as flight and space shuttle simulators. Students can explore complex social problems, such as those proposed in Tom Snyder's role-playing Decisions, Decisions software. This series of software is based on a five-step decision-making model and places students in complex situations that may be drawn from historical events (the Revolutionary War, colonization, the Cold War) or current social concerns (prejudice, substance abuse, violence in the media). The software requires students to collect and analyze data, argue and understand multiple perspectives and viewpoints, and ultimately make predications and draw conclusions. Engaging in the software's activities prepares students to transfer the decision-making model to different settings in order to create possible solutions to different complex problems.

While this section has described specialized modeling and visualization tools that can scaffold learning, keep in mind the many scaffolds in common software applications. Consider how word-processing software identifies misspelled words, can automatically fix typos, makes stylistic suggestions, creates summaries and tables of contents, and can let you determine the reading level of a document you've created. Digital technologies can support student creativity by helping students master concepts and skills that are normally beyond their level of understanding. They help students understand the content and master the skills of a domain so they are better prepared to propose original and creative solutions for problems they might not be able to solve on their own.

Provide Opportunities to Reflect on Student Understanding and Identify Changes in Student Learning

There are many ways that digital tools can support student reflection, but this section focuses on two that I think are most related to promoting student creativity. The first is making thinking visible. While creativity requires some sort of action, it is based on thought—imaginative thought. It requires conceiving of an outcome that is unique, sometimes through the unique combination or juxtaposition of elements. There has been growing emphasis in education on helping students understand what they are learning, the learning and problem-solving strategies they are using, and evaluate whether these are effective. This is an emphasis on metacognition. Simply stated, metacognition is thinking about your thinking.

While concept-mapping strategies do not require digital technologies, the digital tools that support concept mapping are often so easy to use and quick to master that they are helpful for even the youngest of students to determine what they do and maybe even what they do not know. They can be graphic representations of thinking—making thinking visible.

Standard concept maps consist of concepts (nodes, which help identify the components of a concept) and their relationships (links). They may also be called mind maps or schema (based on schema theory). Concept maps can become quite complex. For example, very young students can use one to determine what are and are not characteristics of mammals, while older students can use one to better understand the concept of democracy or civic responsibility. Concept maps can include examples and nonexamples as long as the relationships are clearly expressed.

Related to concept maps are graphic organizers. These allow students to group images of similar elements together under different category headings. For example, students can use freely available clip art to create a graphic organizer about Native Americans using the categories of food, shelter, clothing, and roles in the community.

Concept maps and graphic organizers can help students understand their own thinking and identify all that they know about a concept—essentially representing their known conceptual spaces visually. They can also help teachers identify students' misconceptions. Making the wrong conclusion based on a misconception is not creative; it's a misunderstanding. Students may also be able to identify or at least challenge their own misconceptions when they compare their concept maps to those of an expert, like a teacher, or when they participate in a concept-mapping or mind-mapping activity with the rest of the class, as was described and illustrated in Chapter 1.

A second way that technology can promote reflection may seem obvious: through the use of digital journals or portfolios. There are different types of journals and portfolios, but in an educational setting, reflection is usually an important aspect of each. And while many people keep paper-based journals or portfolios, digital technologies can more easily help make student growth and learning readily apparent.

Most teachers are familiar with paper-based portfolios, but many schools have the means to incorporate digital records of student performance that clearly document changes in student learning. Instead of just a writing portfolio, you can have a reading portfolio, in which you store short recordings of students reading over time. Students and parents can hear students becoming more fluent readers and may even be able to identify growing student vocabularies. You can have a problem-solving portfolio, in which you record students performing a think-aloud in which they explain the strategies they used to solve a math problem or come to a conclusion in a science lab. You can also incorporate digital versions of student work, such as documents they have written (like the math and science problems in their think-aloud activity), presentations they have created, or digital pictures or scanned images of two- or three-dimensional projects. You can also link student work to rubrics or other forms of assessment.

Key to helping students benefit from digital journals and portfolios and to identifying changes in student learning are the reflective activities you incorporate in the process. Students should provide reflections on the artifacts in their journals and portfolios over time. They should identify what strategies and outcomes they had early in the year (or even in previous years if your whole school gets on board) and describe how they do things differently now. What do they know now that they didn't know then? How effective were the strategies they originally used? What strategies do they use now? They may even be able to determine, upon reflection, whether their solutions to problems were creative, based on their expanded understanding of the topics at hand.

Collaborate and Communicate With Others

Creativity can be promoted by sharing ideas and working with others, and communication and collaboration are two real strengths of ICT tools. Communication, literally, is their middle name.

Don't panic, but many people consider communication tools like e-mail and discussion lists old technologies. Schools were late to adopt e-mail, first offering e-mail accounts to administrators and eventually to teachers. Many schools still do not provide e-mail accounts to students, who probably already have multiple personal e-mail accounts or, more likely, multiple MySpace or Facebook accounts. Students are also more likely to instant message or text a friend than send e-mail. Yet from a learning perspective, e-mail still offers some advantages for promoting a culture of collaboration that supports creativity.

An e-mail is usually longer than a text message and is more easily returned to over time. You can also attach documents to e-mail, so it's easier to share more information via e-mail than via text message. Short-term e-mail accounts can be generated for a particular project and can be limited in terms of the recipients. E-mail has also been used successfully through a range of online pen pal programs, such as ePals, that allow students in one school to connect with students in a different state or country. These connections are natural conduits for collaborative activities. Students learn about the social and physical attributes of the communities in which their ePals live and go to school. They learn new perspectives, often related by people their own age, and expand their knowledge through these new perspectives. Collaborating teachers can even develop projects through which students create presentations together on complex issues, either those identified by the teachers and relevant to their course of study or one of the predetermined projects developed by ePals or others, such as global warming or natural disasters.

ICT tools also offer means by which students can connect with experts, including parents and community members. Teachers can take students on virtual field trips to museums, galleries, or businesses where parents or community members work. Students can interact with people and artifacts at distant sites by using audio, video, or web conferencing tools. The rise of low-cost (and even some no-cost) web conferencing tools that support audio and video, like Skype and iChat, has expanded the possibility of reaching experts at distant sites. Web conferencing tools support distant participants at multiple sites in seeing and hearing presentations, interacting through polls and surveys, sharing applications, chatting, and using Webcams.

Social networking tools, which are part of Web 2.0, allow users to post different forms of media on a Web page without having to know any programming languages. Visitors are then able to add comments (if they are granted permission) or create new information. On popular social networking sites like MySpace and Facebook, users can create their own page, post pictures and videos, list their favorite songs, keep track of their whereabouts, accept (or not) friends requests, and send and receive messages. There are social networking sites for a range of products and services, like sharing videos (YouTube and TeacherTube), pictures (Flickr and Shutterfly), and many others.

While some school districts share concerns about social networking sites, especially concerns for student privacy, three types of social networking tools support the kind of collaborations being used by teachers. They can be used for communication with students and parents on the Web or in a protected network simply for class presentations. They share similar features that allow users to create Web pages that contain elements we're used to seeing online, elements like text, images, and hyperlinks. As these technologies evolve, there may someday be little difference between them.

The first tool is a Weblog, commonly called a blog. What makes a blog unique is that it is primarily authored by one person. Think of it in terms of a personal journal. Teachers create blogs for their classes that allow students and parents to access class schedules, announcements, homework assignments, links to helpful resources, and even homework help. People can register to add comments to a blog, but it is primarily a vehicle of communication for one person.

Related to a blog is a wiki, which in Hawaiian means quick. Wikis are a quick way for groups of people to collaborate and post information on a topic or multiple topics. The most popular wiki is probably Wikipedia, which is an online encyclopedia of information that is created by, well, anyone who wants to sign up. Wikis allow users to see who created and modified the record and when. Wikis have also generated a culture that promotes verification. Anyone can post to a wiki, but the content can be marked as unverified or needing proof. Since wikis support collaboration by groups of people, they are tools that groups of students can use to create and post information they have generated together, such as for a class project. However, students don't need to be in the same class (or even school) and can update the information from any computer with Internet access.

A newer social networking tool that has gained some popularity is Ning, a Web site that allows users to create their own social network, which usually focuses on a single topic. Ning is well suited to fan clubs or enthusiasts of a sport, hobby, or profession. Still in the early stages of gaining ground with educators, you're probably more likely to find a group on Ning that is related to an educational topic you might want to participate in than you are to create one for students. But your students may already belong to several groups on Ning, so this tool hold potential for supporting your students' learning.

Creativity has a social and cultural component. Digital technologies make it possible for students to connect with experts and join larger communities interested in particular topics. Learning from these communities and expanding one's exposure to the trends and issues related to these topics adds to and strengthens students' conceptual understanding of a given topic. It is through better understanding of the structures in this conceptual space that the opportunity for greater creative thought and application is promoted.

YOUR TURN

As an individual:

1. Identify one of the five strategies for using technology to promote student creativity that you feel most comfortable with. You may already use this strategy with or without technology. Identify the technologies given as examples, and determine your level of knowledge, skill, and comfort with them. List additional technologies readily available to you that might support this strategy, and consider your knowledge, skill, and comfort with them. Which technology do you want to learn more about in order to support this strategy in your classroom? Which technology do you feel you could use immediately to intentionally address this strategy?

2. Identify one of the five strategies that you either need more information about or do not use as readily in your own instruction. Identify the technologies given as examples as well as others you may have available that can support this strategy. What do you need to learn more about? What resources (people, print, the Internet, etc.) can you turn to in order to learn more about this strategy and better incorporate it into your teaching?

As a teacher team:

1. Have all members of the team identify the standard they feel most comfortable with and one that they either need more information about or have the least familiarity with.

2. Pair up. Teachers who feel most comfortable with a given strategy should connect to those who need more information about that strategy. Have the first teacher share how he or she has used technology to support the strategy. Using examples of technologies commonly available at your school is most beneficial. The second teacher should feel free

to ask questions for clarification and work with the first teacher to identify ways that the first teacher can build his or her skills (see the next section for ideas). Identify any gaps that either teacher has in terms of needing more information or building technology skills. Identify resources (people, print, the Internet, etc.) that can be used to help bridge the gaps. Rotate pairs, and have each person develop a master list to guide future personal and schoolwide staff development.

3. Instead of in pairs, teachers can volunteer to share with the group their experiences with the strategy with which they feel most comfortable. The group should ask questions, identify gaps, and determine resources to support growth. A consensus in an area of need, whether a strategy or the use of technology, is well suited for future staff development opportunities.

BECOMING A MORE CREATIVE TEACHER WITH TECHNOLOGY

Learning new teaching strategies takes time and practice. Throwing technology into the mix raises the intimidation factor for some people. But the technologies and strategies presented here are being used by teachers in classrooms now. You can learn to use them, too. Consider the following recommendations.

1. **Find or create a safe environment in which to develop your technology skills**. Integrating technology in instruction requires that you develop both basic technology skills and pedagogical skills. Teachers report that their limited skills prevent them from using computers more frequently with their students (Becker, 2000). You need to know what success looks like. You'll need time to practice, revise, and hone your skills as you learn new strategies. Some schools provide teachers with a workroom with different technologies to try, or you might be able to schedule a computer lab or even work in your room with new technologies when students aren't around.

2. **Build community support for your efforts**. Community in this sense refers to your teaching and learning community, from the classroom to the entire school. Robinson (2001) notes that creativity is related to culture, and you'll be more successful if you live and teach in a culture that accepts and supports taking risks to learn and try new things, to be creative. A safe environment includes the collegial environment, not just the physical. Pair up with other teachers to learn new technologies. Try to schedule time when you can teach together or observe each other. You'll need to involve school leaders. Let administrators know what you are doing, what you expect to achieve, and how they can help. Collaborate with peers and

colleagues in your school and beyond. Just like your students, you can use technology to communicate and collaborate with others in order to learn about technology.

3. **Learn with your students**. Take advantage of student engagement and curiosity about technology to discover methods and tools that can best support creativity in your classroom. If you wait to learn everything you can about a technology before you use it in class, it may become outdated. Technology is constantly changing. What doesn't change is the need for you and your students to develop flexible learning skills that allow you to use the next new technology effectively and creatively. I've interviewed a lot of teachers about using technology, and those who use it well all tell me they learn new things about technology from their students, even with technologies they've used before. If you learn with your students, you may also be more likely to find more authentic experiences for technology use that better support creativity.

4. **Have a reasonable plan of attack, and pace yourself**. Don't expect to reach the highest levels of technology integration or creativity right out of the gate. Many technology experts agree that teachers go through stages (Dwyer, Ringstaff, & Sandholtz, 1991) or progress along a continuum as they learn to integrate technologies. Robinson (2001) muses that one feature of cultural change is that, for a time, new technologies are used to do old tasks or jobs. Many teachers begin by using technology to replicate or complete tasks they are already familiar with before moving into truly innovative and creative uses of technology. Don't try to do everything at once. You may want to begin by piloting one new activity each grading period or every other grading period. Try modifying or updating an activity you've used in the past rather than trying a bunch of new strategies all at once. When you bring in new lessons or activities, supplant, don't add. If you're constantly adding new lessons without taking anything out of your repertoire, technology use will become a burden.

5. **Document and share what you've learned**. Spread the word at faculty meetings and parent nights or by using one of the many technologies discussed in this chapter. Keep a portfolio or journal, create a class Web page, start a teaching blog, videotape your classes. Share what you've learned at conferences, whether in your district or on a state or national level. Write an article for a school newsletter or Web page, or submit an article to a teaching journal. You may even consider something more formal, such as an action research project. Regardless, by sharing lessons learned you can help others embark on the journey of providing a more creative environment for teaching and learning with technology.

Rules for Lady Teachers in 1915

Before digging into the swirling pool of demands on what the public, the business sector, and even we as teachers want to see as a transformation of the present state of education, let's stop for a moment, take a deep breath, and look at just where we have been. The following set of rules (which are part of a historical display at Halls Gap, Victoria, in Australia) governing the behavior of female teachers close to a century ago can give us a picture of how much change in attitude and expectation has already taken place. Gentlemen, I realize these do not refer to or cover "gentlemen teachers," but it seemed the times were more concerned with female behavior!

1. You will not marry during the term of your contract.

2. You are not to keep company with men.

3. You must be home between the hours of 8 p.m. and 6 a.m. unless attending a school function.

4. You may not loiter downtown in ice-cream parlours.

5. You may not travel beyond the city limits without the permission of the chairman of the board.

6. You may not ride in a carriage or automobile with any man unless he is your father or brother.

7. You may not smoke cigarettes.

8. You may not dress in bright colours.

9. You may under no circumstances dye your hair.

10. You must wear at least two petticoats and your dresses must not be shorter than two inches above the ankle.

11. To keep the school clean you must:

    Sweep the floor at least once daily.

    Scrub the floor with hot soapy water at least once weekly.

    Clean the blackboard at least once a day.

    Start the fire at 7 a.m. so that the room will be warm by 8 a.m.

10

Transforming Teaching Through Creativity for the 21st Century

Human creativity is the ultimate economic resource.

—Richard Florida (2002, p. xiii)

THE LAST TIME

There is a poem by Shel Silverstein, called "The Last Time," that I used to read with my own children years ago. It lists all the "last times" that seem to slip by without our noticing them. Those last times we played hide-and-seek or yelled, "Can Paul come out to play?" or climbed a tree. My youngest vowed he would remember every last time or would refuse to admit there were last times. We laughed at our rebellion against last times through his high school years as he would grab the car keys and tell me he was "going out to play." And I was just as much in denial that last times do eventually slide into all our lives. When visiting an older son living in Texas, I climbed the tree in his backyard and sent a picture to my youngest with the note: "See, I haven't climbed my last tree yet!" As one of the threads in our family's fabric, a consciousness of what time and age and progress does to our lives has always been a curious and shared topic of interest.

Sometimes I've noticed that people don't realize that what they consider the future exists very concretely in the present. When we talk about the needs of learners in the 21st century, we are talking about the needs of learners today, not in some hazy, science fiction version of a problem-free tomorrow. Everything we can imagine that should be part of the perfect picture of tomorrow's education delivery system, tailored to fit the needs of a changing world, is available today. It is available, but probably not yet recognized, acknowledged, utilized, or absorbed into the collective psyche of the mainstream institutional mind. So I'm going to play briefly with the concept of "the last time," both through the lens of my 40 years in education and in terms of what we see as tomorrow but need to become more familiar with as the present.

Those of you who are young teachers might not be able to relate to some of these "last time" examples, but many who are veteran teachers will certainly smile knowingly.

I wonder when I got ink on my hands for the last time from that old, ditto master machine? Or when my students held the paper up to their noses and smelled the fluid from the freshly run purple sheets that I just ran off? When was the last time I showed a 16mm movie in class? Or when a student stuck scraps of paper into the take-up reel to watch them fly out when I rewound the movie? I do remember the last time I wrote a graduate school paper on a typewriter and had to count down the lines to be sure I had enough space for the foot notes. And I remember my professors not looking kindly on the use of Wite-Out on any submitted papers. When was the last time I used an opaque projector to show the class a sample of a student's writing? Those machines were so big, so noisy, so clumsy. For many, the chalk dust clinging to clothes, hair, and hands might now even be a dim memory. That yellow chalk was supposed to be such an innovation from the white, remember? And I—ancient as it might seem—can recall the time I handwrote the grades onto student report cards.

A LOOK AT POSSIBLE FUTURE TRANSFORMATION

Now let's look ahead to see what you just might be writing on your "last time" list a few years from now. Here's a futuristic version of what you might include:

I remember when school districts spent tons of precious assets on heavy, thousand-page textbooks, whereas now they fill a district server with the materials needed for each level and course. I can't believe how much time and energy it took to keep track of all those books, to house them, and how cumbersome it was for children to lug them home in those huge backpacks they carried. Because we have finally cut that umbilical cord that attached all of us to a few dominant textbook companies, we finally can bring the richness of supplementary material into our curriculum. We finally can follow the directions of so many of the studies that recommend our students have access to primary documents and a variety of types of texts and materials.

A Different Classroom

Oh, and remember how our classrooms used to look like little boxed-up containers of children in neat little rows who all supposedly learned at an identical pace? Now, since we've opened our classroom doors as well as our minds, we not only send our students virtually and actually out into the world, we invite the world into our classrooms. Businesses are invited in; adult learners are invited to sign up for courses along with our younger students. The grade march from one year to another faded into the past when they were replaced by levels of expertise and a stronger emphasis on interest, once we truly saw learning as recursive and holistic. What we found when we mixed the populations within a room was a change in the dynamics of learning. Having adult learners mixed in with younger students brought a tremendous shift in the attitudes of both the teachers and the participants and truly a positive change in the learning environment as a whole.

One clear benefit of the shift in our perception of "classroom" has surely been the melting away of teacher isolation that persisted in the old school paradigm. With that gone, the single subject specialization mentality also dropped away. Those attempts at cross-discipline projects in the past were the forerunners of what we all take for granted now as the only sane way to teach. We are all reading teachers, writing teachers, thinking teachers. Yes, we all have our expertise in various areas of learning, but no longer are we segregated specialists. Our work is always in concert with other teachers.

Those early experiments with professional learning communities have now ripened into the norm. We don't remember the last time we tried to solve all our teaching problems alone without utilizing the support and input of our peers. We look back and smile at how fumbling were those first attempts at managing group dynamics—how we had to learn so much about dealing with each other before we could even begin to deal with the issues of education bubbling up around us. Eventually we got there, and consequently no longer do children fail to see the relationship of major concepts as they move from one discipline to another. Student application of essential functions and concepts is far more seamless than in the past. We have learned the hard way, but learned nevertheless, that action is the discussion and simplistic answers are nonexistent. We function as living, flexible teams now, just as people do in the best of the thriving businesses. And our students see us as their models.

Who's Running the Show?

I don't remember quite when schools finally saw the futility of being run by textbook companies, lunch and bus schedules, outside testing mandates, and political agendas, and actually stood up and rebelled against the insanity. Like most social shifts, it happened under the radar, and one day we just looked around and there it was. I think the hallmark of this change was when teachers began demanding that their professional expertise be respected and visibly acknowledged by their institutions as well as the communities they served. With that respect returned the sense of empowerment that we all know is the lifeblood of creative, energetic innovation. Signs of this change showed up in how districts spent their money.

Schools also saw that improvement in student learning meant invest-ing in their teachers first and foremost and not simply in packaged pro-grams that boasted the ability to be delivered by any warm body that could read and follow scripted directions. Programs slowly returned to their rightful place in the hierarchy of importance as tools, not dictators of the classroom. I guess this happened when administrators began to take teacher development seriously and allot time during the day for in-depth conversation, communication, and planning with peers. They began providing the resources necessary to learn how to utilize that time effectively, ensuring not only opportunities for teachers to access state-of-the-art technological equipment but also instruction on how to use it—ongoing instruction, not simply a one-day workshop given by the manufacturer. Now when a district invests in a program, it is one that is given time to grow, develop, and flower. It isn't judged successful or unsuccessful after one or two years of implementation. There is a com-mitment to both the teachers and the fundamental authenticity of a well-built program of learning. Change is no longer seen as having to be mandated in short unreasonable time frames. Thankfully, we have felt the stress brought on by infuriatingly unreasonable demands gradually melt away.

Some of us can remember when we thought of ourselves as the hold-ers of information that needed to be poured out on our students. How dif-ferently we see our roles now. It would be interesting to find out when the concept of teaching as coaching actually took off, but surely as a metaphor it helps define more accurately what we do now than the old "font of infor-mation and wisdom" metaphor we used to embrace. Because we see our-selves as coaches, there is a mix of online, whole, and small learning groups formed and reformed for to tackle learning tasks. We experience firsthand the energy that comes from real-time interactions.

And hasn't communication taken on a more predominant role than in those old days of strictly whole-group instruction? We can't believe that years ago some students could go for weeks without speaking personally to an instructor or even to other members of their classes. The days of the loner slipping through the cracks and failing to be recognized by profes-sionals have long disappeared. We have found personal, frequent confer-ences with students so important for assessing their progress and offering timely feedback. How did we ever really know what they were thinking when we never had time to talk to them or ask them?

A Different Approach to Teaching

Thinking back, I find it hard to believe that students never made con-tact during their education with other people around the world. How did they ever study a foreign country or language without a Webcam? And remember when we considered ourselves so technologically savvy with one computer (ours) in our classrooms and maybe even a SMART Board attached? Our students didn't see us that way at all, did they? Often, they thought of our classes—and their half hour in a computer lab—as educational dinosaurs that hadn't been told their era was over. Until every student had their hands on a computer consistently, one that wasn't necessarily chained down with fear-originating constrictions, we really were simply suffering from the delusion that we were functioning in the computer age in our schools.

Today we find it hard to imagine we ever thought that the same lesson would be effective for 30 students at one time. With what we know now about the difference in the time it takes for individuals to learn specific skills and concepts, we have all come to see and respect the need for differentiation. This isn't a technique we have read about or heard about at a teacher workshop; it is an integral approach born by our working relationship with the young learners assigned to us. Their success is our foremost aim, and together we build the plan, return to the plan, alter the plan, and redefine it as we go. Perhaps it was this basic tenet that forged the successful efforts at decreasing the achievement gap—such a shameful reality in those earlier times. Our understanding of brain functions has finally informed our behaviors in dealing with all children. The myths of why one group of children learns and another group doesn't have almost totally been dissolved.

A Better Idea of Assessing Understanding

Then there is that shiver of pain that resurrects within us as we think back to those days wasted by the runaway testing frenzy that swept the nation during the Bush era. Those days taken from us that needed to be spent on student learning and growth, and authentic assessments. Our methods of assessing and evaluating are so different now. We probe with our questions, we stimulate more curiosity and open doors for further investigation. We observe students. We set up opportunities for them to apply what they are learning in order to show us evidence of thorough learning. Because we have dropped the old Cartesian view of separation of mind and body, we no longer view ourselves as "filling their heads with facts," nor have we continued to disregard research on the importance of taking the body into consideration when attempting to teach. We have definitely

Emotion is the superhighway between facts and understanding... use it.

moved toward a deeper understanding of and respect for educating the whole person. We actually do more than simply pay lip service to the findings of Maslow and Dewey, Darwin and Piaget, Gardner, Bloom, Gregoric, Marzano and Costa, Tomlinson and Sprenger, Wiggins and McTighe, Tileston, Jensen, and Wolf.

Our assessments are much more deeply informed than they were when we were required by many states to judge a student's ability or progress from a one-shot test given in extremely stressful circumstances. And let me emphasize here how good it is that we have finally returned to that original vision about the construction and use of standards that we had when we first began using them to guide our teaching. Our work and our early vision of how we needed standards to inform that work were pure and reasonable. We started with the realization that we were trying to do too much without having strong guiding principles to direct us. Our early work on standards construction and implementation was filled with enthusiasm and energy. It fostered a bottom-up flow as opposed to a top-down set of regulations. Somehow it all got sullied as the punitive conditions of government mandates began to infiltrate our efforts. Gratefully, I can say we have returned to our original clarity of purpose.

And finally, can you remember the last time you used a Scantron machine? I think I saw one packed away in a closet a few years ago. Those machines could be the lasting artifacts symbolizing the existence of the veneer education mentality. They could easily symbolize the mind-set most of us had that was characterized by the belief that good education was found in covering huge quantities of material, having our students accumulate mammoth stockpiles of facts that would be spewed out in the form of darkened circles on answer sheets. We were so bent on coverage that was neatly spelled out for us in pacing guides that we seldom had the opportunity to really focus on student understanding. No wonder so many teachers at that time were suffering from stress and a feeling of helplessness. Thank goodness we somehow saw the light and moved from *covering* to *uncovering* as the focus of our planning. And remember when quietly and with no fanfare we saw Bloom's Taxonomy revised to place creativity at the very top of the chart? We no longer see creativity as a stepchild in our instruction but as a fundamental consideration in equipping students with the ability to use their whole brains to solve problems that haven't even arisen yet. We frame opportunities now to strengthen and generate creative behaviors both for ourselves and for our students. We teach them both lateral and vertical thinking skills so they can function in this world that is so different from the one we grew up in.

So there it is, a brief look into the kaleidoscope of the future informed by the present. What have I missed? What would you have written?

YOUR TURN

As an individual:

1. This imaginary look into the future covers quite a lot of educational ground. Highlight five of the statements that represent what you would like to see happen.

2. Of those five that you highlighted, which ones to your knowledge are actually beginning to take a foothold in educational discussions, books, or articles?

3. Choose one specific area to research, and find out what is going on across the country in practice and educational forums. Pass on this information to some others in your school. Talk about it with them.

4. Pretend that you are me, and write another section that you feel was missing from my look at the future.

5. If possible, copy this section and use it as the basis for discussion at a faculty meeting. Choose one or two points to focus on with your professional learning communities.

As a teacher team:

1. This imaginary look into the future covers quite a lot of educational ground. Highlight five of the statements that represent what you would like to see happen. Share and discuss the relevancy of these statements together.

2. Of the five that each of you highlighted, which ones did you have in common? Which ones to your knowledge are actually beginning to take a foothold in educational discussions, books, or articles? Which ones are more relevant to your situation?

3. Each member of the team should choose one specific area to research and find out what is going on across the country in practice and educational forums. Discuss this information as a team at a follow-up meeting.

4. Pretend that you are me. I'd like each of you to write another section that you feel was missing from my look at the future. Share these with each other.

5. If possible, copy this section and use it as the basis for discussion at a faculty meeting. Choose one or two points to focus on with your professional learning communities.

THE PAST AS OF 1970

I'm sure we all got a good laugh at the prologue to this chapter, which listed the behavior that was expected of certain female teachers in 1915. Indeed this appears to be ancient history. But having been a "lady teacher" for many years, I can make an even more interesting list of rules that governed my early teaching career less than 40 years ago. Almost all of these were put in writing; all were my personal experiences:

1. You could expect to be asked in your interview if you have a steady boyfriend and if you intend to marry in the near future (a mark against you if answered *yes*).

2. Your interview process consisted of a 20-minute talk with the school principal. You were hired or not hired immediately.

3. You might teach six years before being formally evaluated.

4. You were not allowed to wear slacks or pants of any kind to class.

5. If pregnant, you had to resign your position when you got to the point at which you had to wear maternity clothes.

6. You were not covered by insurance for your pregnancy and delivery because you were not technically sick.

7. If you missed school to deliver your child, your pay was docked for each day absent since you could not use your sick days.

8. Men's salaries were usually higher than women's despite level of education or years of experience since they were considered "heads of households."

9. Extra-duty positions were never compensated but were expected to be performed as part of the job.

10. A teacher's children could qualify for free and reduced lunch status because of your level of salary.

11. You could be the teacher of the year one year and not rehired the next because a board member's relative needed a job. (The superintendent's explanation: you're a good teacher, you'll get a job somewhere else; she isn't very talented and has no experience, so no one will hire her.)

12. There were no curriculum guides, orientations, professional development opportunities, or mentoring systems for new teachers entering the field.

YOUR TURN

As an individual:

1. If you had to pick a rule from both the 1915 and 1970 lists that you feel were simply outrageous, what would they be? Write down some of the reasons for your outrage.

2. Almost all of us can think back to a few similar circumstances that could be added to my list. What would a couple of yours be? When did these change?

(Continued)

(Continued)

3. Most of these rules have nothing specifically to say about teaching students. What does this omission say about attitudes toward education in years past?

4. What are the major areas of change that have brought about more positive circumstances for teachers today? Where did these originate?

As a teacher team:

1. If you had to pick a rule from both the 1915 and 1970 lists that you feel were simply outrageous, what would they be? Write down some of the reasons for your outrage. Discuss the rules each of you chose and what you think about them.

2. Almost all of us can think back to a few similar circumstances that could be added to my list. What would a couple of yours be? When did these change? Share some of these experiences that now seem like ancient history.

3. Most of these rules have nothing specifically to say about teaching students. What does this omission say about attitudes toward education in years past?

4. What are the major areas of change that have brought about more positive circumstances for teachers today? Where did these originate?

WHAT DOES THE PUBLIC THINK WE SHOULD BE DOING?

After having looked into both the past and the future, we might be more prepared to set our focus on our current situations and the push for in-depth change. This movement through transformation is always a duality—the change occurring within ourselves soon being reflected and acting as the vehicle for transformation outside ourselves. Linguistically, thanks to Wikipedia, I can venture to say that the verb *transform* originated in 14th-century Middle English, based on Latin. The definitions speak of both an interior and an exterior change usually resulting in a higher degree of form, nature, or function. A transformer is more that an agent of change. This is because the change that a transformer brings about is never superficial. It's a saturating, lifting-up process resulting in a higher, more perfected condition.

Then there is the transformer, the device, whose function is defined as transferring electrical energy from one circuit to another through inductively coupled electrical conductors. It doesn't take much of a metaphorical stretch to see this in terms of the teacher and a class of students. We are indeed the transferring mechanism of energy that ignites even more energy in those we are teaching.

So why the definitions? Because it seems that the country as a whole is becoming more and more aware of the need not just for change but for transformation in the way we go about educating our young. The answer that is coming from discussions on what needs to be done is not simply newer, sleeker buildings filled with the latest technology (although many of our schools could definitely benefit from such changes). The call is for deeper, substantial shifts in our very thinking about what we mean by education. The call is for transformation. We have all seen what happens when the technology changes but the mind-set of the user, the teacher, doesn't. I've walked by classrooms where teachers are posting notes on expensive SMART Boards that are to be copied by students in the same way that they might have copied notes posted on the overhead or written on the good old blackboard. We need transformation in the mind, not just the tools.

Technology changes, but not the teacher.

Many groups are joining this conversation on what all of this will mean, what it should look like, and how it can be attained. The Partnership for 21st Century Skills is one such group. Its report titled *Beyond the Three Rs: Voter Attitudes Toward 21st Century Skills* (2007a) begins with this statement: "A virtually unanimous 99 percent of voters say that teaching students a wide range of 21st century skills—including critical thinking and problem-solving skills, computer and technology skills, and communication and self-direction skills—is important to our country's future economic success" (p. 1). It's no small matter that the revised Bloom's Taxonomy of critical thinking has placed creativity in the highest strata of skills that reflect in-depth critical thinking. It's no small matter that students are in need of being taught how to problem solve by learning lateral as well as vertical methods of thinking. To solve problems that we have never anticipated, why on earth aren't we instructing our children in how to use every method at their disposal? Creative thinking is a potent addition to the logical, sequential, scientific method and a necessary addition to the needs that these children will face in the immediate as well as long-term future. Figure 10.1 shows an example of the broader range of skills that need to be the focus of educational emphasis in order to more adequately address and prepare both today's and tomorrow's learners.

Figure 10.1   enGauge 21st Century Skills Chart

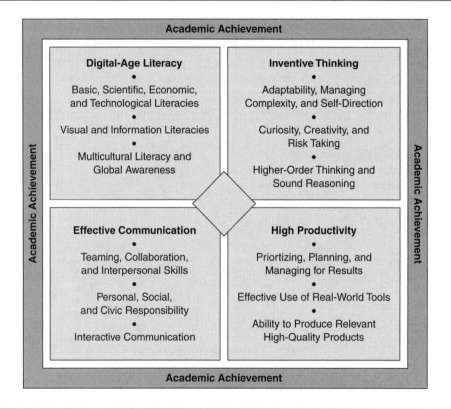

Source: Copyright © 2003 North Central Regional Educational Laboratory and the Metiri Group. All rights reserved. Reprinted with permission of Learning Point Associates.

The national poll that the Partnership for 21st Century Skills (2007a) report is based on, conducted by Public Opinion Strategies and Peter D. Hart Research Associates, reflects a shift from the "back to basics" movement of the 1990s. More that 74 percent of those polled thought that much more was needed than an emphasis on math, reading, and science for our children to compete in the world of tomorrow. They felt that an equal emphasis on 21st-century skills was needed. Half of the country believes that we are headed in the wrong direction with the current educational system. Moreover, "an overwhelming 80 percent of voters say that the kind of skills students need to learn to be prepared for the jobs of the 21st century is different from what they needed 20 years ago" (Partnership for 21st Century Skills, 2007a, p. 1). As far as creativity and innovation are concerned, 43 percent of the eight hundred people polled felt that these are indeed important skills, but only 5 percent felt that our schools are addressing this need. The public seems to know what we in education haven't caught on to yet: as Dan Pink (2005a) says, "the future no longer belongs to people who can reason with computer-like logic, speed, and precision. It belongs to a different kind of person with a different kind of mind" (¶ 3). It's the "right brainers" who need to take the lead and step up to meet the demands of this new world that we are entering into.

The Conference Board (2008) concludes that "innovation is crucial to competition, and creativity is integral to innovation" (p. 1). Having surveyed public school superintendents and American business executives (employers) to identify and compare their views surrounding creativity, the Conference Board found that

> overwhelmingly, both the superintendents who educate future workers and the employers who hire them agree that creativity is increasingly important in U.S. workplaces. . . . Yet, there is a gap between understanding this truth and putting it into meaningful practice. . . . Other results of this survey:
>
> - Eighty-five percent of employers concerned with hiring creative people say they can't find the applicants they seek.
> - Employers concerned with hiring creative people rarely use profile tests to assess the creative skills of potential employees. . . . Instead, they rely on face-to-face interviews.
> - While 97 percent of employers say creativity is of increasing importance, only 72 percent say that hiring creative people is a primary concern. (p. 1)

It seems that, as a country, we have yet to place enough emphasis and focus on creativity to be able to articulate what it is or how to recognize it in potential employees. We know it's important, but we don't know how to talk about it intelligently. In a *Teacher Magazine* article titled "Courting Creativity," Bob Watt, vice president of government and community relations at Boeing, is quoted as saying, "We make our living imagining things that never before existed. . . . Creativity is at the heart of what Boeing does" (¶ 11). The article goes on to say that, "in addition to trying to hire creative people, Watt says Boeing encourages its employees to continue their education and potentially gain more inspiration by offering to pay their college tuition to study anything they want, whether it's related to building airplanes or not"(¶ 12). The same article attributes this wisdom to Bob Drewel, former president of Everett Community College who now runs the Puget Sound Regional Council: "It's important to teach children both how to think and that there are different ways to think. . . . Public education may have to change to make room for more creativity. . . . [T]eachers aren't always given the time or the freedom to use their creative energy in a way that inspires children" (¶ 13–14).

WELCOME TO OUR BRAVE NEW RIGHT-BRAINED WORLD

In "Revenge of the Right Brain," Dan Pink (2005a) sums up the situation this way:

> Until recently, the abilities that led to success in school, work, and business were characteristic of the left hemisphere. They were the sorts of linear, logical, analytical talents measured by SATs and deployed by CPAs. Today, those capabilities are still necessary. But they're no longer sufficient. In a world upended by outsourcing, deluged with data, and choked with choices, the abilities that matter most are now closer in spirit to the specialties of the right hemisphere—artistry, empathy, seeing the big picture, and pursuing the transcendent. (¶ 5)

If these qualities are taken seriously, a tremendous shift needs to be made in the traditional educational framework that has been in place since the 18th century—the factory model. Pink continues, saying that

> to flourish in this age, we'll need to supplement our well-developed high tech abilities with aptitudes that are "high concept" and "high touch." High concept involves the ability to create artistic and emotional beauty, to detect patterns and opportunities, to craft a satisfying narrative, and to come up with inventions the world didn't know it was missing. High touch involves the capacity to empathize, to understand the subtleties of human interaction, to find joy in one's self and to elicit it in others, and to stretch beyond the quotidian in pursuit of purpose and meaning. (¶ 23)

Reteaching and valuing these attributes are part of what makes us human and competent in this age of conceptualism as opposed to simply information gathering.

Where do we start to begin forming the kind of changes that Pink and others like him envision? It's more than just adding equipment or new courses. It's really centered in a transformation of what we value, what we see as our role as educators, what we have come to see as necessary for our students' well-being. Yet this transformation can come only after we accept ourselves as capable and able to function in this role. It starts with us, with our willingness to articulate what we know is genuine, our willingness to take risks and together lead our students through the potential minefield that is the future. Our transformation as people sold on the benefit of addressing the whole person's needs, acknowledging and working to better the myriad strengths and shortcomings of ourselves as well as our students, is what will always come first.

There will be no change in our educational structure if there is no change in us. As Linda Darling-Hammond (2007) explains,

> part of the problem is that the standards used to guide teaching in many states are a mile wide and an inch deep: Most high-achieving countries teach (and test) fewer topics each year and teach them more thoroughly so students build a stronger foundation for their learning. Whereas students in most parts of the United States are typically asked simply to recognize a single fact they have memorized from a list of answers, students in high-achieving countries are asked to apply their knowledge in the ways that writers, mathematicians, historians and scientists do. (¶ 8–9)

Creativity in thinking, in producing, needs time and focus. Until the perception that curriculum "a mile wide and an inch deep" isn't consistent with quality learning and understanding, teachers will be pulled apart trying to teach the way they know is effective while still meeting the directives and requirements of their local schools and districts.

EVERY TEACHER A CREATIVE TEACHER

Curtis Sittenfeld (2000) paraphrases Stanford Graduate School of Business professor Michael Ray when he says, "When people can't tap into their creativity . . . that doesn't mean that it's not there; it's just being suppressed by what [Ray] calls the 'voice of judgment,' or VOJ—that pesky internal self-esteem destroyer, heavily influenced by both society and parents, that says you can't, you shouldn't, and you're going to look stupid if you try" (¶ 25). To counter this negativity and "internal self-esteem destroyer," one really could benefit from training. Tom Peters (2003), internationally renowned author who writes and speaks about personal and business empowerment and problem-solving methodologies, agrees that "training in Creativity is important, in general. But it is absolutely essential in this Age of Intangibles & Intellectual Capital" (p. 278). His particular vision of what school systems should embody is one most of us could and should buy into: "a school system that recognizes that learning is natural, that a love of learning is normal, and that real learning is passionate learning; a school curriculum that values questions above answers, creativity above fact, regurgitation, individuality above uniformity and excellence above standardized performance [and] a society that respects its teachers and principals, pays them well, and grants them the autonomy to do their job as the creative individuals they are, and for the creative individuals in their charge" (p. 268). This vision is the one that requires transformers—creative teachers in every classroom, creative administrators in every central office. That's the purpose of this book: to begin that conversation that will generate understanding of the need for and power of creativity in transforming our classrooms to meet the needs of the 21st century.

YOUR TURN

As an individual or as a teacher team:

1. Write an "elevator talk" about what you have gotten out of dipping into this book. (The definition of an "elevator talk" is found in the preface.)

2. Thinking over ideas is good, but planning to do something about them is better. List five specific actions you intend to take in order to build, use, and amplify your own creativity.

3. We make far better strides in learning and developing patterns if we work in community. Find a partner or partners who want to systematically work on becoming more creative teachers. Set an on-going, recurring meeting time to compare efforts and energize your commitment to expanding your creativity.

References

Angelou, M. (1997). *Even the stars look lonesome.* New York: Random House.

Appalachia Regional Comprehensive Center. (2005–2006). *Technology proficiency: A moving target.* Retrieved February 24, 2009, from www.edvantia.org/publications/arccwebcast/october07/

Becker, H. J. (2000). *Findings from the teaching, learning, and computing survey: Is Larry Cuban right?* University of California at Irvine. Retrieved February 24, 2009, from http://www.crito.uci.edu/tlc/findings/ccsso.pdf

Block, P. (2002). *The answer to how is yes: Acting on what matters.* San Francisco: Berrett-Koelher.

Bloom, B. S. (1956). *Taxonomy of educational objectives: The classification of educational goals.* New York: Longmans, Green.

Boddy-Evans, M. (2009). *Right brain and left brain inventory.* Retrieved February 17, 2009, from http://painting.about.com/library/blpaint/blrightbraintable.htm

Bransford, J., Brown, A., & Cocking, R. (Eds.). (2000). *How people learn: Brain, mind, experience, and school.* Washington, DC: National Academies Press.

Brown, D. G., & Ellison, C. W. (1991). What is active learning? In S. R. Hatfield (Ed.), *The seven principles in action: Improving undergraduate education* (pp. 39–53). Bolton, MA: Anker.

Brown, J., & Moffett, C. (1999). *The hero's journey: How educators can transform schools and improve learning.* Alexandria, VA: Association for Supervision and Curriculum Development.

Buzan, T. (2003). *Mind maps for kids: The shortcut to success at school.* London: Thorsons.

Caine, G., & Caine, R. N. (Eds.). (1991). *Making connections: Teaching and the human brain.* Alexandria, VA: Association for Supervision and Curriculum Development.

Calkins, L. M. (with Harwayne, S.). (1991). *Living between the lines.* Portsmouth, NH: Heinemann.

Cameron, J. (1992). *The artist's way.* New York: Penguin-Putman.

Campbell, J. (with Moyers, B.). (1991). *The power of myth.* New York: Anchor Books.

Card, O. S. (1991). *Ender's game.* New York: Tom Doherty Associates.

Cennamo, K., Ross, P., & Ertmer, P. (2009). *Technology integration for meaningful classroom use: A standards-based approach.* Belmont, CA: Cengage Learning/Wadsworth.

Cherry, D., & Spiegel, J. (2006). *Leadership, myth, and metaphor: Finding common ground to guide effective school change.* Thousand Oaks, CA: Corwin.

Conference Board. (2008). *Ready to innovate: Key findings.* New York: Author.

Connell, D. (2009–1996). *Left brain/right brain: Pathways to reach every learner.* Retrieved February 17, 2009, from http://content.scholastic.com/browse/article.jsp?id=3629

Costa, A. L. (1989). Re-assessing assessment. *Educational Leadership, 46*(7), 2.

Costa, A. L. (1995, January). *Habits of mind.* Keynote address at the National Middle School Conference, Phoenix, AZ.

Costa, A. L., & Kallick, B. (2008). *Learning and leading with habits of mind: 16 essential characteristics for success.* Alexandria, VA: Association for Supervision and Curriculum Development.

Courting creativity. (2007, December 3). *Teacher Magazine.*

Cox, W. M., Alm, R., & Holmes, N. (2004, May 13). Where the jobs are. *New York Times,* p. A27.

Creativity Matters. (2007). *About.* Retrieved February 12, 2009, from http://creativitymatters .net/about.php

Csikszentmihalyi, M. (1997). *Creativity: Flow and psychology of discovery and invention.* New York: HarperPerennial.

Cullum, A. (1971). *The geranium on the window sill just died, but teacher you went right on.* London: Harlin Quist.

D'Acquisto, L. (2006). *Learning on display: Student-created museums that build understanding.* Alexandria, VA: Association for Supervision and Curriculum Development.

Darling-Hammond, L. (2007, October 14). *High-quality standards, a curriculum based on critical thinking can enlighten our students.* Retrieved February 25, 2009, from http://sfgate .com/cgi-bin/article.cgi?f=/c/a/2007/10/14/IN9GSOEUC.DTL

Debold, E. (2002). Flow with soul: An interview with Dr. Mihaly Csikszentmihalyi. *What Is Enlightenment? 21.* Retrieved February 23, 2009, from http://www.enlightennext.org/ magazine/j21/csiksz.asp?pf=1

de Bono, E. (1970). *Lateral thinking: Creativity step by step.* New York: Harper & Row.

de Bono, E. (1988). Serious creativity. *Journal for Quality and Participation, 11*(3). Retrieved February 16, 2009, from http://www.debonogroup.com/serious_creativity.htm

de Bono, E. (1992). *Serious creativity: Using the power of lateral thinking to create new ideas.* New York: Harper Business.

DeBono, T., & Rosen, S. (Directors). (2001). *Accidental hero: Room 408.* United States: KQED.

de Geus, A. (2002). *The living company: Habits for survival in a turbulent business environment.* Boston: Harvard Business School Press.

Diamond, M., & Hopson, J. (1998). *Magic trees of the mind.* New York: Dutton Books.

Dooling, D. M. (1987). *A way of working* (2nd ed.). New York: Anchor Press/Doubleday.

Draper, S. (1998). *Forged by fire.* New York: Aladdin.

Draper, S. (2001). *Not quite burned out but crispy around the edges.* Portsmouth, NH: Heinemann.

Dwyer, D. C., Ringstaff, C., & Sandholtz, J. H. (1991). Changes in teachers' beliefs and practices in technology-rich classrooms. *Educational Leadership, 48*(8), 45–52.

Faucette, R. (1997). Using Play-Doh to teach the writing process. In *Ideas Plus: Book 15* (pp. 1–4). Urbana, IL: National Council of Teachers of English.

Florida, R. (2002). *The rise of the creative class: And how it's transforming work, leisure, community and everyday life.* New York: Basic Books.

The Freedom Writers (with Gruwell, E.). (1999). *The freedom writers diary: How a teacher and 150 teens used writing to change themselves and the world around them.* New York: Broadway Books.

Friedman, T. L. (2005). *The world is flat: A brief history of the twenty-first century.* New York: Farrar, Straus and Giroux.

Gardner, H. (2006). *Multiple intelligences: New horizons in theory and practice.* New York: Basic Books.

Gund, C. (Producer), & Sullivan, L. A. (Director). (2005). *Touch of greatness.* United States: Public Broadcasting Service.

Guthrie, J. T. (2002). Preparing students for high-stakes test taking in reading. In A. E. Farstrup & S. J. Samuels (Eds.), *What research has to say about reading instruction* (3rd ed., pp. 370–391). Newark, DE: International Reading Association.

Hedrick, W. B. (2007). Bumps in the road: Test madness. *Voices From the Middle, 15*(2), 64–65.

International Society for Technology in Education. (2007). *National educational technology standards for students.* Eugene, OR: Author.

International Society for Technology in Education. (2008). *National educational technology standards for teachers.* Eugene, OR: Author.

Jenkins, H. (2004, January 2). Media literacy goes to school. *Technology Review.* Retrieved February 19, 2009, from http://www.technologyreview.com/biomedicine/13429/

Jensen, E. (1998). *Teaching with the brain in mind.* Alexandria, VA: Association for Supervision and Curriculum Development.

Jones, C. F. (1991). *Mistakes that worked: 40 familiar inventions and how they came to be.* New York: Delacorte Press.

Kabat-Zin, J. (2005). *Wherever you go there you are: Mindfulness meditation in everyday life.* New York: Hyperion.

Kay, M. (2008, September 14). Teaching without a script. *New York Times.* Retrieved February 17, 2009, from http://lessonplans.blogs.nytimes.com/2008/09/14/script-free-teaching/?ei=5070&emc=eta

Koetsch, P., D'Acquisto, L., Kurin, A., Juffer, S., & Goldberg, L. (2002). Schools into museums. *Educational Leadership, 60*(1), 74–78.

Kotulak, R. (1997). *Inside the brain: Revolutionary discoveries of how the mind works.* Kansas City, MO: Andrews McMeel.

Lackney, J. A. (n.d.). *12 design principles based on brain-based learning research.* Retrieved February 12, 2009, from http://www.designshare.com/Research/BrainBasedLearn98.htm

Lakoff, G. (2002). *Moral politics: How liberals and conservatives think.* Chicago: University of Chicago Press.

Lakoff, G. (2008). *The political mind: Why you can't understand 21st-century American politics with an 18th-century brain.* New York: Viking.

Lakoff, G., & Johnson, M. (1980). *Metaphors we live by.* Chicago: University of Chicago Press.

Louv, R. (2006). *Last child in the woods: Saving our children from nature-deficit disorder.* New York: Algonquin Books.

McCaw, D. (2007). Dangerous intersection ahead. *School Administrator, 64*(2), 32–38.

Michalko, M. (2006). *Thinkertoys: A handbook of creative-thinking techniques.* Berkeley, CA: Ten Speed Press.

Morris, W. (2006). *Creativity: Its place in education.* Retrieved February 12, 2009, from http://www.jpb.com/creative/Creativity_in_Education.pdf

Mundow, A. (2007, October 21). The advocate of teaching over testing. *Boston Globe.* Retrieved February 17, 2009, from http://www.boston.com/ae/books/articles/2007/10/21/the_advocate_of_teaching_over_testing/?page=2

Nadia, S. (1993 December 15). Kids' brain power. *The Oregonian,* pp. 12–15.

National Research Council. (2000). *How people learn: Brain, mind, experience, and school.* Washington, DC: National Academies Press.

Ornstein, R. (1997). *The right mind: Making sense of the hemispheres.* New York: Harcourt Brace.

Palmer, P. J. (1997). *The heart of a teacher: Identity and integrity in teaching.* Retrieved February 22, 2009, from http://www.newhorizons.org/strategies/character/palmer.htm

Partnership for 21st Century Skills. (2007a). *Beyond the three Rs: Voter attitudes toward 21st century skills.* Tucson, AZ: Author.

Partnership for 21st Century Skills. (2007b). *Framework for 21st century learning.* Tucson, AZ: Author.

Pert, C. (Speaker). (2008). *Psychosomatic wellness: Guided meditations, affirmations and music to heal your bodymind* (CD). Louisville, CO: Sounds True.

Peters, T. (2003). *Re-imagine! Business excellence in a disruptive age.* London: DK.

Peterson, K. D., & Deal, T. E. (2002). *The shaping school culture fieldbook.* San Francisco: Jossey-Bass.

Pink, D. H. (2005a). Revenge of the right brain. *Wired, 13*(2). Retrieved February 25, 2009, from http://www.wired.com/wired/archive/13.02/brain.html

Pink, D. H. (2005b). *A whole new mind: Moving from the information age to the conceptual age.* New York: Riverhead Books.

Popham, J. (2008). Ask about accountability: When the test says you're not so smart. *Educational Leadership, 65*(7), 87–88.

Rae-Dupree, J. (2008, May 4). Can you become a creature of new habits? *New York Times.* Retrieved February 23, 2009, from http://www.nytimes.com/2008/05/04/business/04unbox.html

Richards, S. (2007). The last word: An interview with Arthur L. Costa. *Journal of Advanced Academics, 18,* 313–327.

Robinson, K. (2001). *Out of our minds: Learning to be creative.* West Sussex, UK: Capstone.

Ryan, M. J. (2006). *This year I will . . . : How to finally change a habit, keep a resolution, or make a dream come true.* New York: Broadway Books.

Saskatchewan Education. (n.d.). *Understanding the common essential learnings: A handbook for teachers.* Regina, Saskatchewan, Canada: Author. Retrieved February 23, 2009, from http://www.sasklearning.gov.sk.ca/docs/policy/cels/index.html

Schmoker, M. (2001, October 20). The "Crayola Curriculum." *Education Week,* pp. 42–44. Retrieved February 10, 2009, from http://mikeschmoker.com/crayola-curriculum.html

Schon, D. A. (1993). Generative metaphor: A perspective on problem-setting in social policy. In A. Ortony (Ed.), *Metaphor and thought* (2nd ed., pp. 137–163). Cambridge, UK: Cambridge University Press.

Sitomer, A., & Cirelli, M. (2004). *Hip-hop poetry and the classics for the classroom.* Beverly Hills, CA: Milk Mug.

Sittenfeld, C. (2000). The most creative man in Silicon Valley. *Fast Company, 35.* Retrieved February 25, 2009, from http://www.fastcompany.com/node/40613/print

Smith, M. W., & Wilhelm, J. D. (2006). *Going with the flow: How to engage boys (and girls) in their literacy learning.* Portsmouth, NH: Heinemann.

Spires, E. (& Nivola, C., Illus.). (2001). *The mouse of Amherst.* New York: Farrar, Straus and Giroux.

Sprenger, M. (2008). *Differentiation through learning styles and memory.* Thousand Oaks, CA: Corwin.

Swanson, C. B. (2008). *Cities in crisis: A special analytic report on high school graduation.* Bethesda, MD: Editorial Projects in Education.

Thomas, J. W. (2000). *A review of research on project-based learning.* San Rafael, CA: Autodesk.

Tileston, D. W. (2003). Increase your brain power. *Virginia Journal of Education* (October). Retrieved February 18, 2009, from http://www.veanea.org/vea-journal/0310/October2003-IncreaseYourBrainPower.html

Tomlinson, C. A., & Kalbfleisch, M. L. (1998). Teach me, teach my brain: A call for differentiated classrooms. *Educational Leadership, 56*(3), 52–55.

Tovani, C. (2000). *I read it, but I don't get it: Comprehension strategies for adolescent readers.* Portland, ME: Stenhouse.

Ulrich, D. (2002). *The widening stream: The seven stages of creativity.* Hillsboro, OR: Beyond Words.

Vakos, P. (2008). *Why the blank stare? Strategies for visual learners.* Retrieved February 18, 2009, from http://www.phschool.com/eteach/social_studies/2003_05/essay.html

Viadero, D. (2008, April 14). Black-white gap widens faster for high achievers. *Education Week.* Retrieved February 17, 2009, from http://www.edweek.org/ew/articles/2008/04/16/33gap_ep.h27.html

Wahl, M. (1999). *Math for humans: Teaching math through 8 intelligences.* Langley, WA: LivnLern Press.

Wiggins, G. (1998). *Educative assessment: Designing assessments to inform and improve student performance.* San Francisco, California: Jossey-Bass.

Wiggins, G., & McTighe, J. (2005). *Understanding by design* (Expanded 2nd ed.). Alexandria, VA: Association for Supervision and Curriculum Development.

Wilhelm, J. D. (1997). *"You gotta BE the book": Teaching engaged and reflective reading with adolescents.* New York: Teachers College Press.

Wilhelm, J. D. (2002). *Action strategies for deepening comprehension: Role-plays, text structure tableaux, talking statues and other enactment techniques that engage students with text.* New York: Scholastic.

Wilhelm, J. D. (2007a). Beyond programs: Asserting our authority as teachers. *Voices From the Middle, 14*(3), 50–52.

Wilhelm, J. D. (2007b). *Engaging readers and writers with inquiry: Promoting deep understandings in language arts and the content areas with guiding questions.* New York: Scholastic.

Wilson, L. O. (2005). *Thinking patterns that help create new ideas.* Retrieved February 23, 2009, from https://www.uwsp.edu/education/lwilson/creativ/thinking.htm

Woodbury, L. (1991). *The concept of school as a factory.* Retrieved February 22, 2009, from http://www.strugglingteens.com/archives/1991/4/oe02.html

Yatvin, J. (2007). 2007 NCTE presidential address: Where ignorant armies clash by night. *Council Chronicle, 17*(4), 25–31.

Index